# SPIDEY

## FIRST DAY

### ROBBIE THOMPSON
WRITER

WITHDRAWN

**ISSUES #1-3**

---

**ISSUES #4-6**

---

### NICK BRADSHAW
ARTIST

### ANDRÉ LIMA ARAÚJO
ARTIST

**JIM CAMPBELL** WITH
**RACHELLE ROSENBERG** (#3)
COLOR ARTISTS

**RACHELLE ROSENBERG** (#4)
& **JIM CAMPBELL** (#5-6) WITH
**JAVA TARTAGLIA** (#5)
COLOR ARTISTS

**NICK BRADSHAW** &
**JIM CAMPBELL**
COVER ART

**NICK BRADSHAW** &
**JIM CAMPBELL** (#4 & #6) AND
**ANDRE LIMA ARAÚJO** &
**JIM CAMPBELL** (#5)
COVER ART

**SPIDER-MAN** CREATED BY **STAN LEE** & **STEVE DITKO**

COLLECTION EDITOR: **JENNIFER GRÜNWALD**
ASSOCIATE EDITOR: **SARAH BRUNSTAD**
EDITOR, SPECIAL PROJECTS: **MARK D. BEAZLEY**
VP, PRODUCTION & SPECIAL PROJECTS: **JEFF YOUNGQUIST**
SVP PRINT, SALES & MARKETING: **DAVID GABRIEL**
BOOK DESIGNER: **ADAM DEL RE**

CHIEF CREATIVE OFFICER: **JOE QUESADA**
PUBLISHER: **DAN BUCKLEY**
EXECUTIVE PRODUCER: **ALAN FINE**

**SPIDEY VOL. 1: FIRST DAY.** Contains material originally published in magazine form as SPIDEY #1-6. First printing 2016. ISBN# 978-0-7851-9675-4. Published by MARVEL WORLDWIDE, INC., a subsidiary of MARVEL ENTERTAINMENT, LLC. OFFICE OF PUBLICATION: 135 West 50th Street, New York, NY 10020. Copyright © 2016 MARVEL No similarity between any of the names, characters, persons, and/or institutions in this magazine with those of any living or dead person or institution is intended, and any such similarity which may exist is purely coincidental. **Printed in Canada.** ALAN FINE, President, Marvel Entertainment; DAN BUCKLEY, President, TV, Publishing & Brand Management; JOE QUESADA, Chief Creative Officer; TOM BREVOORT, SVP of Publishing; DAVID BOGART, SVP of Business Affairs & Operations, Publishing & Partnership; C.B. CEBULSKI, VP of Brand Management & Development, Asia; DAVID GABRIEL, SVP of Sales & Marketing, Publishing; JEFF YOUNGQUIST, VP of Special Projects; DAN CARR, Executive Director of Publishing Technology; ALEX MORALES, Director of Publishing Operations; SUSAN CRESPI, Production Manager; STAN LEE, Chairman Emeritus. For information regarding advertising in Marvel Comics or on Marvel.com, please contact Vit DeBellis, Integrated Sales Manager, at vdebellis@marvel.com. For Marvel subscription inquiries, please call 888-511-5480. **Manufactured between 6/17/2016 and 7/25/2016 by SOLISCO PRINTERS, SCOTT, QC, CANADA.**

10 9 8 7 6 5 4 3 2 1

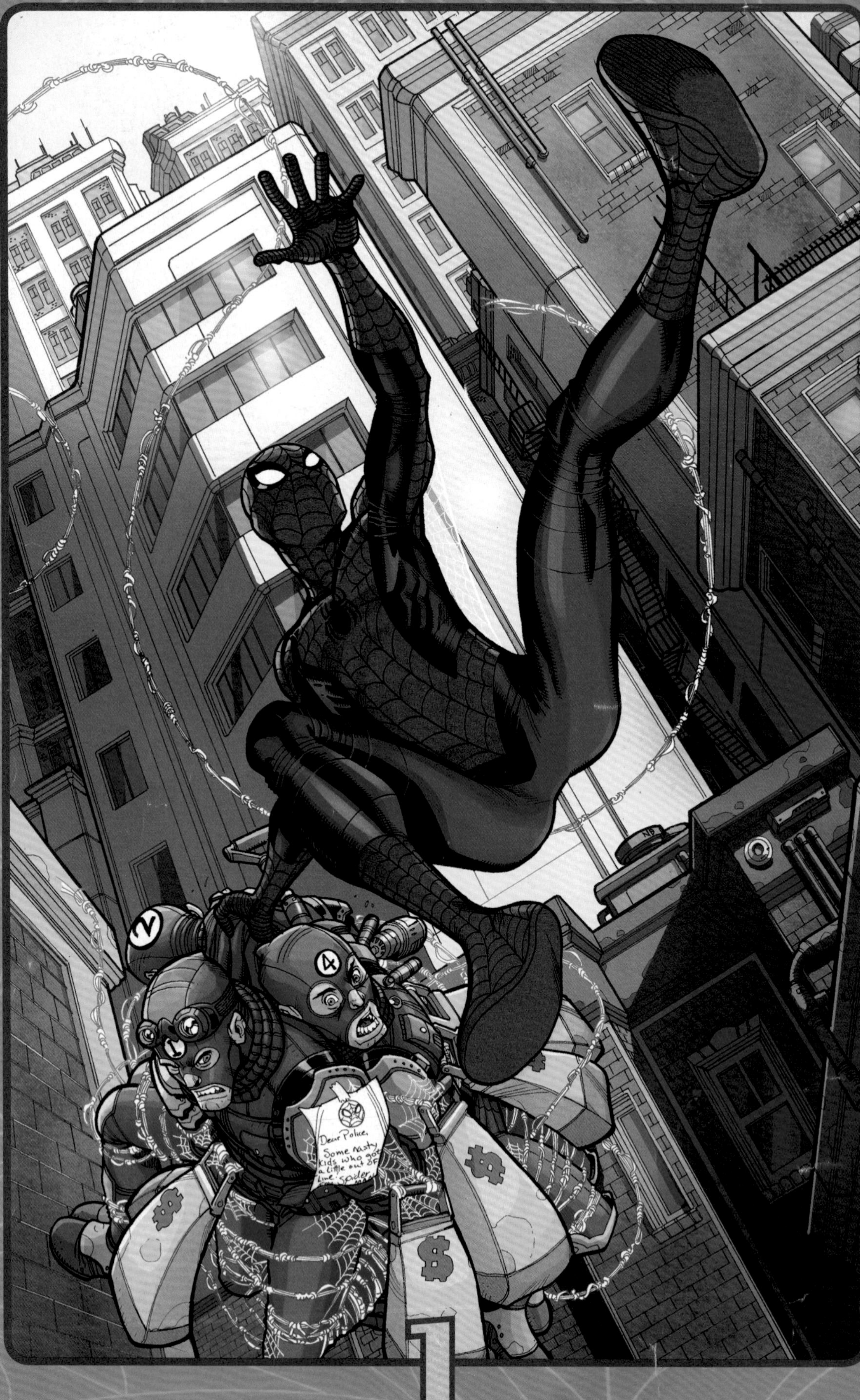
Dear Police,
Some nasty kids who got a little out of Line.
Spider

# 1

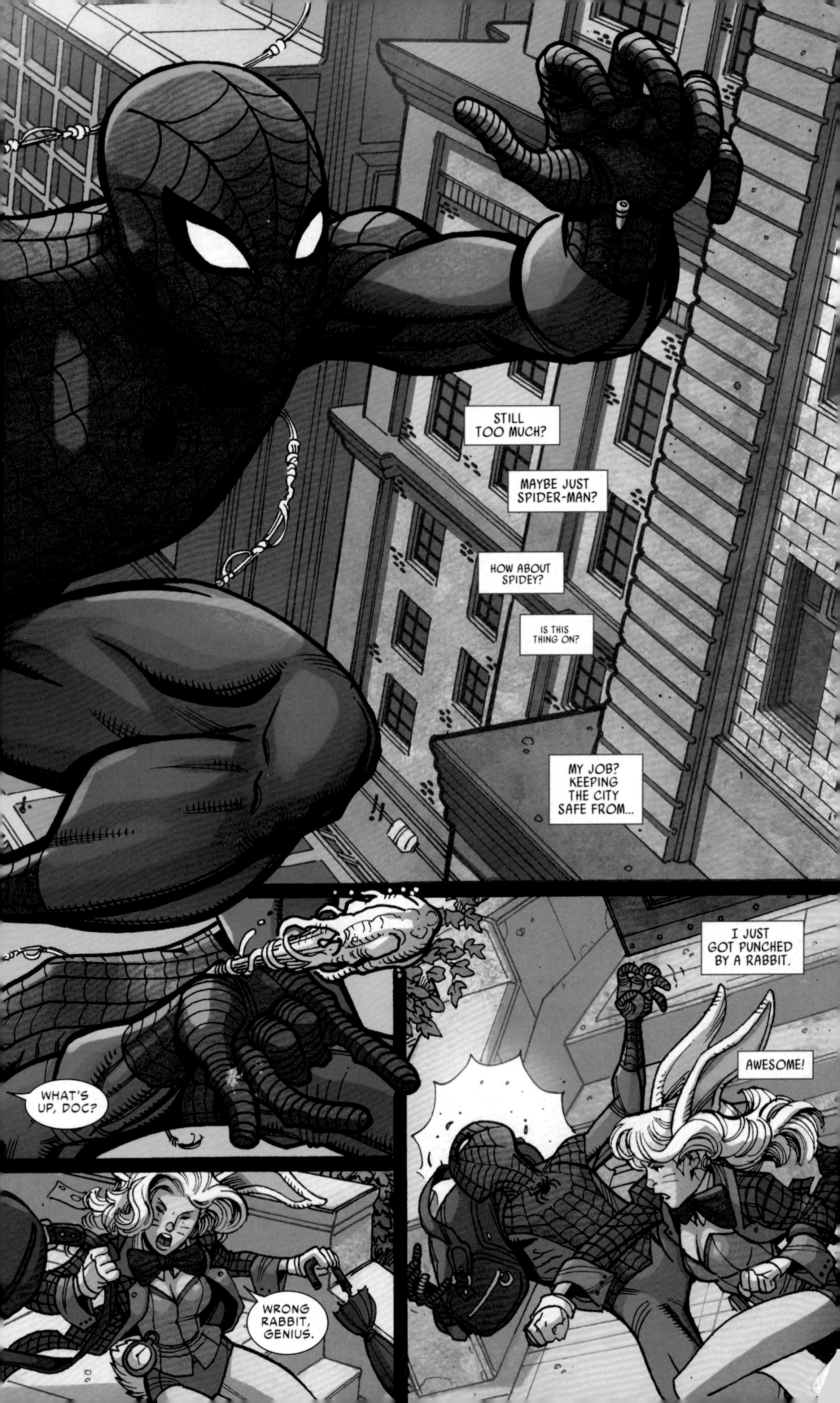
STILL TOO MUCH?
MAYBE JUST SPIDER-MAN?
HOW ABOUT SPIDEY?
IS THIS THING ON?
MY JOB? KEEPING THE CITY SAFE FROM...
WHAT'S UP, DOC?
WRONG RABBIT, GENIUS.
I JUST GOT PUNCHED BY A RABBIT.
AWESOME!

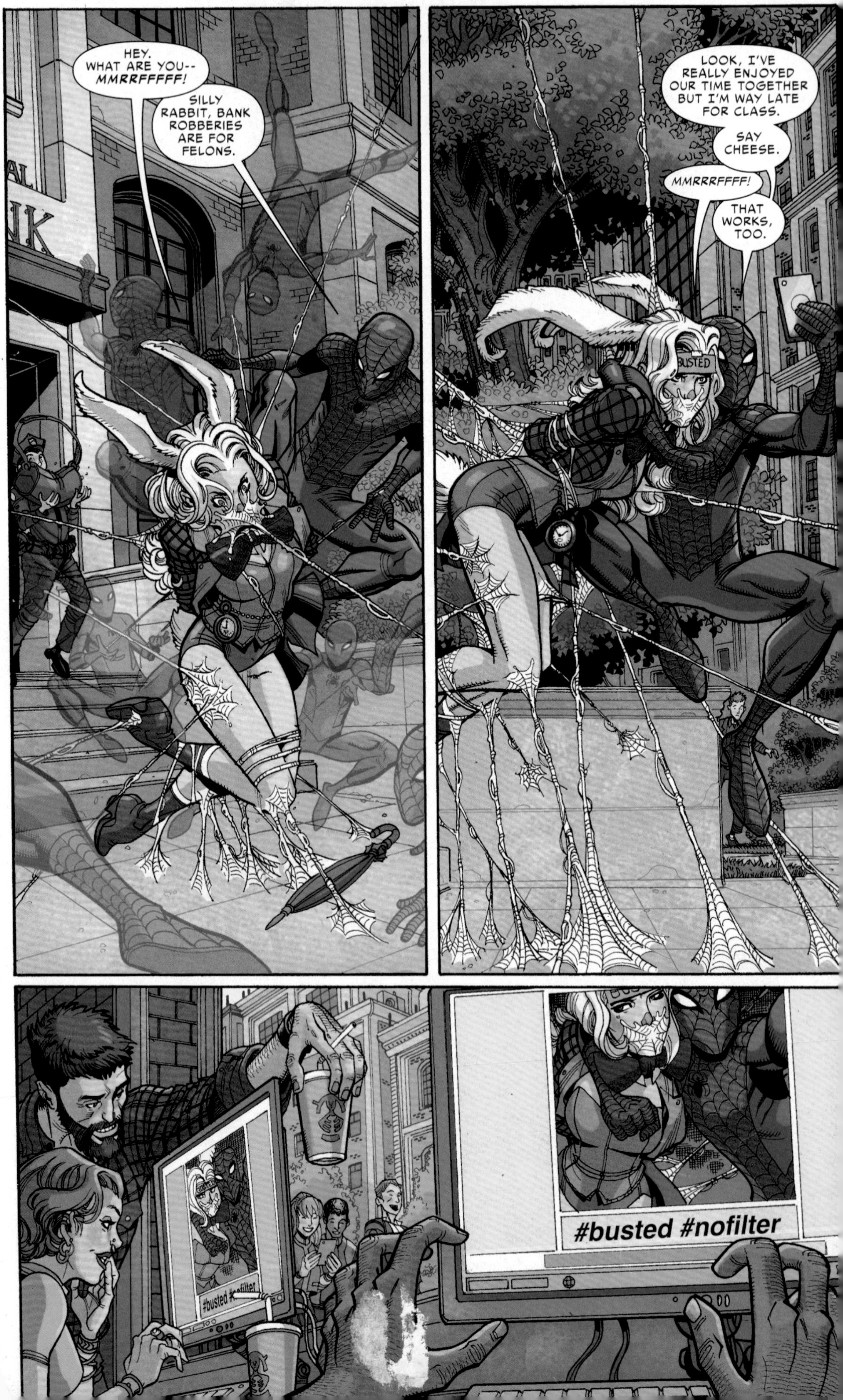

HEY. WHAT ARE YOU-- MMRRFFFFF!
SILLY RABBIT, BANK ROBBERIES ARE FOR FELONS.
LOOK, I'VE REALLY ENJOYED OUR TIME TOGETHER BUT I'M WAY LATE FOR CLASS.
SAY CHEESE.
MMRRRFFFF!
THAT WORKS, TOO.
BUSTED
#busted #nofilter

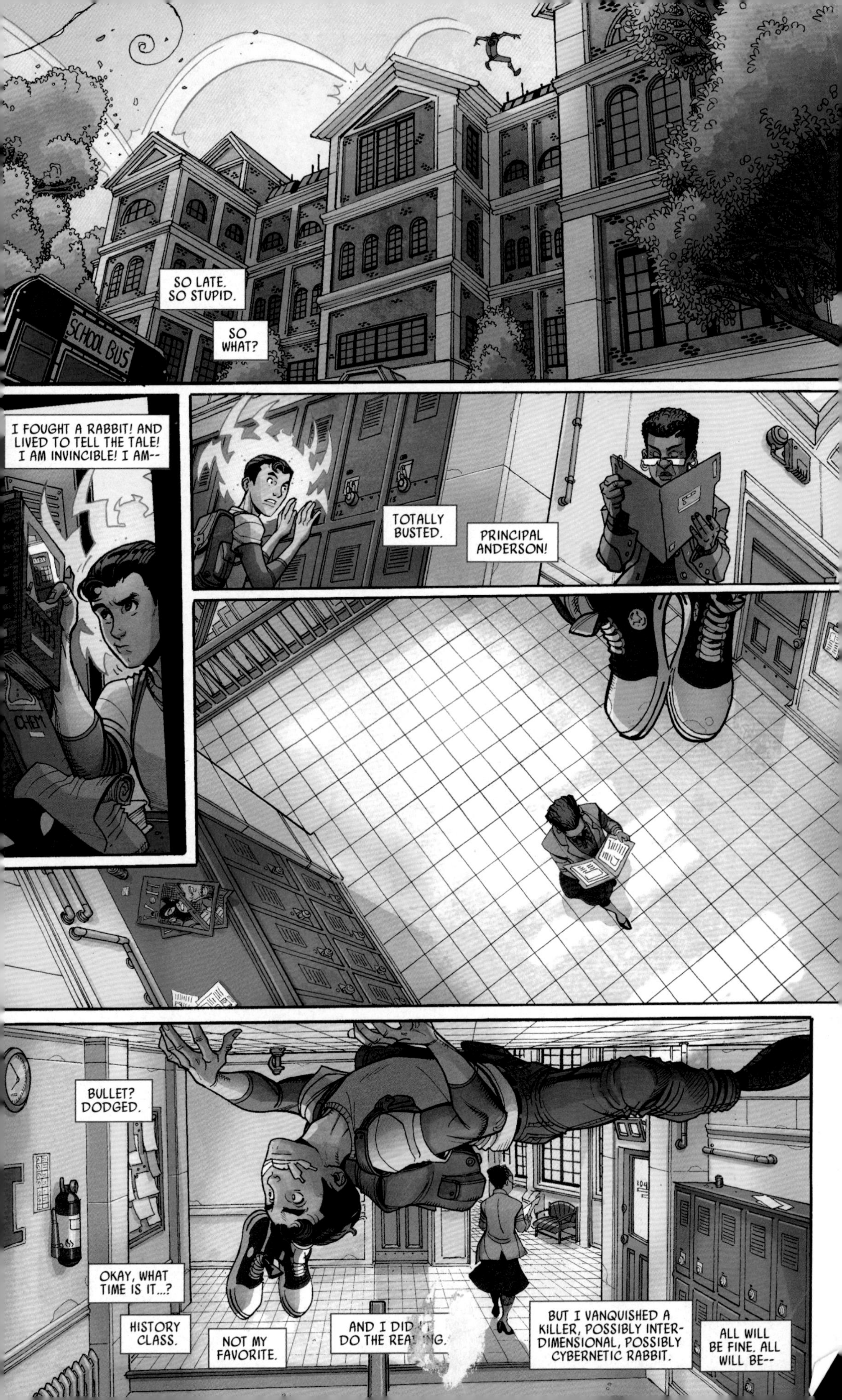
SO LATE.
SO STUPID.
SO
WHAT?
SCHOOL BUS
I FOUGHT A RABBIT! AND LIVED TO TELL THE TALE! I AM INVINCIBLE! I AM--
TOTALLY BUSTED.
PRINCIPAL ANDERSON!
CHEM
BULLET? DODGED.
OKAY, WHAT TIME IS IT...?
HISTORY CLASS.
NOT MY FAVORITE.
BUT I VANQUISHED A KILLER, POSSIBLY INTER-DIMENSIONAL, POSSIBLY CYBERNETIC RABBIT.
ALL WILL BE FINE. ALL WILL BE--

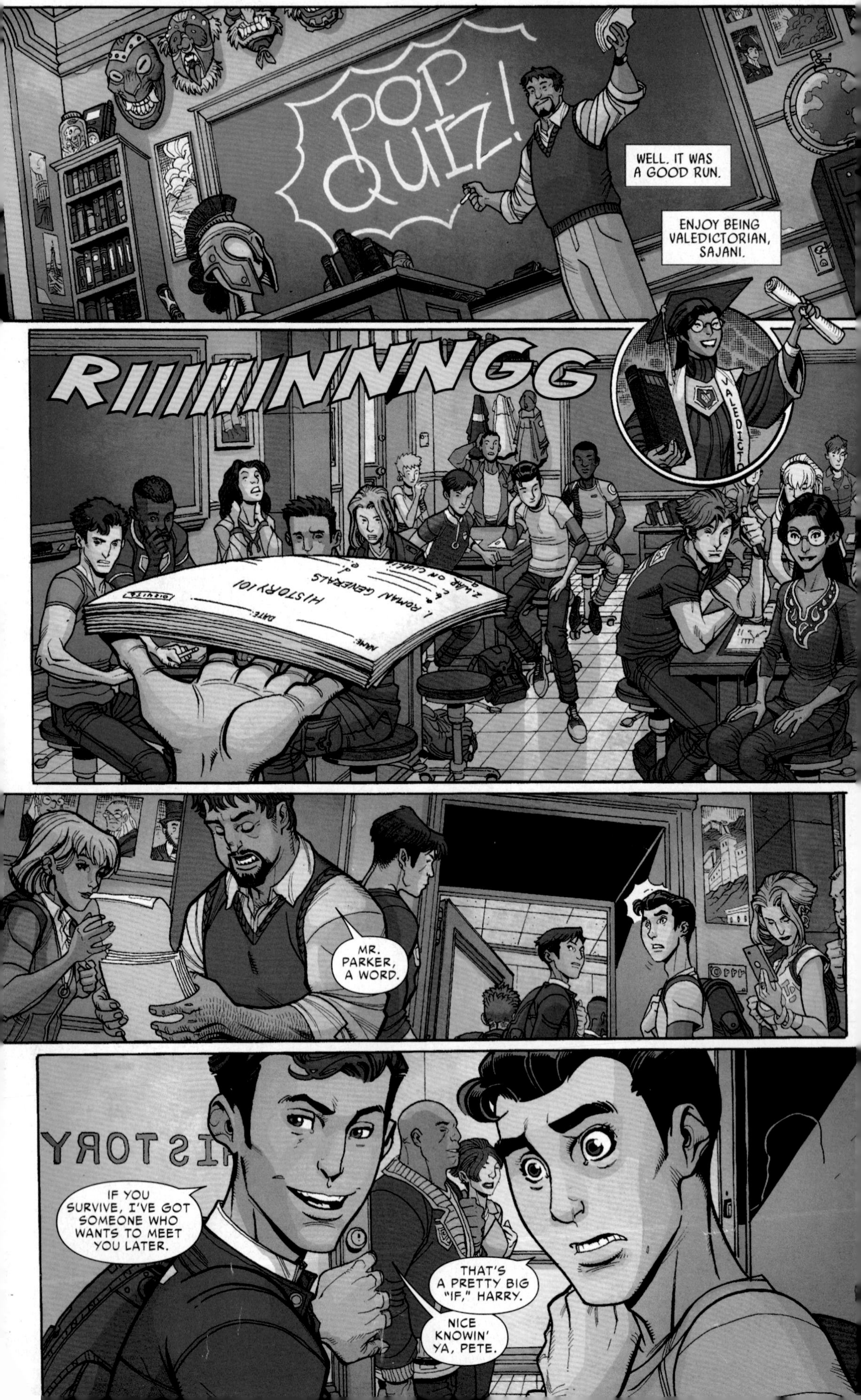

POP QUIZ!
WELL. IT WAS A GOOD RUN.
ENJOY BEING VALEDICTORIAN, SAJANI.
VALEDICTO
RIIIIIINNNNGG
HISTORY 101
1. ROMAN GENERALS
2. WAR ON CURLL
MR. PARKER, A WORD.
HISTORY
IF YOU SURVIVE, I'VE GOT SOMEONE WHO WANTS TO MEET YOU LATER.
THAT'S A PRETTY BIG "IF," HARRY.
NICE KNOWIN' YA, PETE.

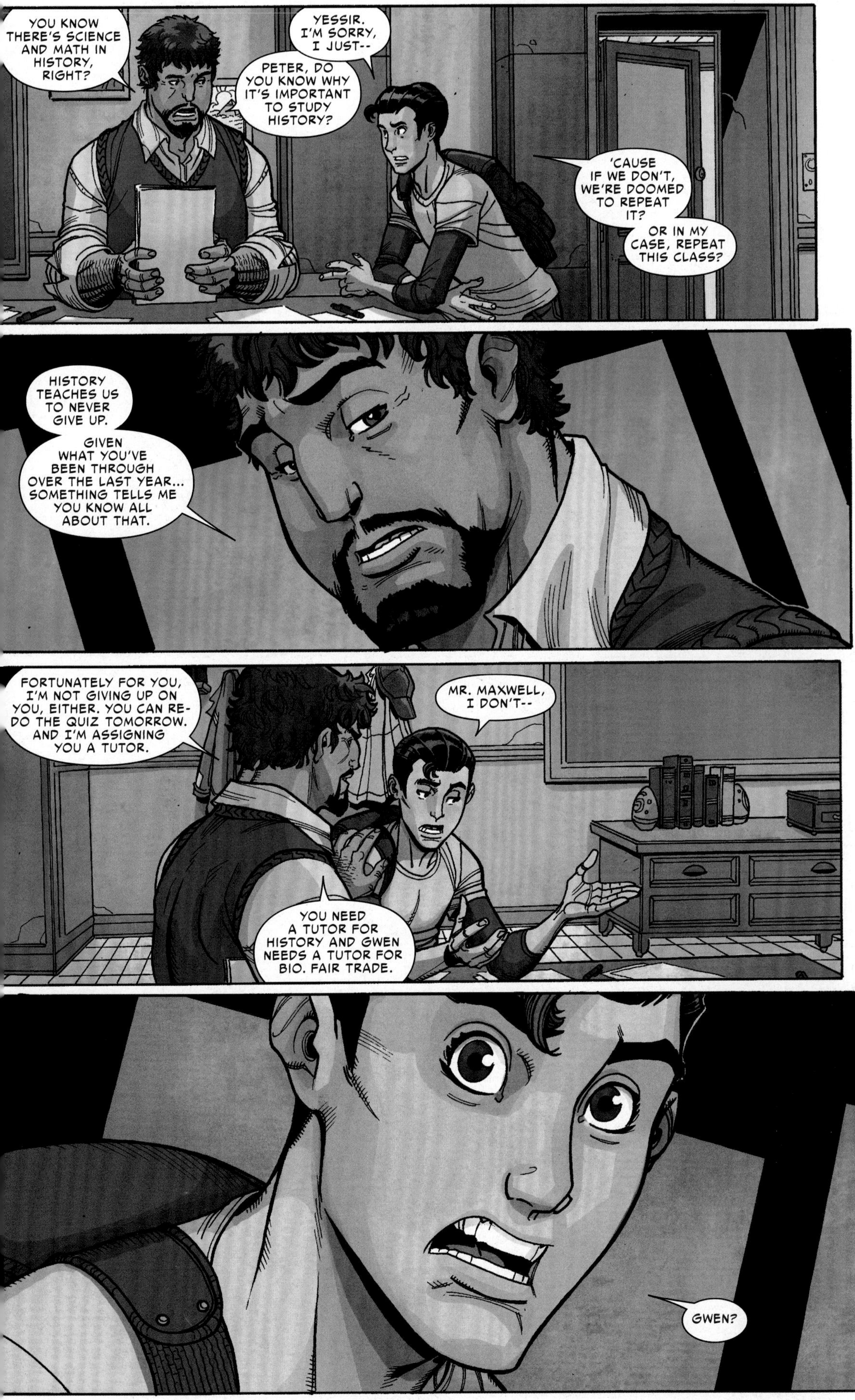

YOU KNOW THERE'S SCIENCE AND MATH IN HISTORY, RIGHT?
YESSIR. I'M SORRY, I JUST--
PETER, DO YOU KNOW WHY IT'S IMPORTANT TO STUDY HISTORY?
'CAUSE IF WE DON'T, WE'RE DOOMED TO REPEAT IT?
OR IN MY CASE, REPEAT THIS CLASS?
HISTORY TEACHES US TO NEVER GIVE UP.
GIVEN WHAT YOU'VE BEEN THROUGH OVER THE LAST YEAR... SOMETHING TELLS ME YOU KNOW ALL ABOUT THAT.
FORTUNATELY FOR YOU, I'M NOT GIVING UP ON YOU, EITHER. YOU CAN RE-DO THE QUIZ TOMORROW. AND I'M ASSIGNING YOU A TUTOR.
MR. MAXWELL, I DON'T--
YOU NEED A TUTOR FOR HISTORY AND GWEN NEEDS A TUTOR FOR BIO. FAIR TRADE.
GWEN?

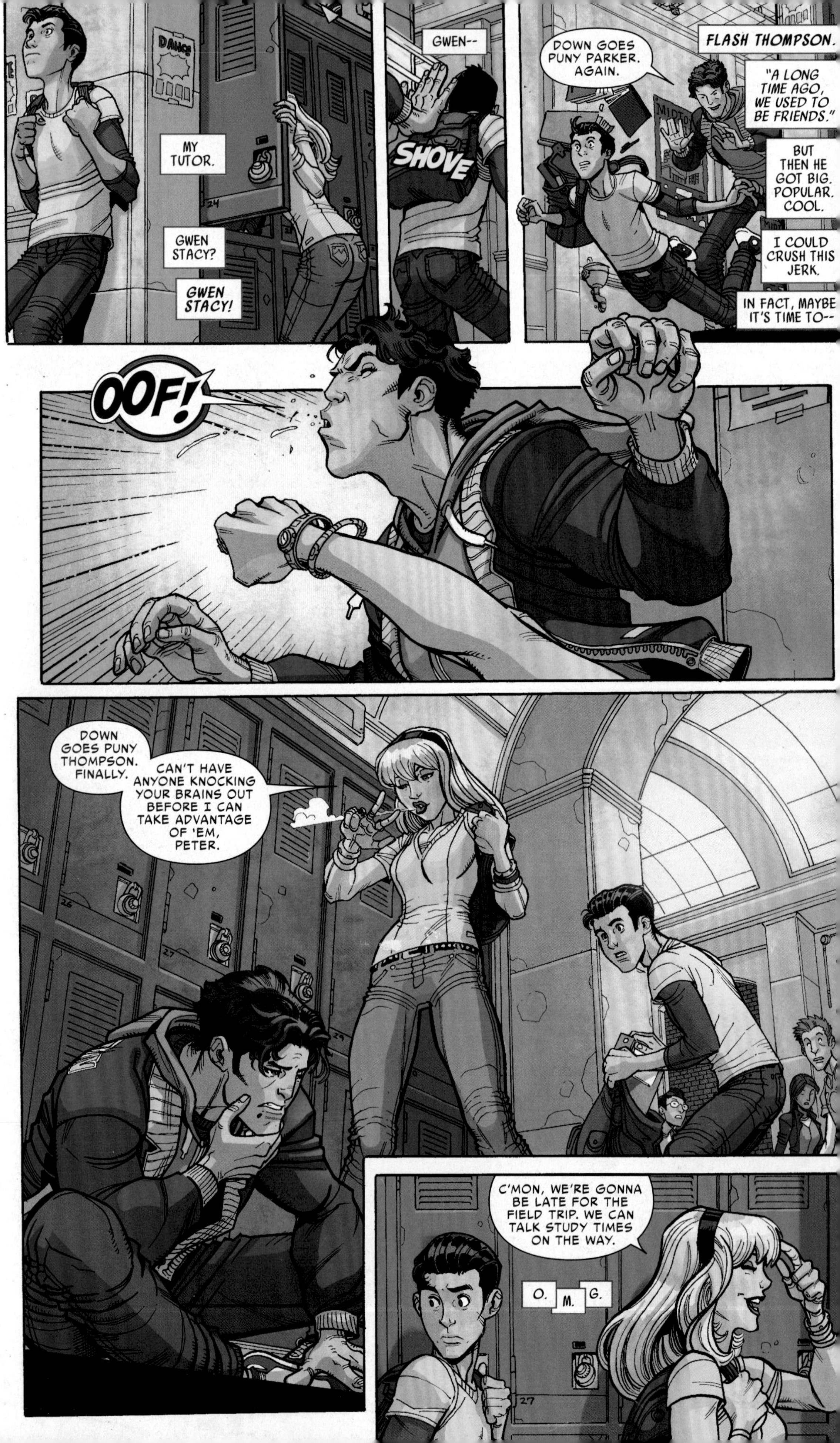

MY TUTOR.
GWEN STACY?
GWEN STACY!
GWEN--
SHOVE
DOWN GOES PUNY PARKER. AGAIN.
FLASH THOMPSON.
"A LONG TIME AGO, WE USED TO BE FRIENDS."
BUT THEN HE GOT BIG. POPULAR. COOL.
I COULD CRUSH THIS JERK.
IN FACT, MAYBE IT'S TIME TO--
OOF!
DOWN GOES PUNY THOMPSON. FINALLY.
CAN'T HAVE ANYONE KNOCKING YOUR BRAINS OUT BEFORE I CAN TAKE ADVANTAGE OF 'EM, PETER.
C'MON, WE'RE GONNA BE LATE FOR THE FIELD TRIP. WE CAN TALK STUDY TIMES ON THE WAY.
O.
M.
G.

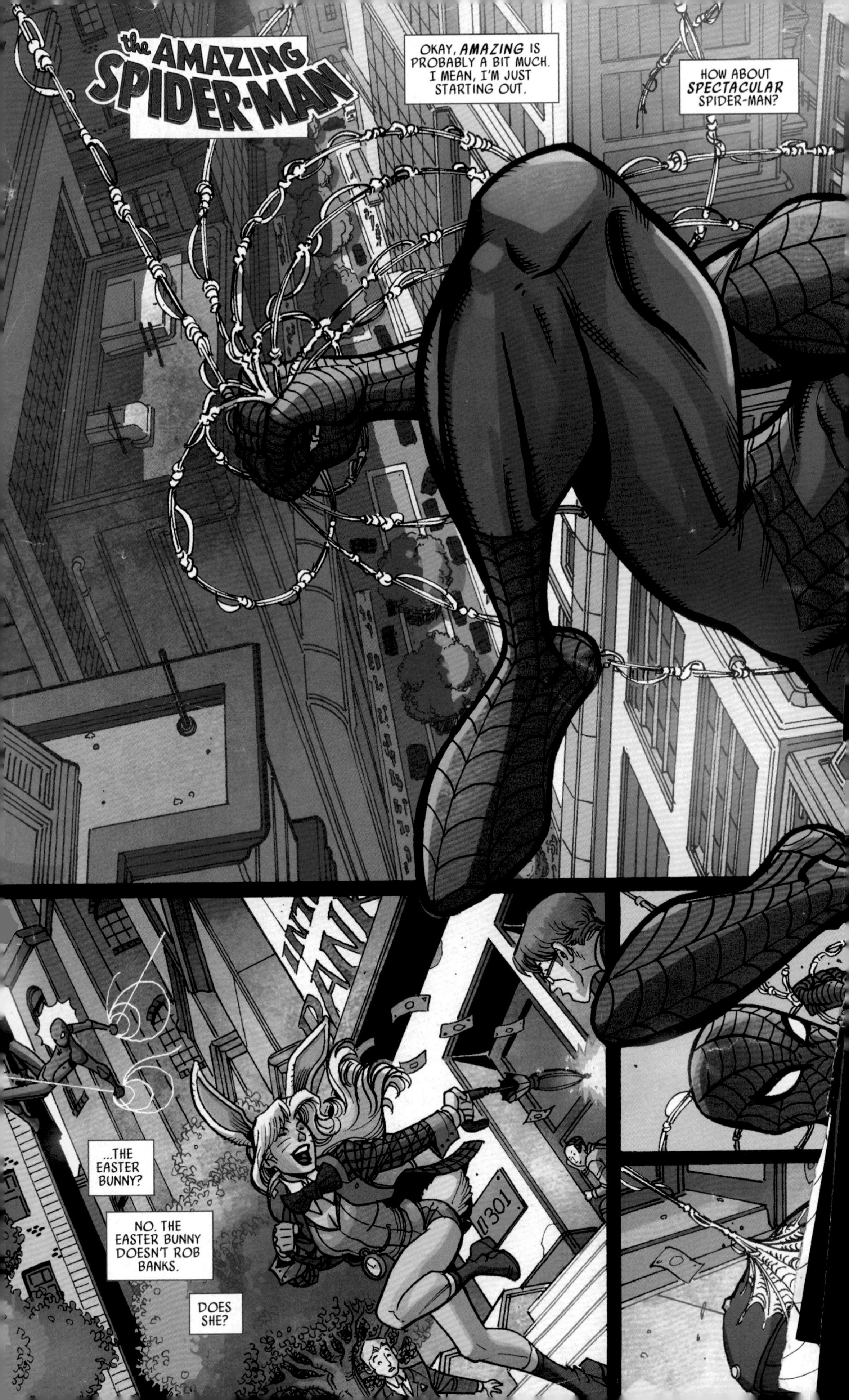
the AMAZING SPIDER-MAN
OKAY, AMAZING IS PROBABLY A BIT MUCH. I MEAN, I'M JUST STARTING OUT.
HOW ABOUT SPECTACULAR SPIDER-MAN?
...THE EASTER BUNNY?
NO. THE EASTER BUNNY DOESN'T ROB BANKS.
DOES SHE?
1301

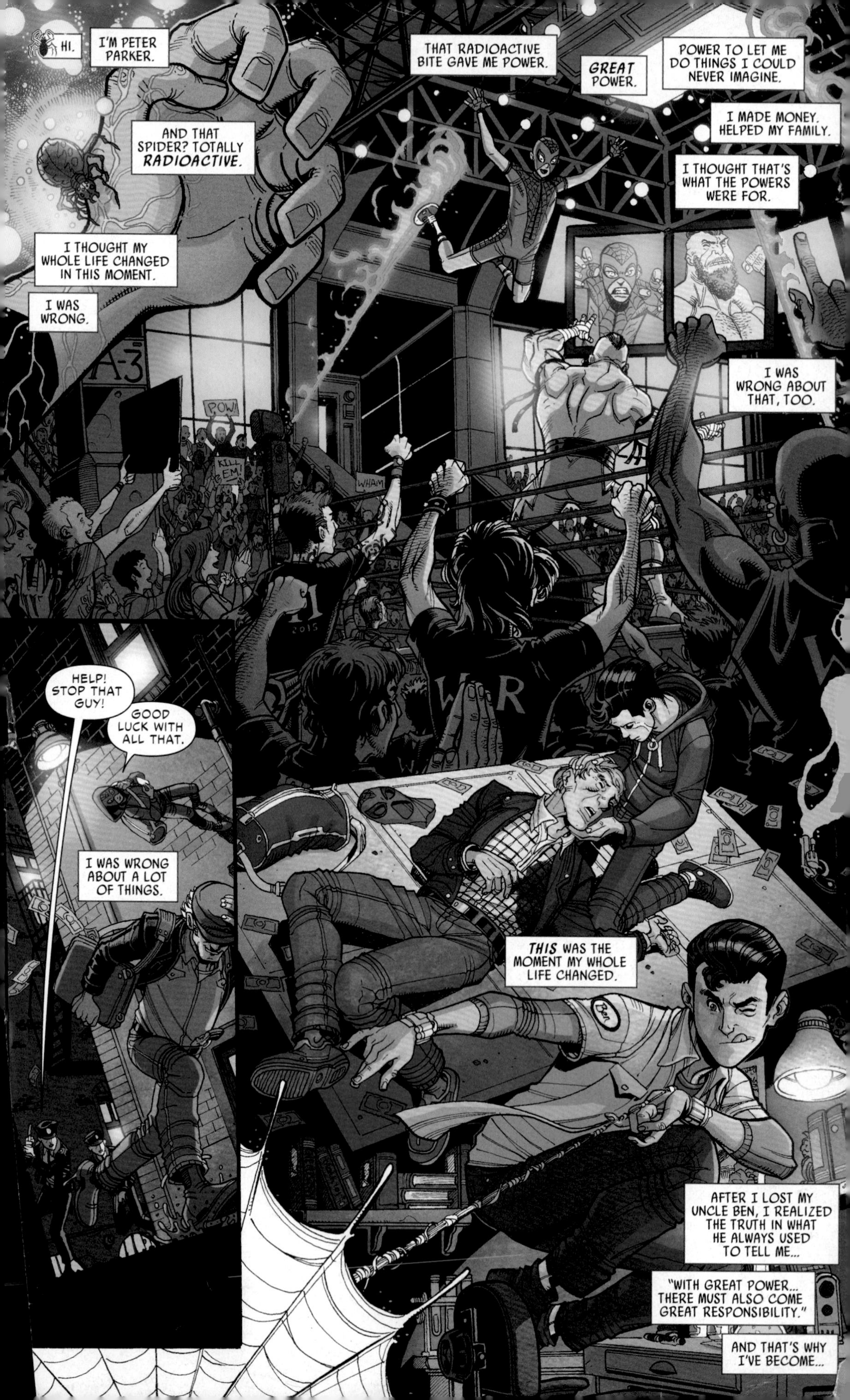
HI.
I'M PETER PARKER.
AND THAT SPIDER? TOTALLY *RADIOACTIVE.*
I THOUGHT MY WHOLE LIFE CHANGED IN THIS MOMENT.
I WAS WRONG.
THAT RADIOACTIVE BITE GAVE ME POWER.
*GREAT* POWER.
POWER TO LET ME DO THINGS I COULD NEVER IMAGINE.
I MADE MONEY. HELPED MY FAMILY.
I THOUGHT THAT'S WHAT THE POWERS WERE FOR.
POW!
KILL EM!
WHAM
I WAS WRONG ABOUT THAT, TOO.
HELP! STOP THAT GUY!
GOOD LUCK WITH ALL THAT.
I WAS WRONG ABOUT A LOT OF THINGS.
*THIS* WAS THE MOMENT MY WHOLE LIFE CHANGED.
AFTER I LOST MY UNCLE BEN, I REALIZED THE TRUTH IN WHAT HE ALWAYS USED TO TELL ME...
"WITH GREAT POWER... THERE MUST ALSO COME GREAT RESPONSIBILITY."
AND THAT'S WHY I'VE BECOME...

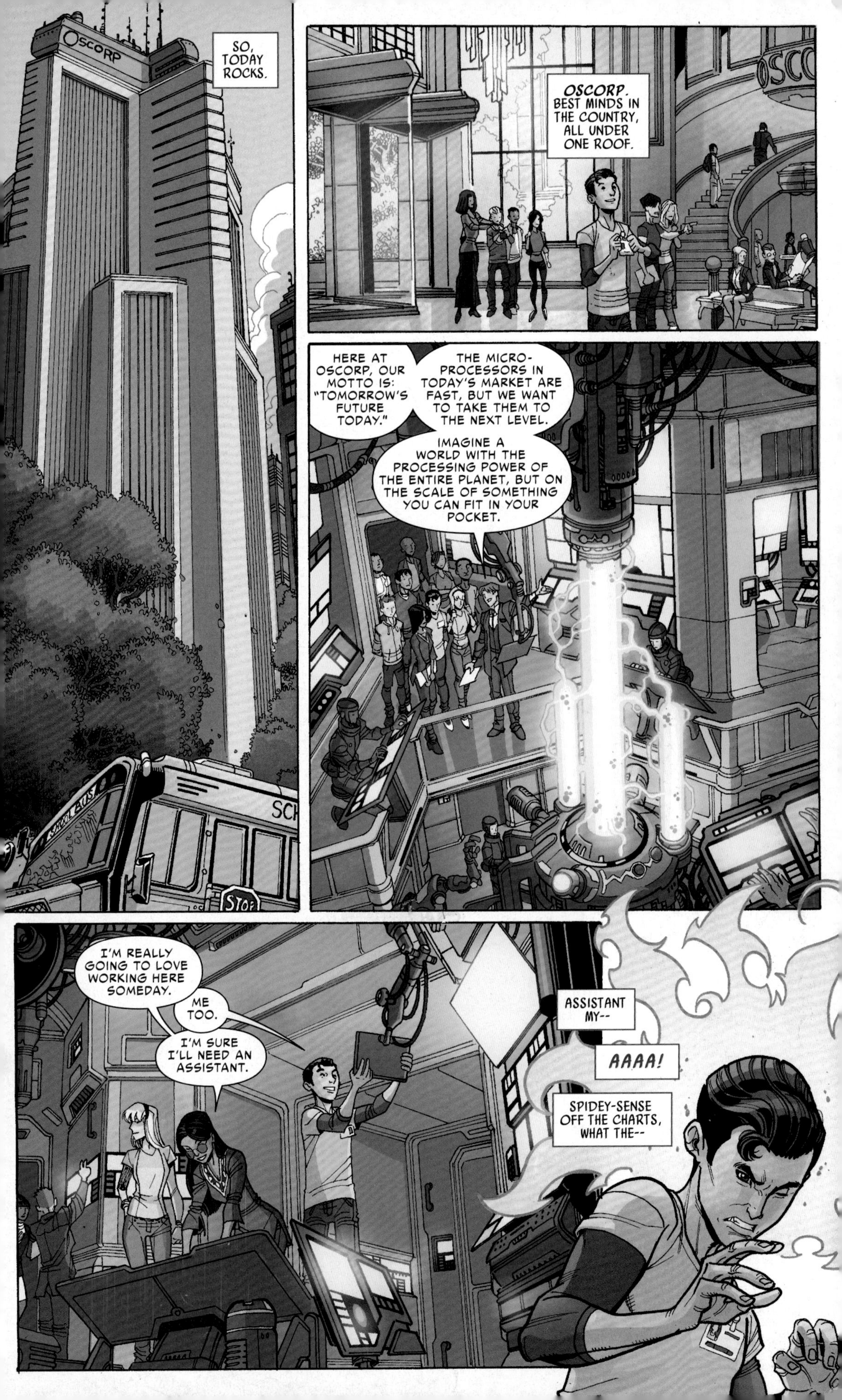

OSCORP
SO, TODAY ROCKS.
OSCORP. BEST MINDS IN THE COUNTRY, ALL UNDER ONE ROOF.
HERE AT OSCORP, OUR MOTTO IS: "TOMORROW'S FUTURE TODAY."
THE MICRO-PROCESSORS IN TODAY'S MARKET ARE FAST, BUT WE WANT TO TAKE THEM TO THE NEXT LEVEL.
IMAGINE A WORLD WITH THE PROCESSING POWER OF THE ENTIRE PLANET, BUT ON THE SCALE OF SOMETHING YOU CAN FIT IN YOUR POCKET.
STOP
I'M REALLY GOING TO LOVE WORKING HERE SOMEDAY.
ME TOO.
I'M SURE I'LL NEED AN ASSISTANT.
ASSISTANT MY--
AAAA!
SPIDEY-SENSE OFF THE CHARTS, WHAT THE--

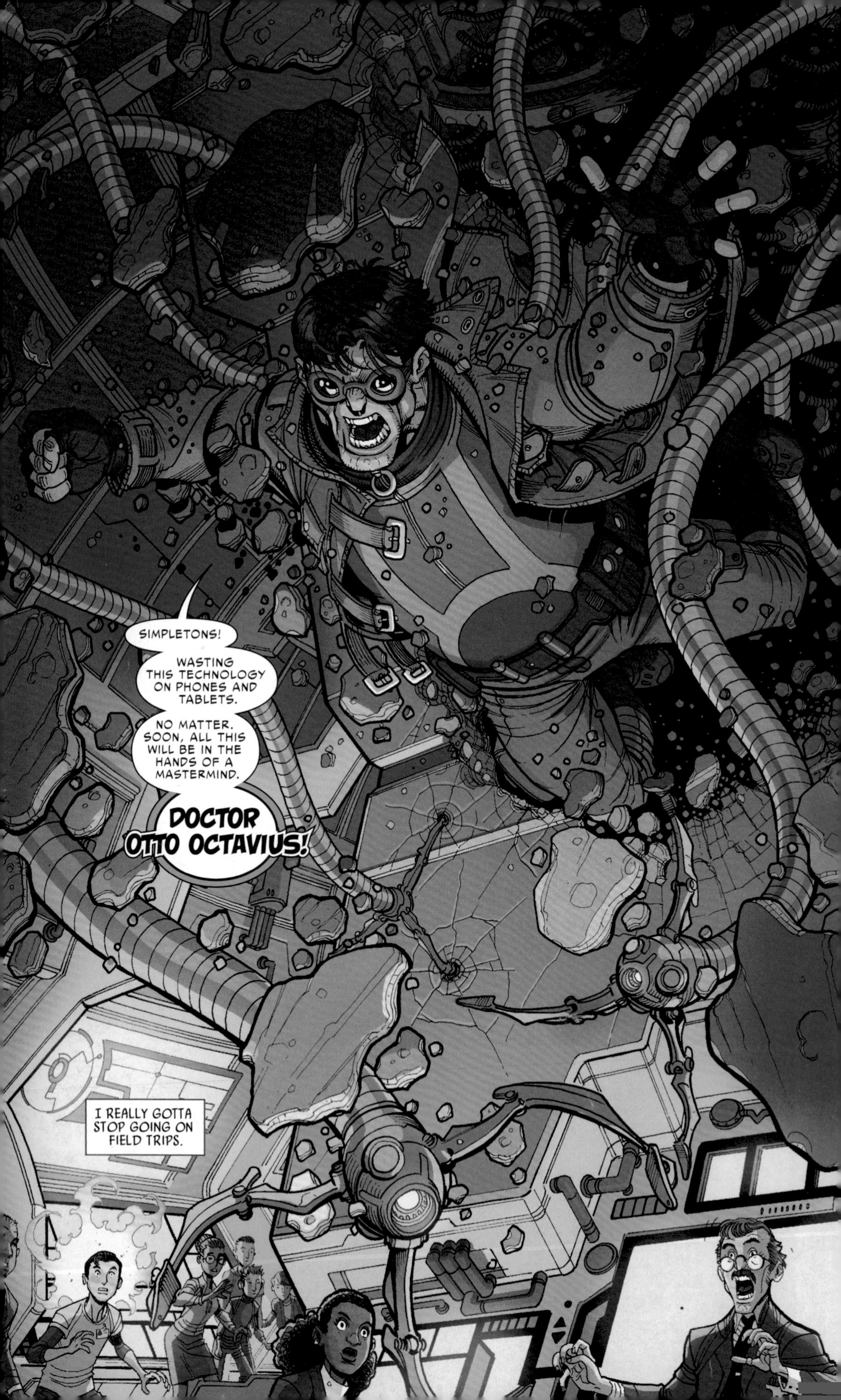

SIMPLETONS!
WASTING THIS TECHNOLOGY ON PHONES AND TABLETS.
NO MATTER. SOON, ALL THIS WILL BE IN THE HANDS OF A MASTERMIND.
DOCTOR OTTO OCTAVIUS!
I REALLY GOTTA STOP GOING ON FIELD TRIPS.

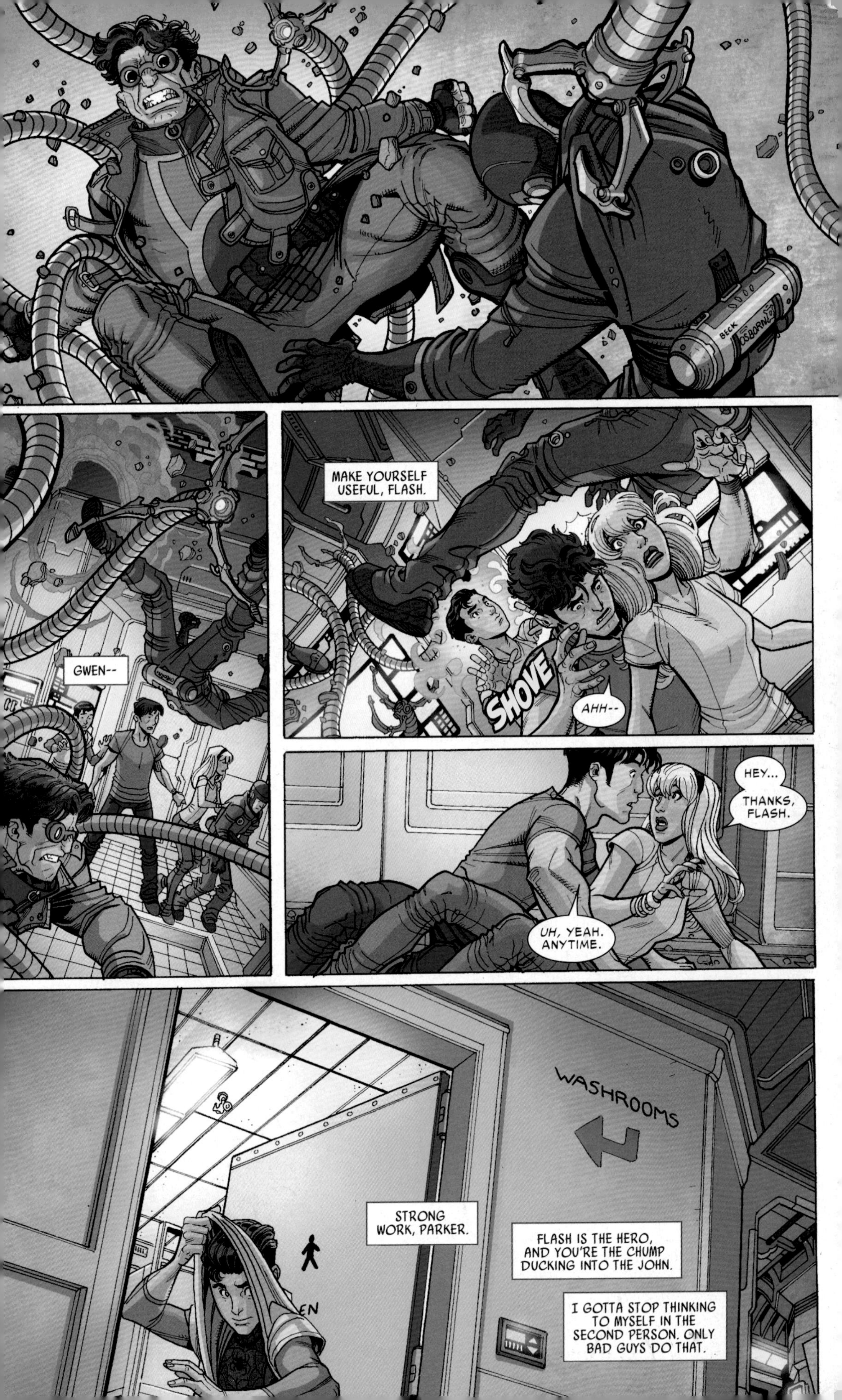
BECK
OSBORN
GWEN--
MAKE YOURSELF USEFUL, FLASH.
SHOVE
AHH--
HEY... THANKS, FLASH.
UH, YEAH. ANYTIME.
WASHROOMS
STRONG WORK, PARKER.
FLASH IS THE HERO, AND YOU'RE THE CHUMP DUCKING INTO THE JOHN.
I GOTTA STOP THINKING TO MYSELF IN THE SECOND PERSON. ONLY BAD GUYS DO THAT.

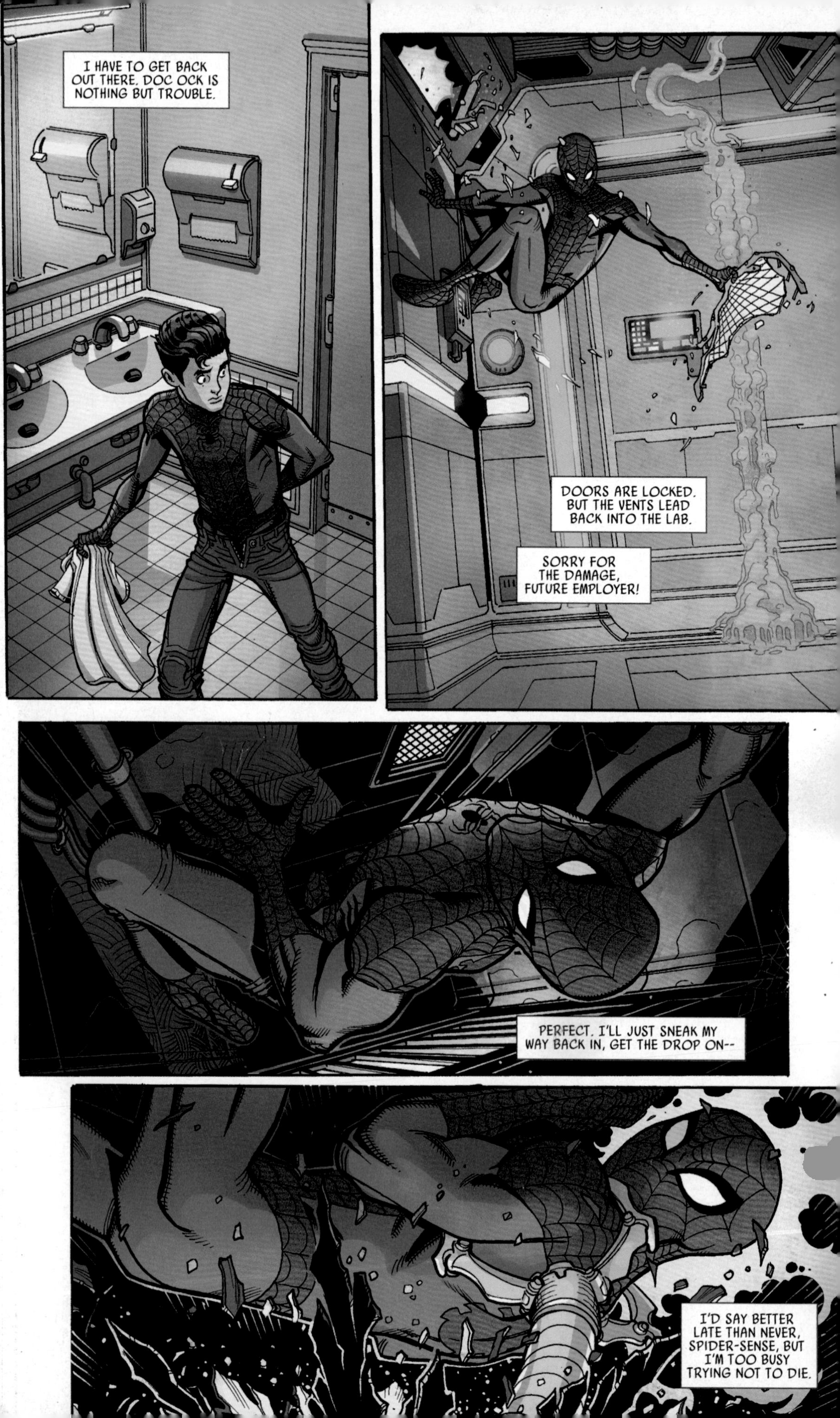
I HAVE TO GET BACK OUT THERE. DOC OCK IS NOTHING BUT TROUBLE.
DOORS ARE LOCKED. BUT THE VENTS LEAD BACK INTO THE LAB.
SORRY FOR THE DAMAGE, FUTURE EMPLOYER!
PERFECT. I'LL JUST SNEAK MY WAY BACK IN, GET THE DROP ON--
I'D SAY BETTER LATE THAN NEVER, SPIDER-SENSE, BUT I'M TOO BUSY TRYING NOT TO DIE.

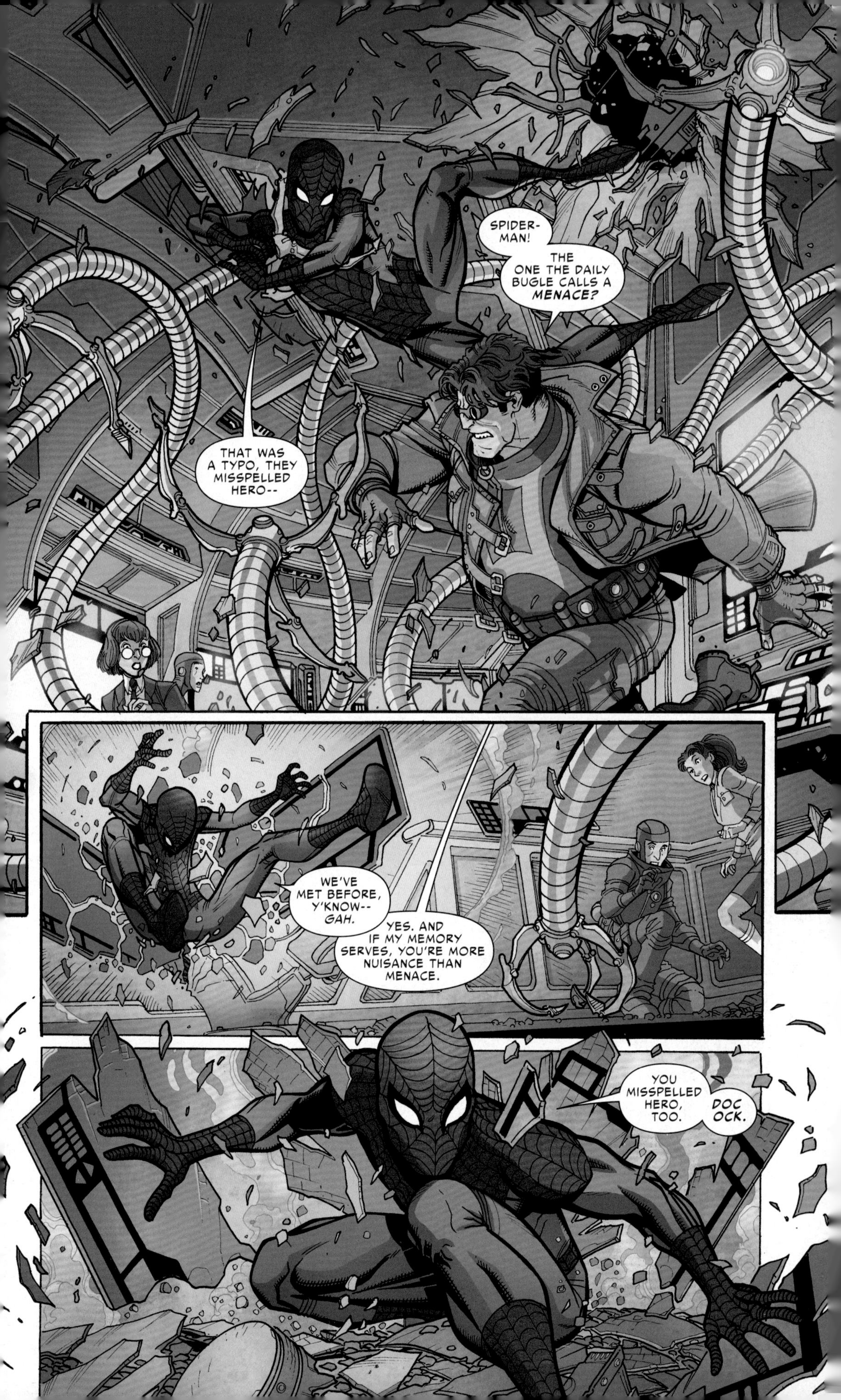
SPIDER-MAN!
THE ONE THE DAILY BUGLE CALLS A MENACE?
THAT WAS A TYPO, THEY MISSPELLED HERO--
WE'VE MET BEFORE, Y'KNOW-- GAH.
YES. AND IF MY MEMORY SERVES, YOU'RE MORE NUISANCE THAN MENACE.
YOU MISSPELLED HERO, TOO.
DOC OCK.

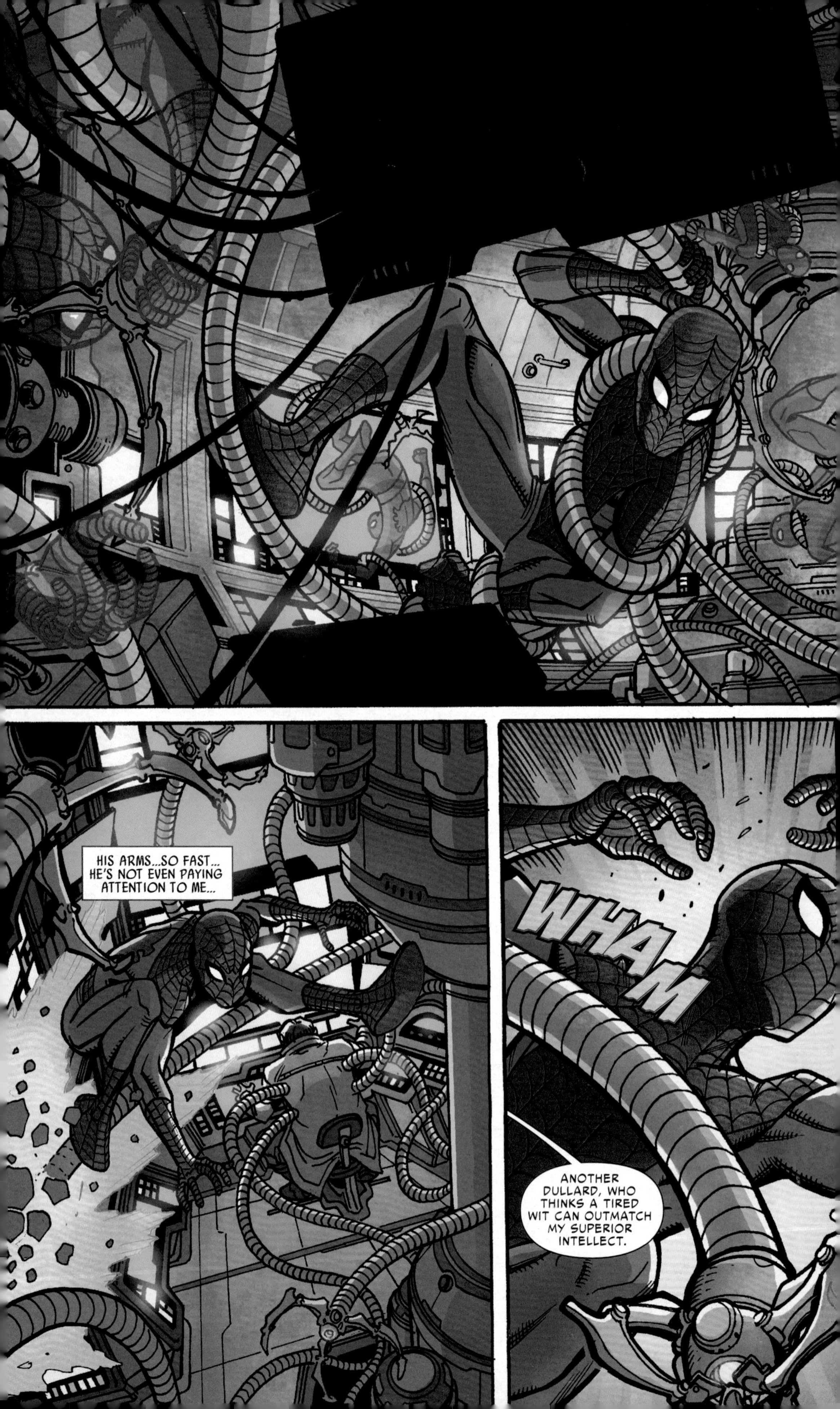
HIS ARMS...SO FAST... HE'S NOT EVEN PAYING ATTENTION TO ME...
WHAM
ANOTHER DULLARD, WHO THINKS A TIRED WIT CAN OUTMATCH MY SUPERIOR INTELLECT.

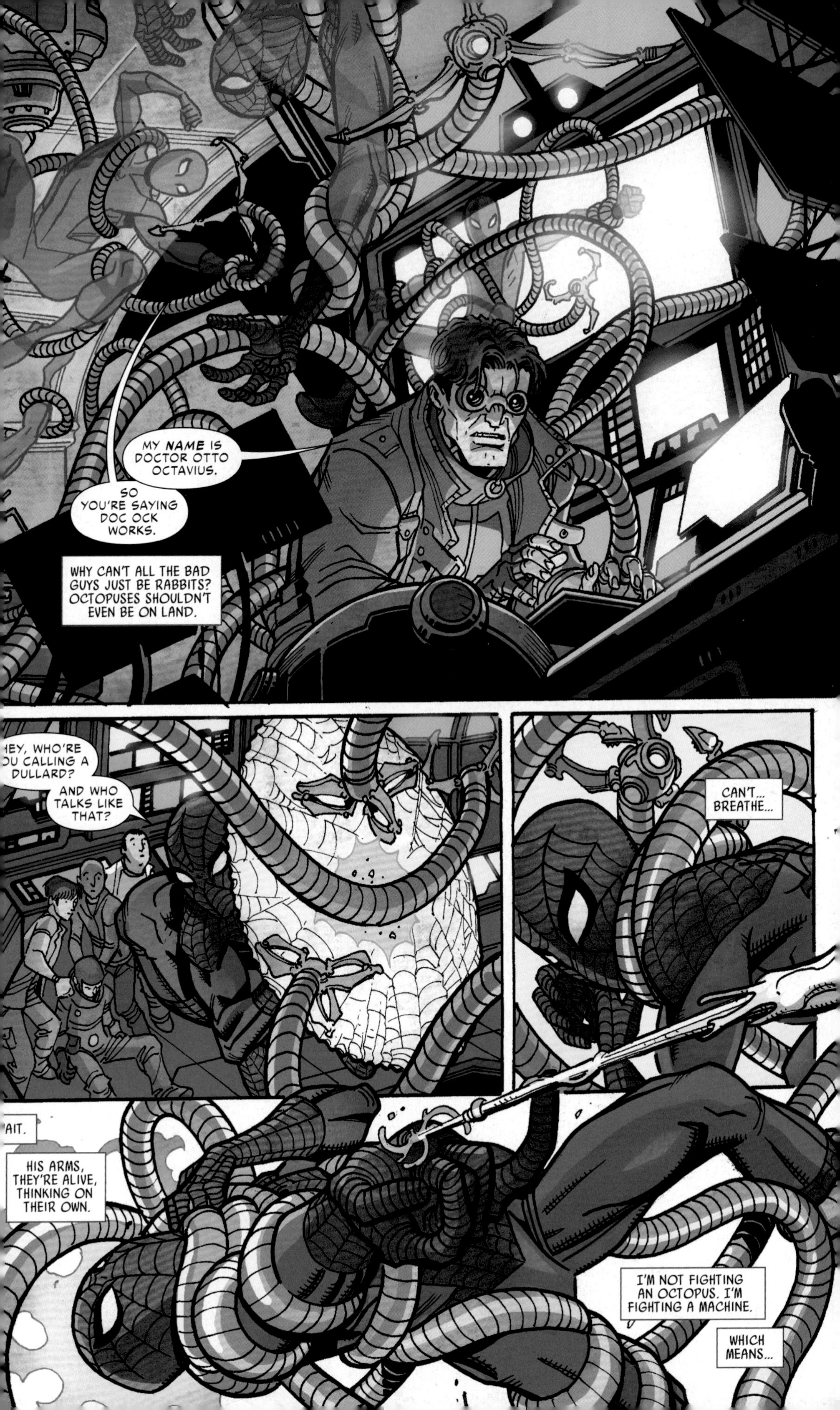

MY NAME IS DOCTOR OTTO OCTAVIUS.
SO YOU'RE SAYING DOC OCK WORKS.
WHY CAN'T ALL THE BAD GUYS JUST BE RABBITS? OCTOPUSES SHOULDN'T EVEN BE ON LAND.
HEY, WHO'RE YOU CALLING A DULLARD?
AND WHO TALKS LIKE THAT?
CAN'T... BREATHE...
AIT.
HIS ARMS, THEY'RE ALIVE, THINKING ON THEIR OWN.
I'M NOT FIGHTING AN OCTOPUS. I'M FIGHTING A MACHINE.
WHICH MEANS...

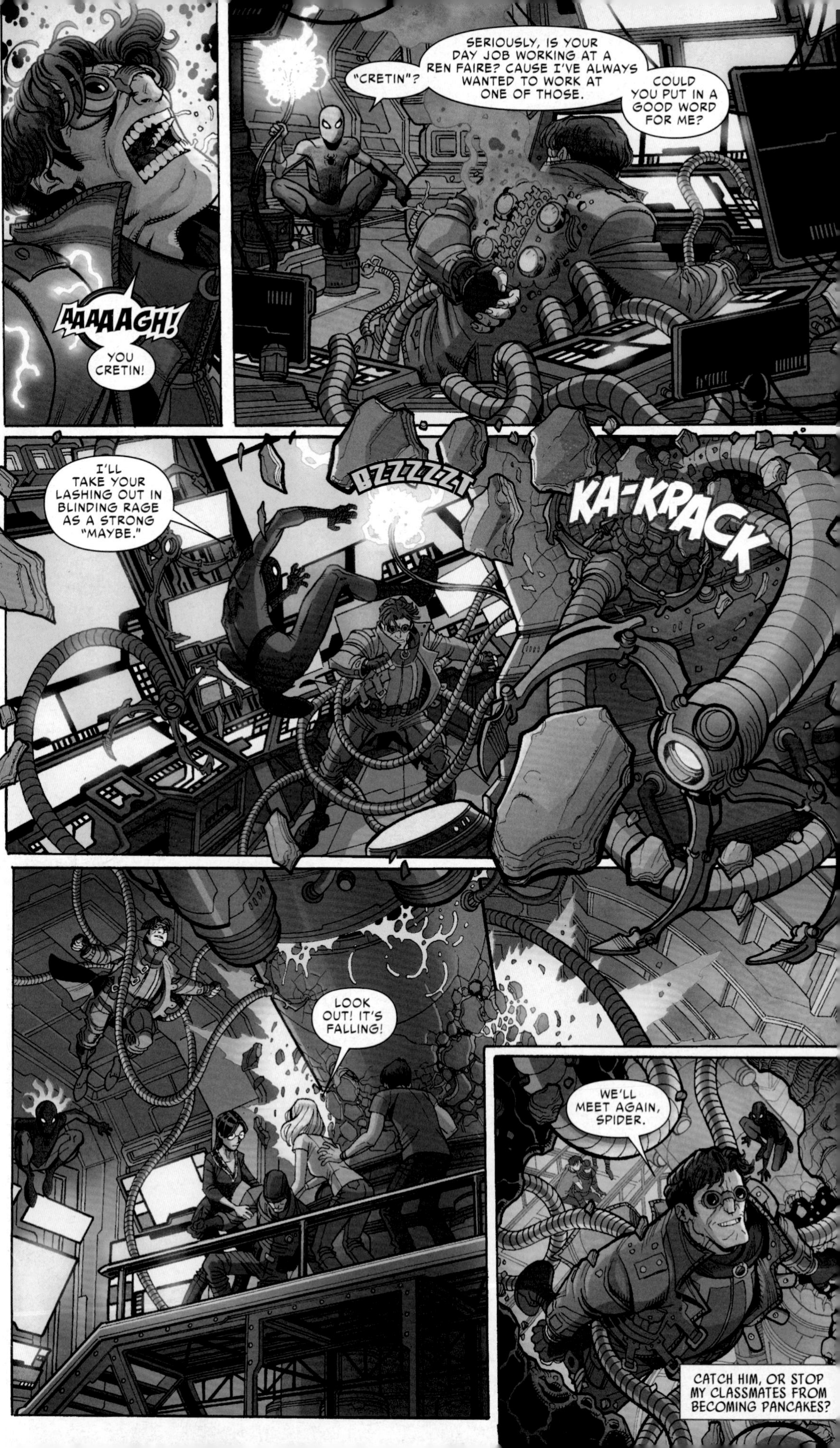
AAAAAGH!
YOU CRETIN!
"CRETIN"?
SERIOUSLY, IS YOUR DAY JOB WORKING AT A REN FAIRE? CAUSE I'VE ALWAYS WANTED TO WORK AT ONE OF THOSE.
COULD YOU PUT IN A GOOD WORD FOR ME?
I'LL TAKE YOUR LASHING OUT IN BLINDING RAGE AS A STRONG "MAYBE."
BZZZZZZT
KA-KRACK
LOOK OUT! IT'S FALLING!
WE'LL MEET AGAIN, SPIDER.
CATCH HIM, OR STOP MY CLASSMATES FROM BECOMING PANCAKES?

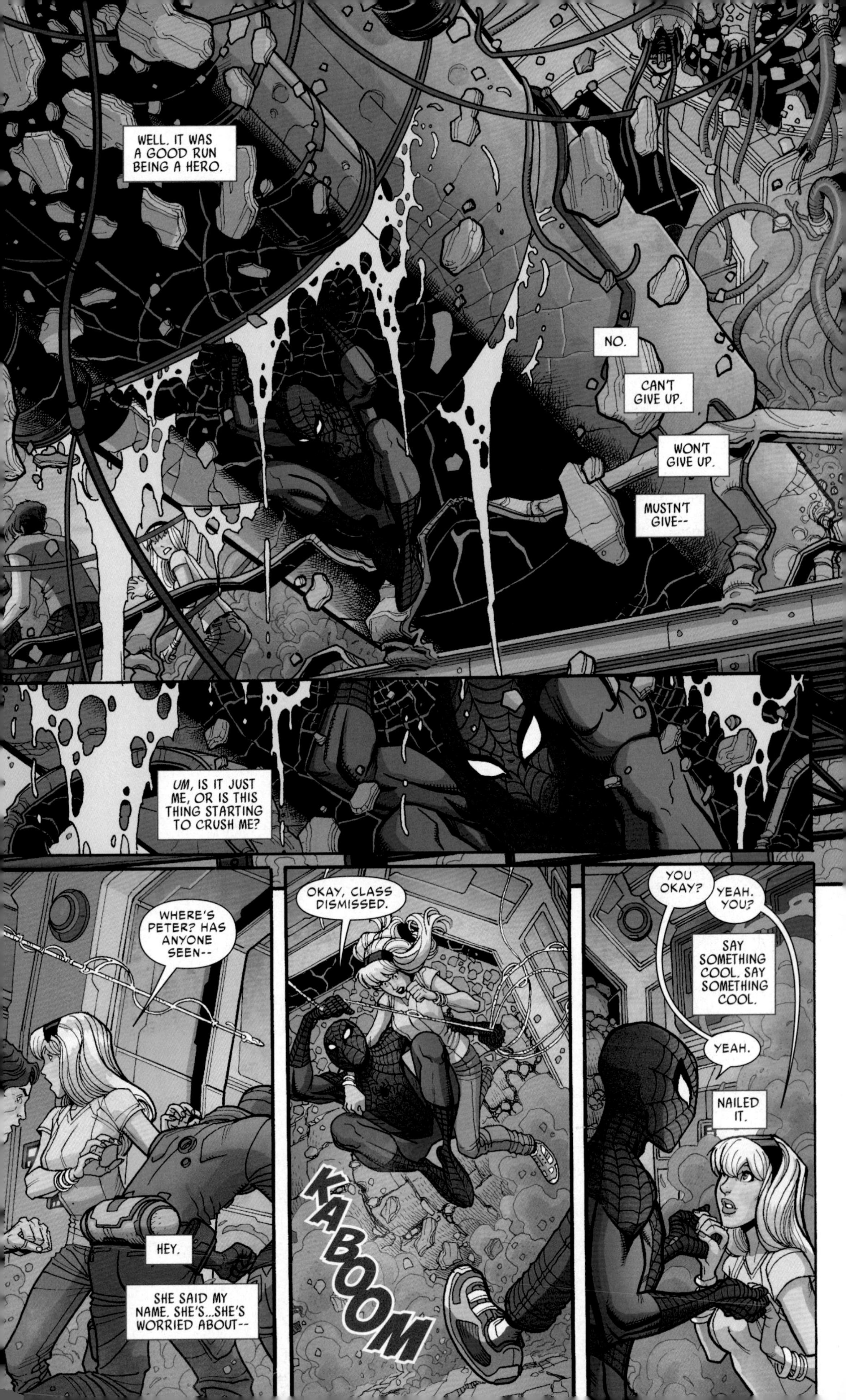
WELL. IT WAS A GOOD RUN BEING A HERO.
NO.
CAN'T GIVE UP.
WON'T GIVE UP.
MUSTN'T GIVE--
UM, IS IT JUST ME, OR IS THIS THING STARTING TO CRUSH ME?
WHERE'S PETER? HAS ANYONE SEEN--
HEY.
SHE SAID MY NAME. SHE'S...SHE'S WORRIED ABOUT--
OKAY, CLASS DISMISSED.
KABOOOM
YOU OKAY?
YEAH. YOU?
SAY SOMETHING COOL. SAY SOMETHING COOL.
YEAH.
NAILED IT.

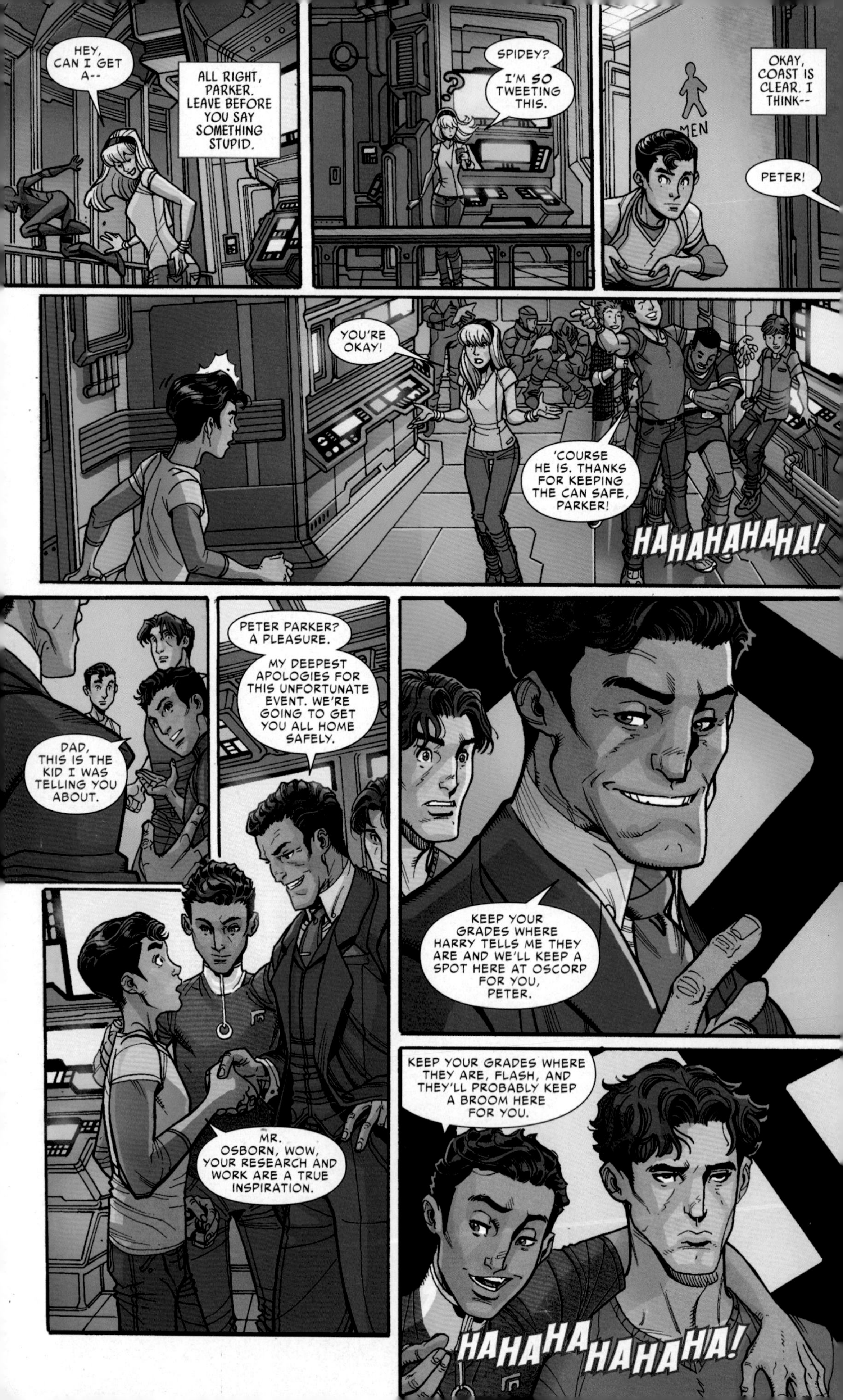
HEY, CAN I GET A--
ALL RIGHT, PARKER. LEAVE BEFORE YOU SAY SOMETHING STUPID.
SPIDEY?
I'M SO TWEETING THIS.
MEN
OKAY, COAST IS CLEAR. I THINK--
PETER!
YOU'RE OKAY!
'COURSE HE IS. THANKS FOR KEEPING THE CAN SAFE, PARKER!
HAHAHAHAHA!
DAD, THIS IS THE KID I WAS TELLING YOU ABOUT.
PETER PARKER? A PLEASURE.
MY DEEPEST APOLOGIES FOR THIS UNFORTUNATE EVENT. WE'RE GOING TO GET YOU ALL HOME SAFELY.
MR. OSBORN, WOW, YOUR RESEARCH AND WORK ARE A TRUE INSPIRATION.
KEEP YOUR GRADES WHERE HARRY TELLS ME THEY ARE AND WE'LL KEEP A SPOT HERE AT OSCORP FOR YOU, PETER.
KEEP YOUR GRADES WHERE THEY ARE, FLASH, AND THEY'LL PROBABLY KEEP A BROOM HERE FOR YOU.
HAHAHA HAHAHA!

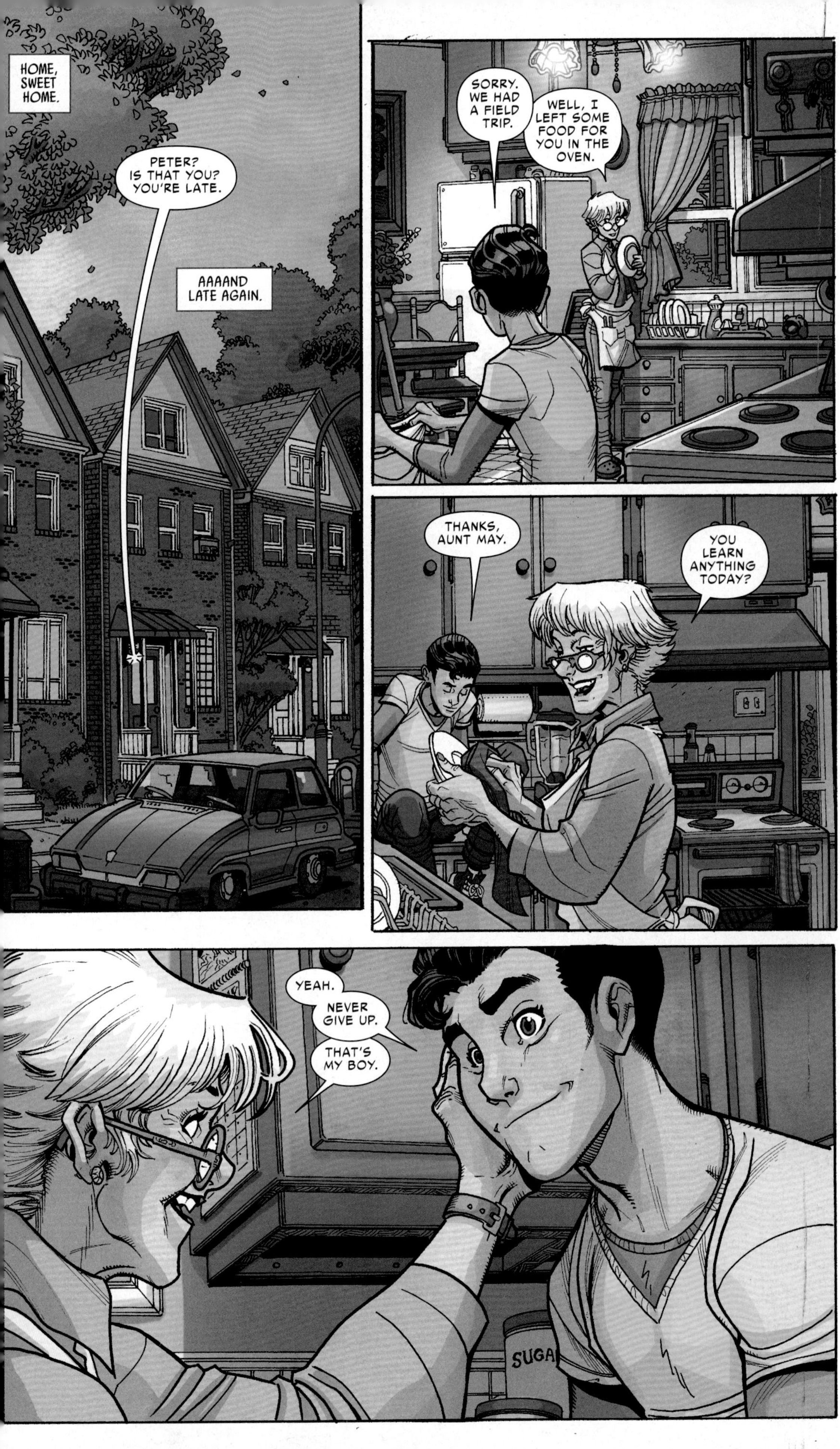
HOME, SWEET HOME.
PETER? IS THAT YOU? YOU'RE LATE.
AAAAND LATE AGAIN.
SORRY. WE HAD A FIELD TRIP.
WELL, I LEFT SOME FOOD FOR YOU IN THE OVEN.
THANKS, AUNT MAY.
YOU LEARN ANYTHING TODAY?
YEAH.
NEVER GIVE UP.
THAT'S MY BOY.
SUGA

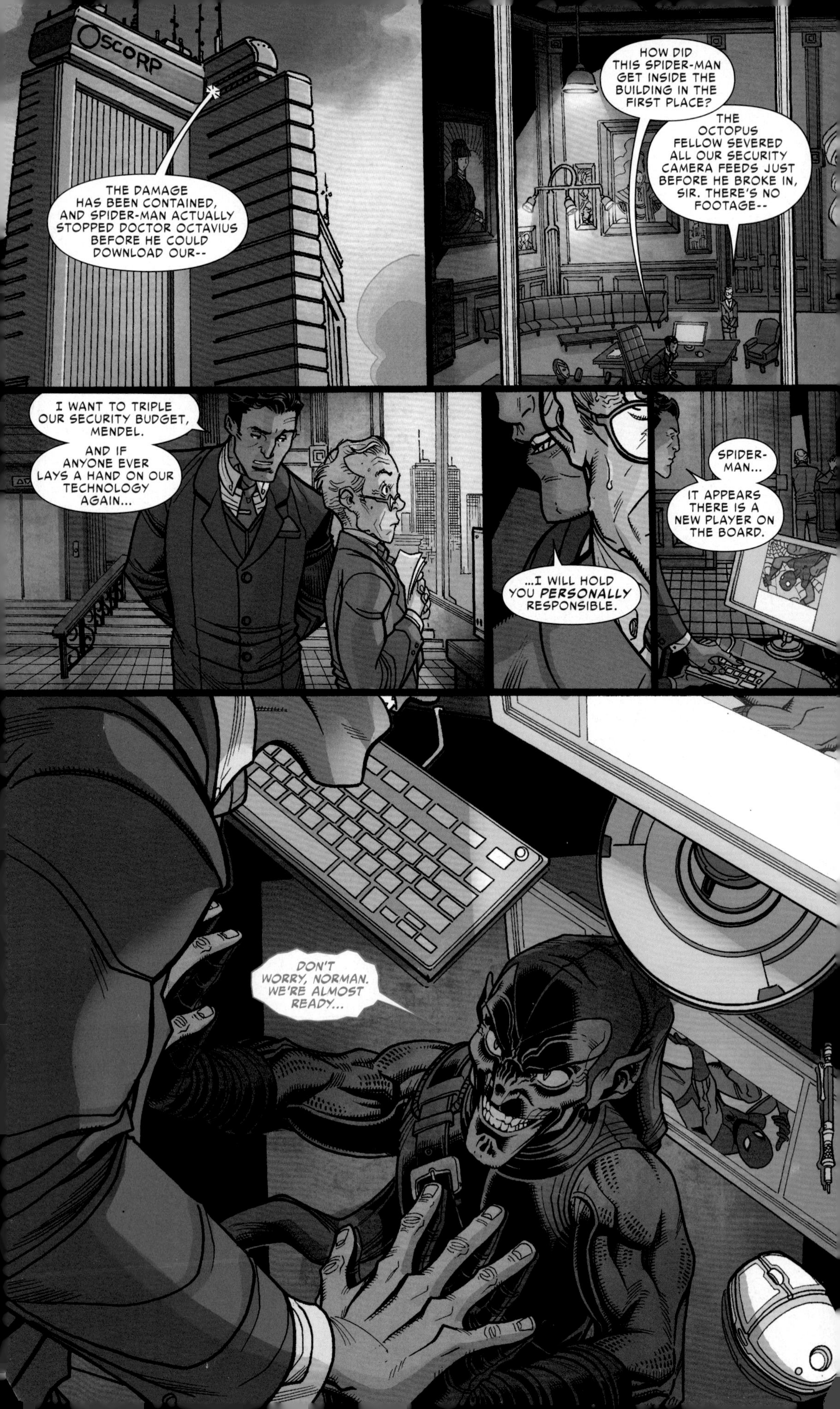

THE DAMAGE HAS BEEN CONTAINED, AND SPIDER-MAN ACTUALLY STOPPED DOCTOR OCTAVIUS BEFORE HE COULD DOWNLOAD OUR--
HOW DID THIS SPIDER-MAN GET INSIDE THE BUILDING IN THE FIRST PLACE?
THE OCTOPUS FELLOW SEVERED ALL OUR SECURITY CAMERA FEEDS JUST BEFORE HE BROKE IN, SIR. THERE'S NO FOOTAGE--
I WANT TO TRIPLE OUR SECURITY BUDGET, MENDEL.
AND IF ANYONE EVER LAYS A HAND ON OUR TECHNOLOGY AGAIN...
...I WILL HOLD YOU PERSONALLY RESPONSIBLE.
SPIDER-MAN...
IT APPEARS THERE IS A NEW PLAYER ON THE BOARD.
DON'T WORRY, NORMAN. WE'RE ALMOST READY...

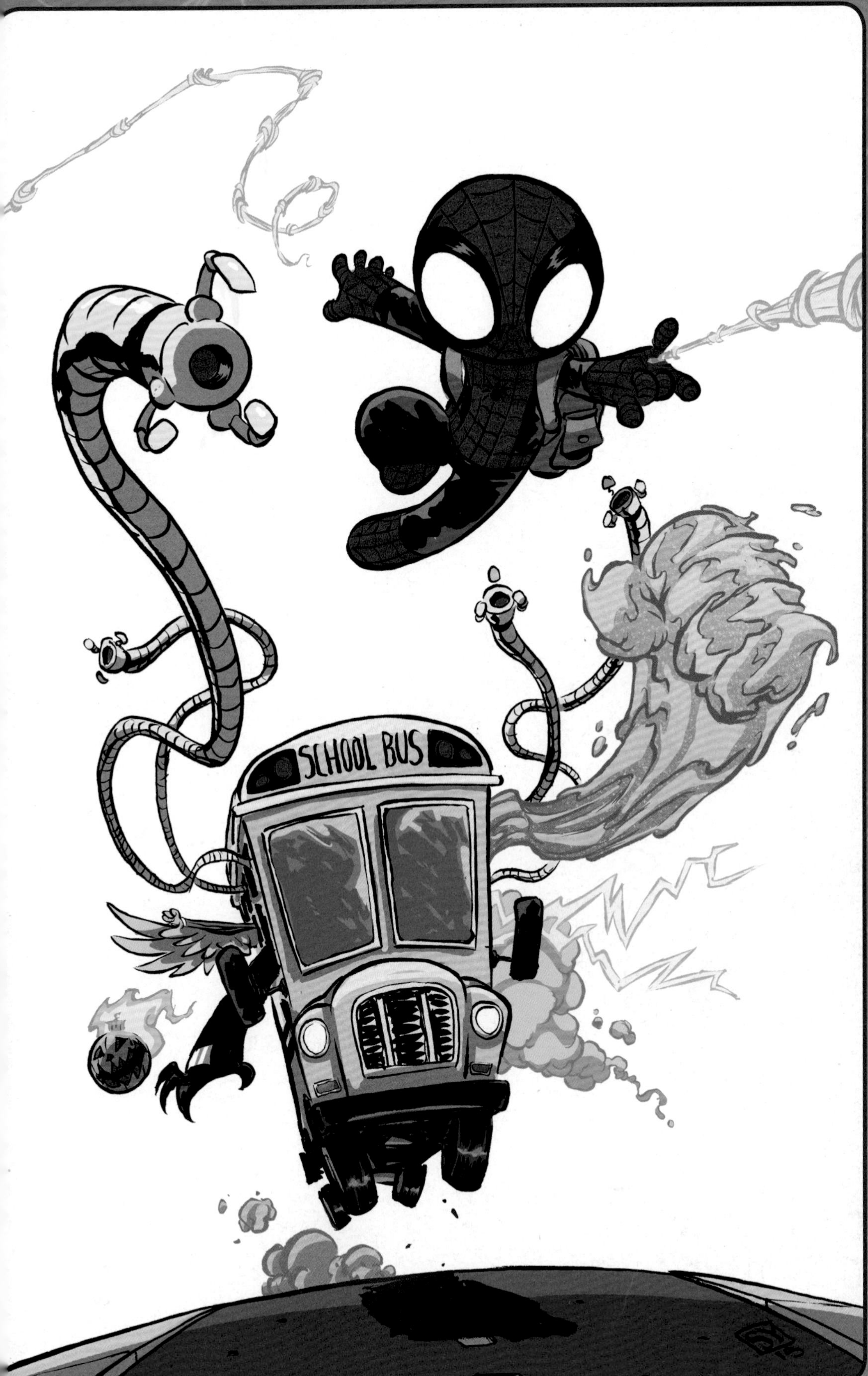
SCHOOL BUS

**SKOTTIE YOUNG**
**1 VARIANT**

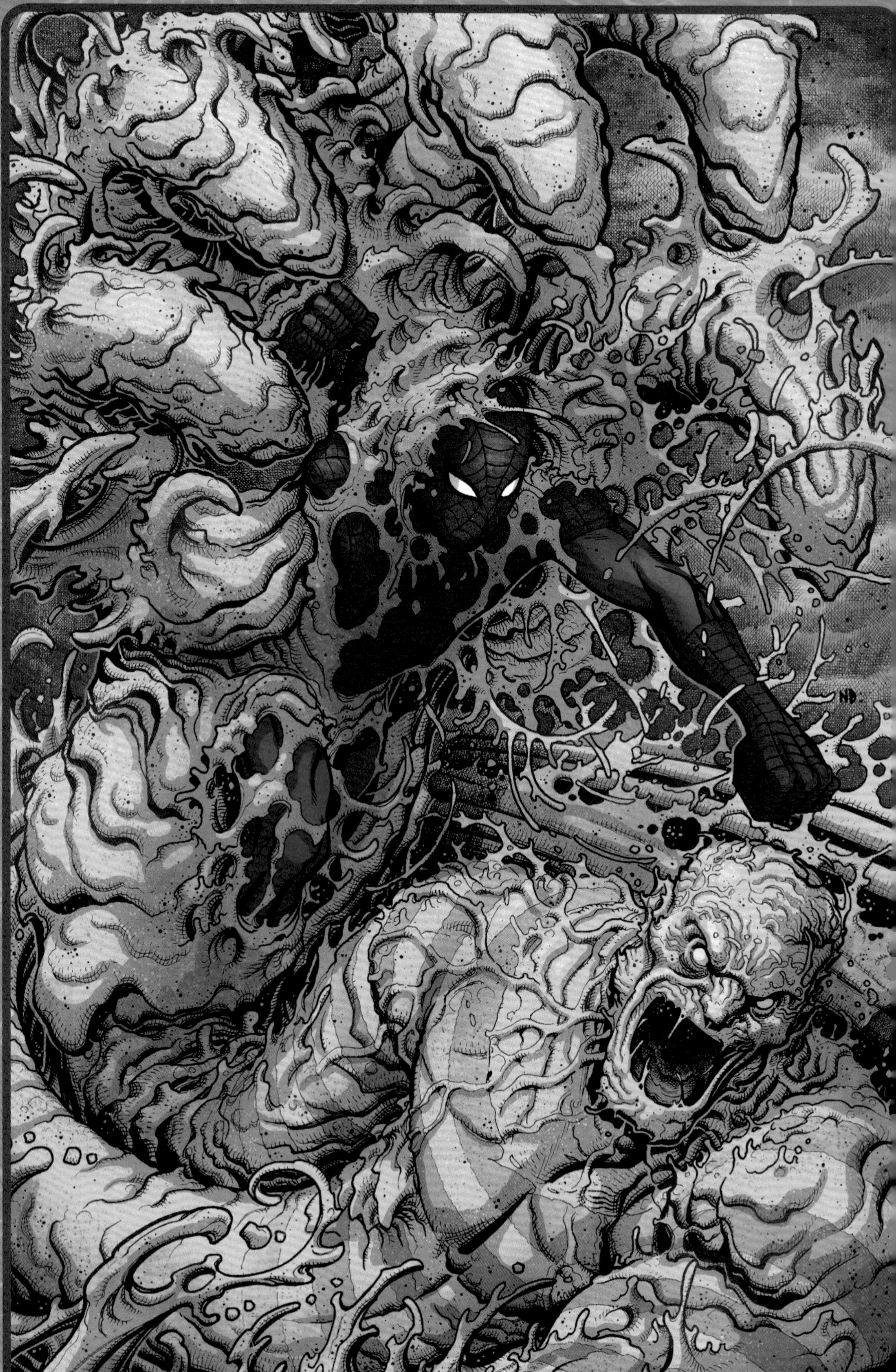

# 2

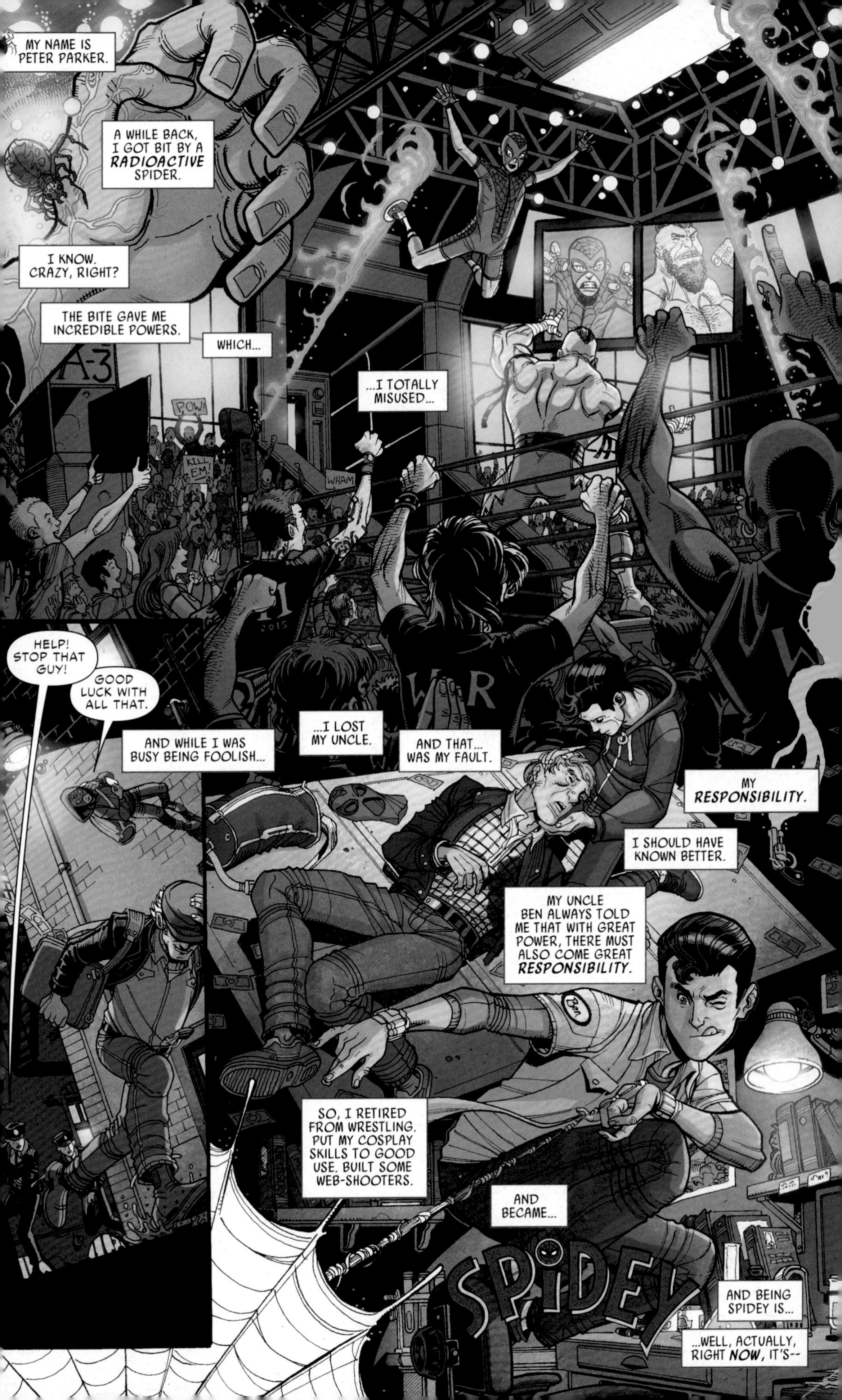
MY NAME IS PETER PARKER.
A WHILE BACK, I GOT BIT BY A RADIOACTIVE SPIDER.
I KNOW. CRAZY, RIGHT?
THE BITE GAVE ME INCREDIBLE POWERS.
WHICH...
...I TOTALLY MISUSED...
POW
KILL EM!
WHAM
HELP! STOP THAT GUY!
GOOD LUCK WITH ALL THAT.
AND WHILE I WAS BUSY BEING FOOLISH...
...I LOST MY UNCLE.
AND THAT... WAS MY FAULT.
MY RESPONSIBILITY.
I SHOULD HAVE KNOWN BETTER.
MY UNCLE BEN ALWAYS TOLD ME THAT WITH GREAT POWER, THERE MUST ALSO COME GREAT RESPONSIBILITY.
SO, I RETIRED FROM WRESTLING. PUT MY COSPLAY SKILLS TO GOOD USE. BUILT SOME WEB-SHOOTERS.
AND BECAME...
SPIDEY
AND BEING SPIDEY IS...
...WELL, ACTUALLY, RIGHT NOW, IT'S--

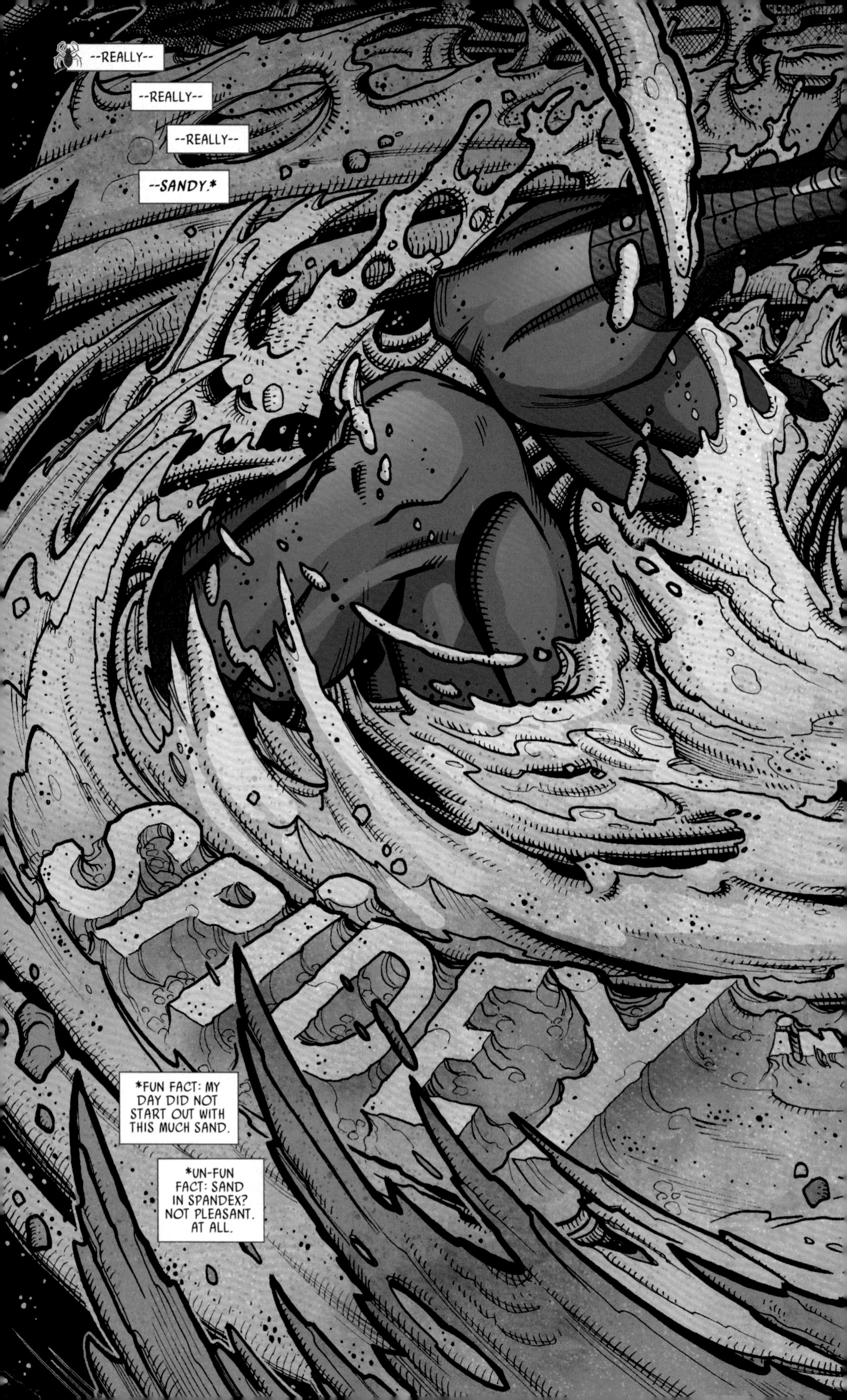
--REALLY--
--REALLY--
--REALLY--
--SANDY.*
*FUN FACT: MY DAY DID NOT START OUT WITH THIS MUCH SAND.
*UN-FUN FACT: SAND IN SPANDEX? NOT PLEASANT. AT ALL.

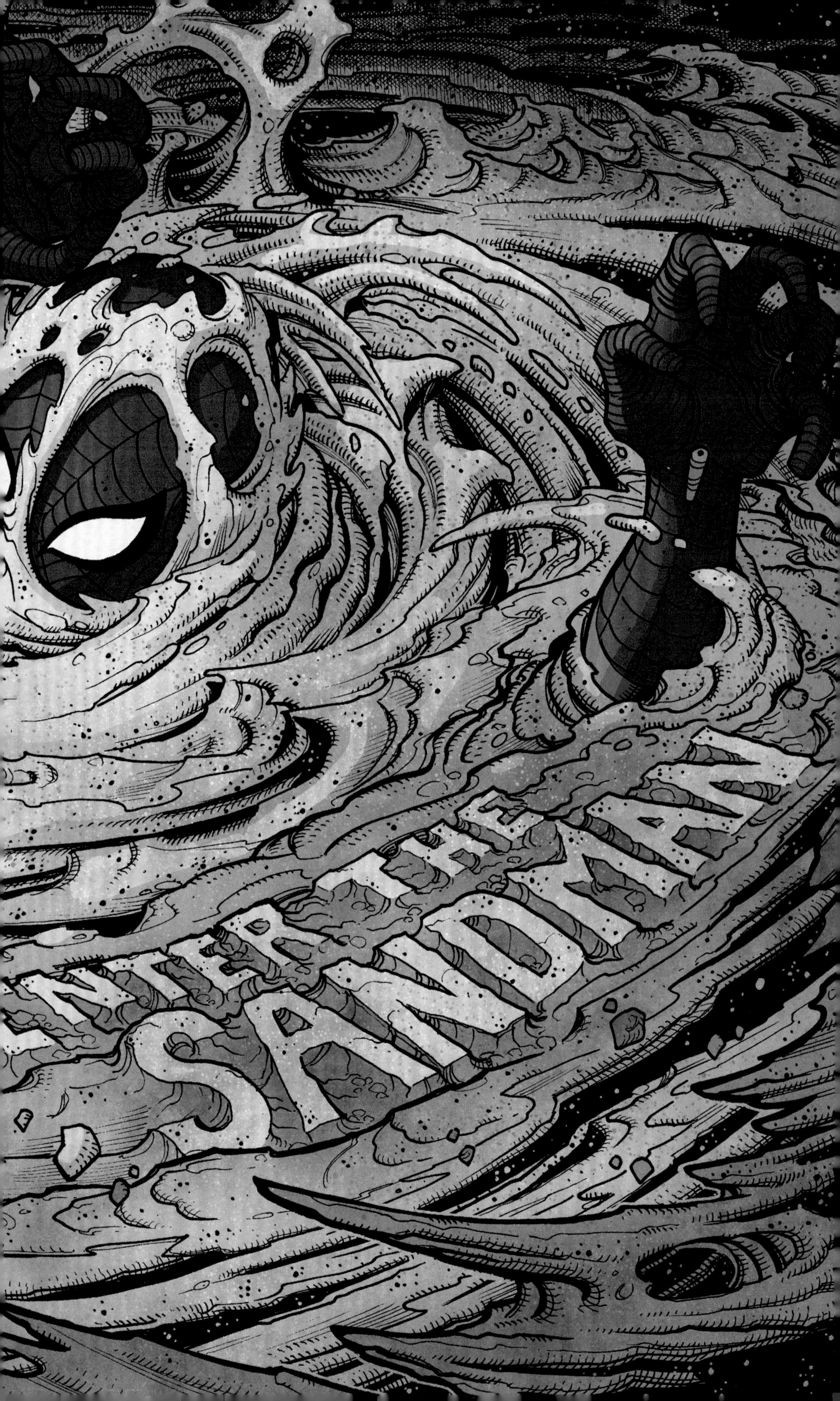
SANDMAN

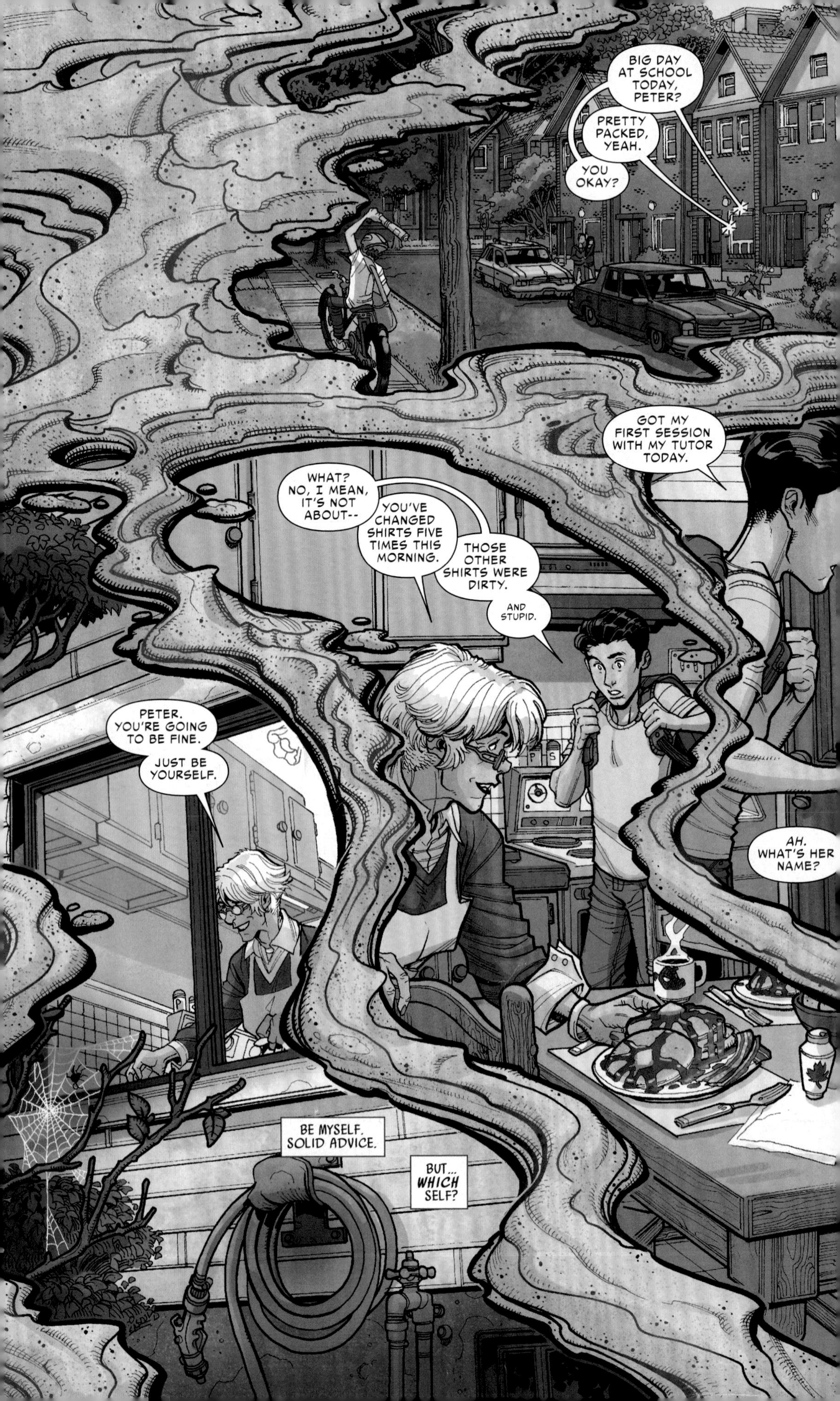
BIG DAY AT SCHOOL TODAY, PETER?
PRETTY PACKED, YEAH.
YOU OKAY?
GOT MY FIRST SESSION WITH MY TUTOR TODAY.
WHAT? NO, I MEAN, IT'S NOT ABOUT--
YOU'VE CHANGED SHIRTS FIVE TIMES THIS MORNING.
THOSE OTHER SHIRTS WERE DIRTY.
AND STUPID.
AH. WHAT'S HER NAME?
PETER. YOU'RE GOING TO BE FINE.
JUST BE YOURSELF.
BE MYSELF. SOLID ADVICE.
BUT... WHICH SELF?

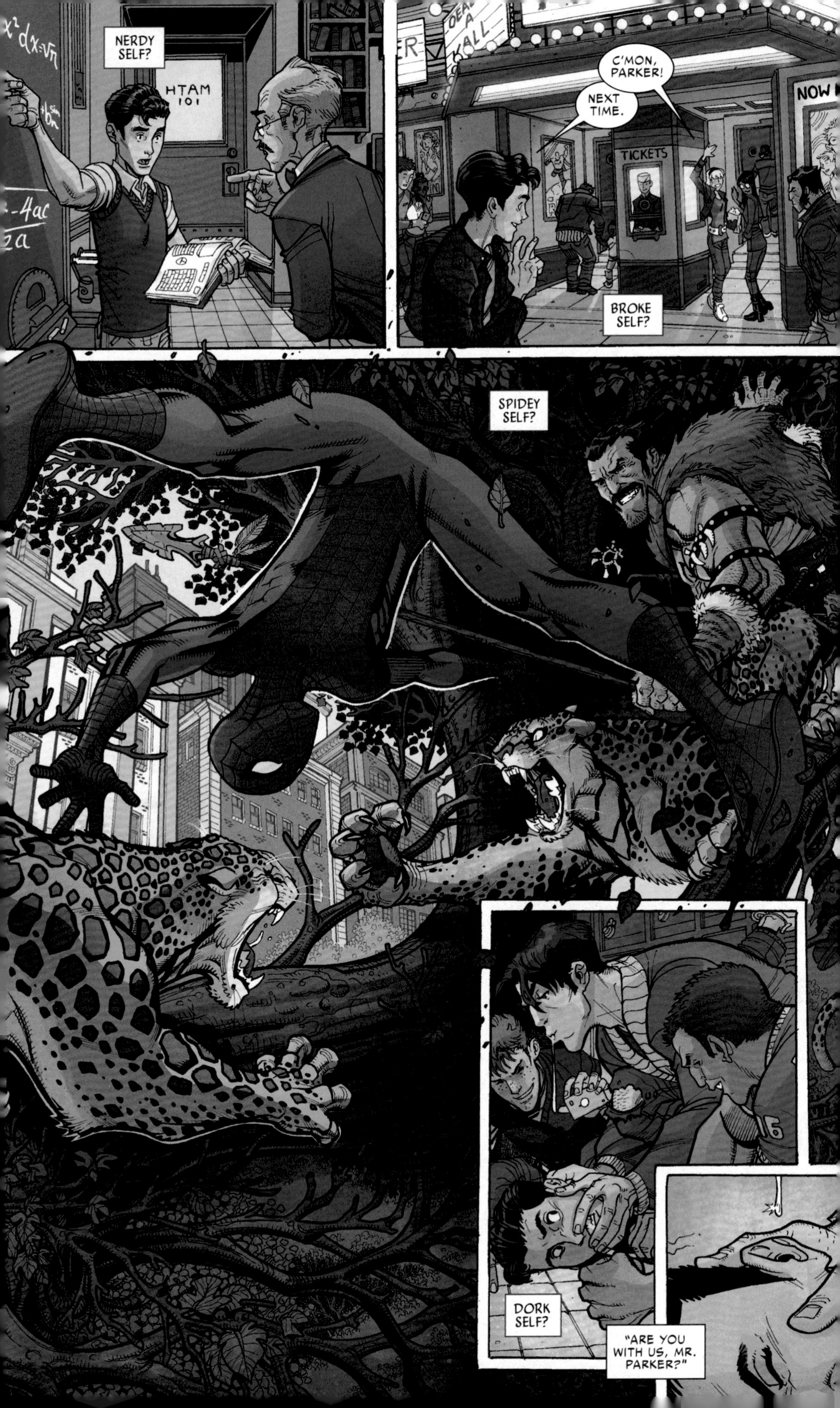

NERDY SELF?
HTAM 101
C'MON, PARKER!
NEXT TIME.
TICKETS
NOW
BROKE SELF?
SPIDEY SELF?
DORK SELF?
"ARE YOU WITH US, MR. PARKER?"

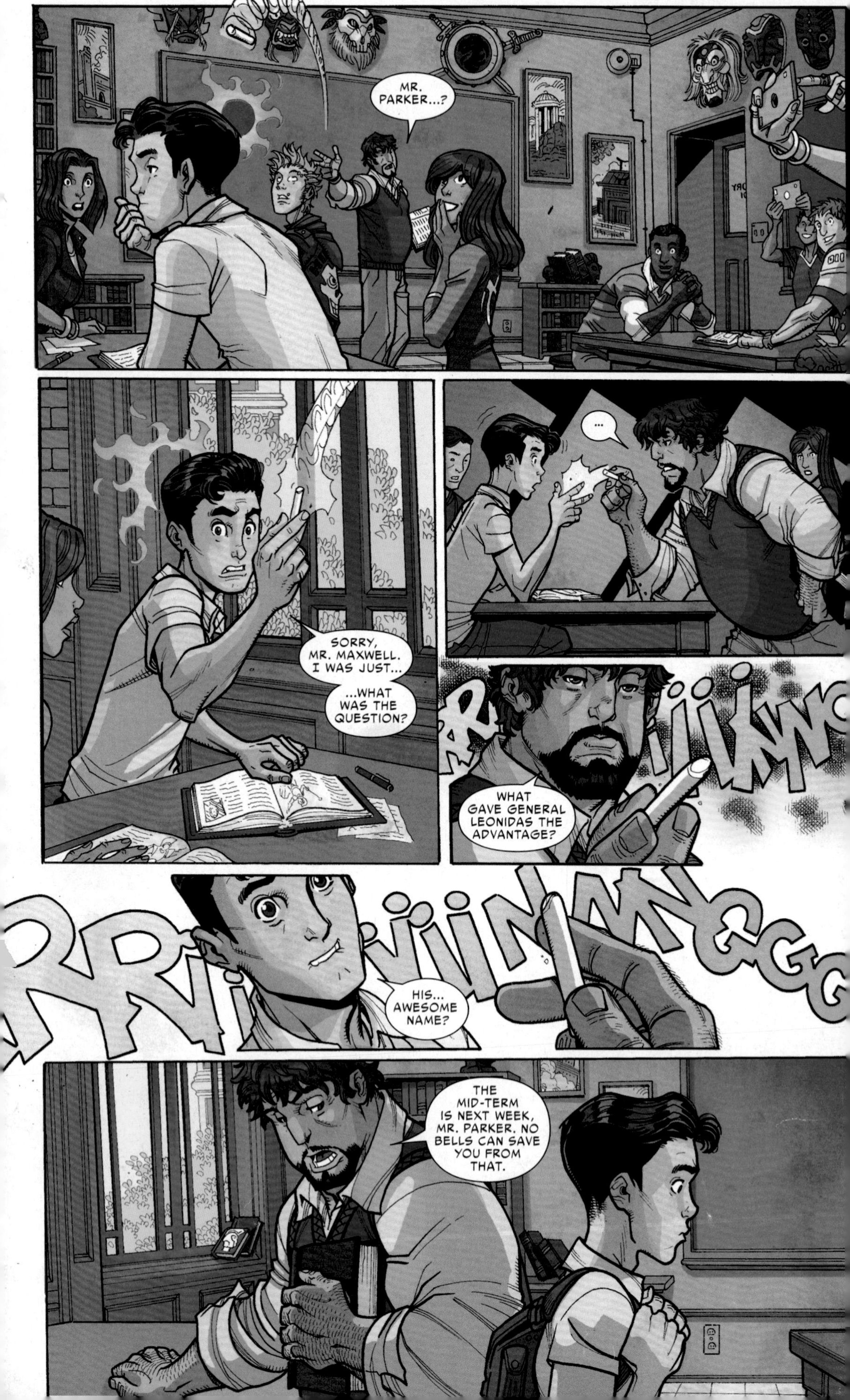
MR. PARKER...?
SORRY, MR. MAXWELL. I WAS JUST...
...WHAT WAS THE QUESTION?
...
WHAT GAVE GENERAL LEONIDAS THE ADVANTAGE?
HIS... AWESOME NAME?
RRRIIIINNNGGG
THE MID-TERM IS NEXT WEEK, MR. PARKER. NO BELLS CAN SAVE YOU FROM THAT.

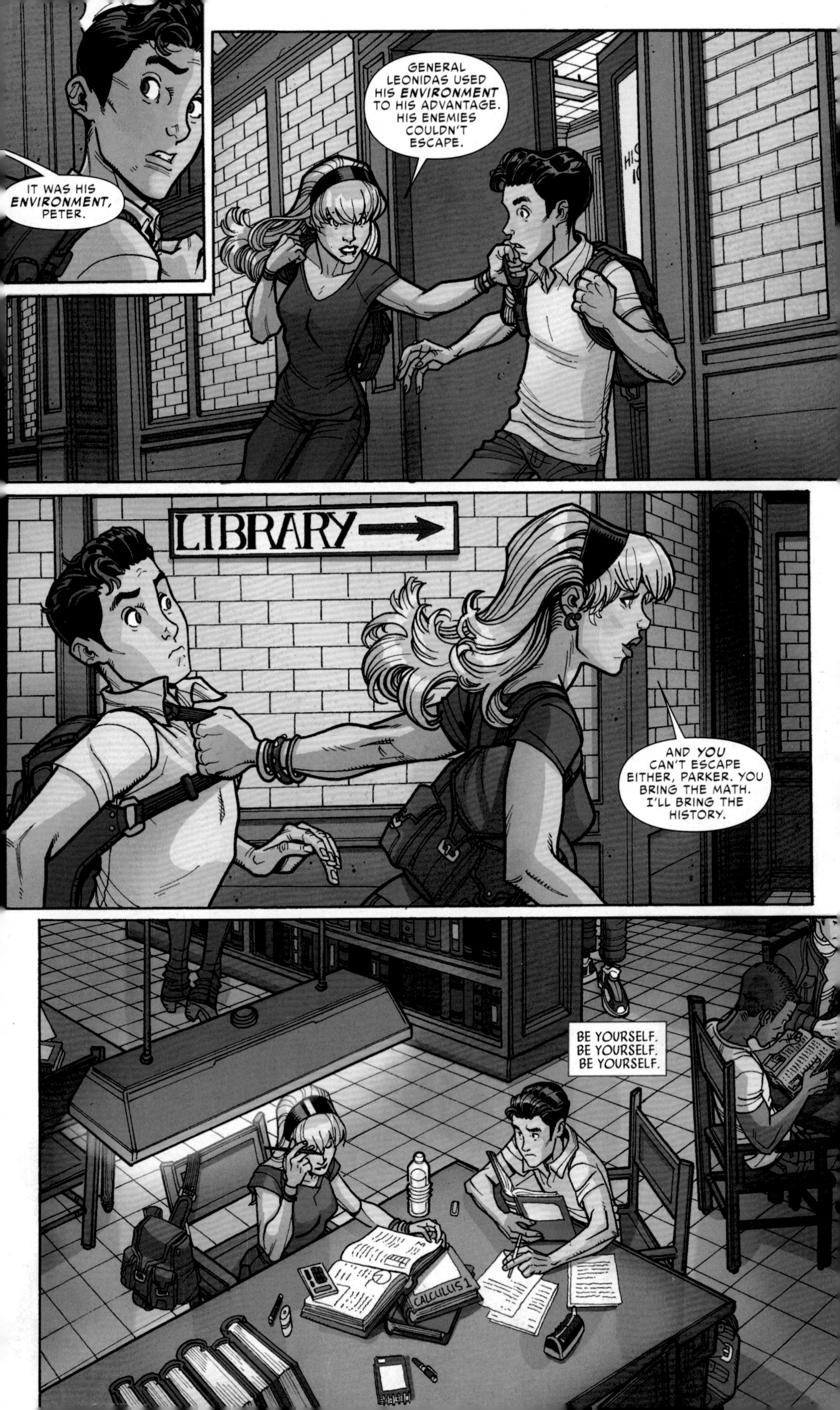

IT WAS HIS *ENVIRONMENT*, PETER.
GENERAL LEONIDAS USED HIS *ENVIRONMENT* TO HIS ADVANTAGE. HIS ENEMIES COULDN'T ESCAPE.
LIBRARY
AND *YOU* CAN'T ESCAPE EITHER, PARKER. YOU BRING THE MATH. I'LL BRING THE HISTORY.
BE YOURSELF. BE YOURSELF. BE YOURSELF.
CALCULUS 1

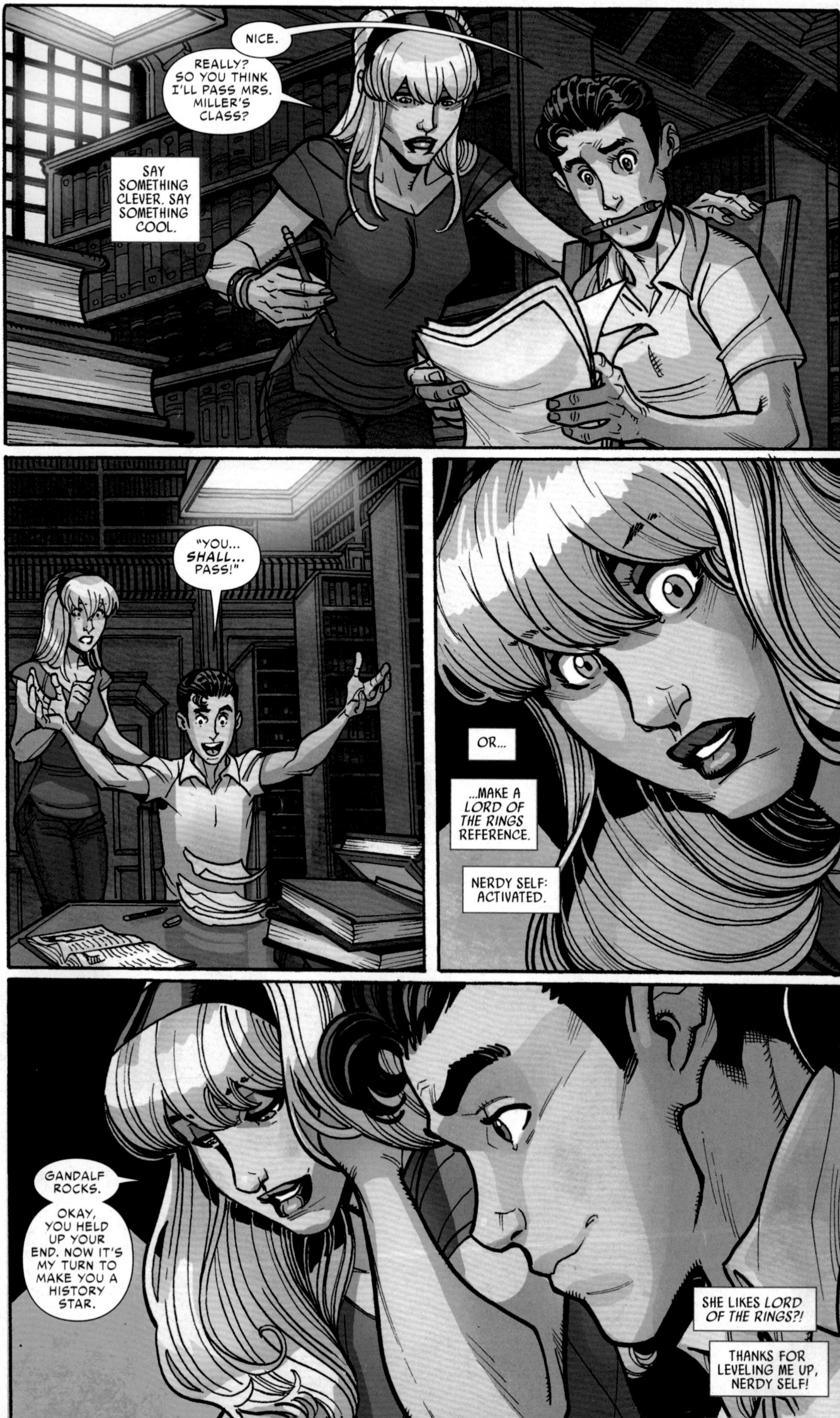
NICE.
REALLY? SO YOU THINK I'LL PASS MRS. MILLER'S CLASS?
SAY SOMETHING CLEVER. SAY SOMETHING COOL.
"YOU... SHALL... PASS!"
OR...
...MAKE A LORD OF THE RINGS REFERENCE.
NERDY SELF: ACTIVATED.
GANDALF ROCKS.
OKAY, YOU HELD UP YOUR END. NOW IT'S MY TURN TO MAKE YOU A HISTORY STAR.
SHE LIKES LORD OF THE RINGS?!
THANKS FOR LEVELING ME UP, NERDY SELF!

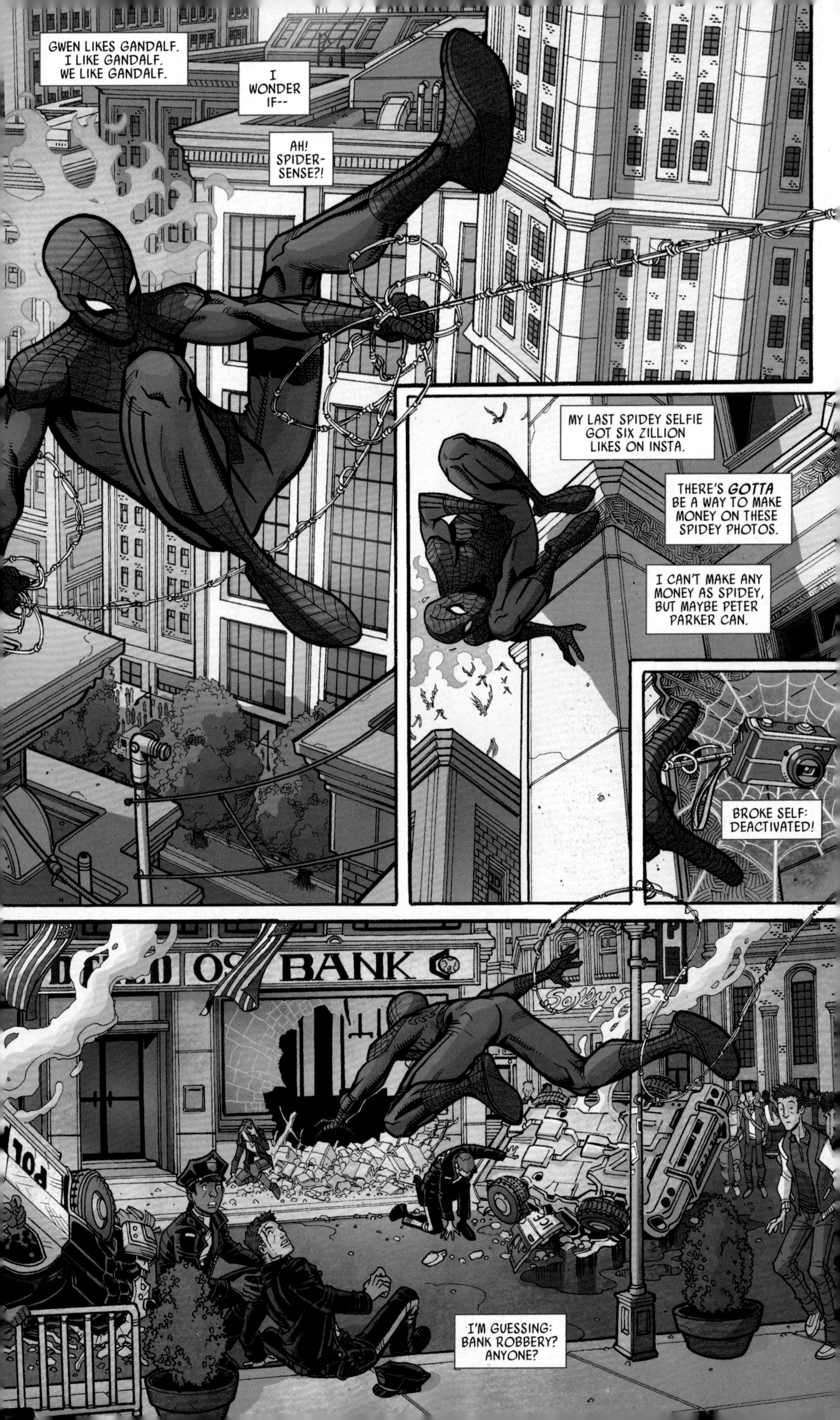
GWEN LIKES GANDALF. I LIKE GANDALF. WE LIKE GANDALF.
I WONDER IF--
AH! SPIDER-SENSE?!
MY LAST SPIDEY SELFIE GOT SIX ZILLION LIKES ON INSTA.
THERE'S GOTTA BE A WAY TO MAKE MONEY ON THESE SPIDEY PHOTOS.
I CAN'T MAKE ANY MONEY AS SPIDEY, BUT MAYBE PETER PARKER CAN.
BROKE SELF: DEACTIVATED!
BANK
I'M GUESSING: BANK ROBBERY? ANYONE?

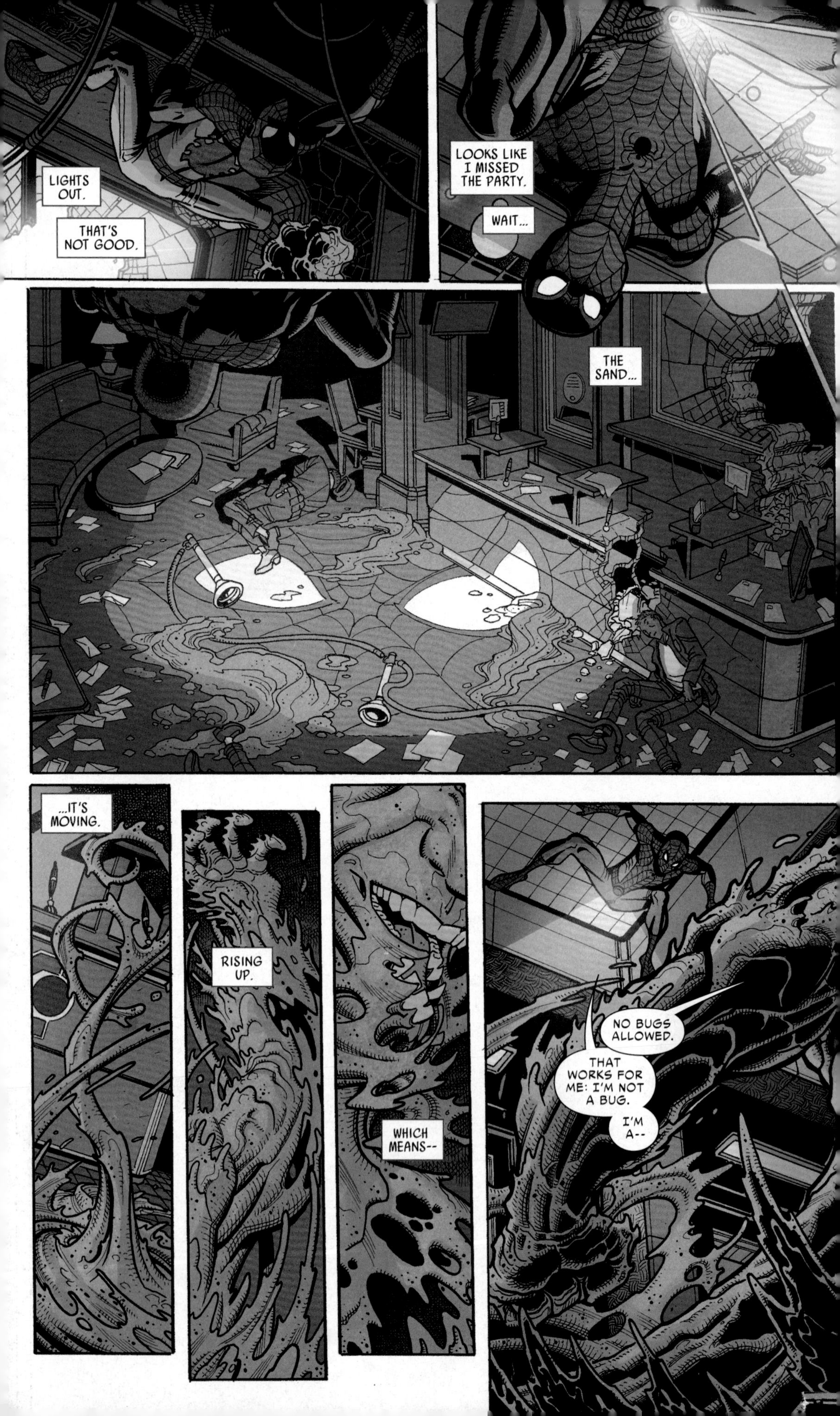

LIGHTS OUT.
THAT'S NOT GOOD.
LOOKS LIKE I MISSED THE PARTY.
WAIT...
THE SAND...
...IT'S MOVING.
RISING UP.
WHICH MEANS--
NO BUGS ALLOWED.
THAT WORKS FOR ME: I'M NOT A BUG.
I'M A--

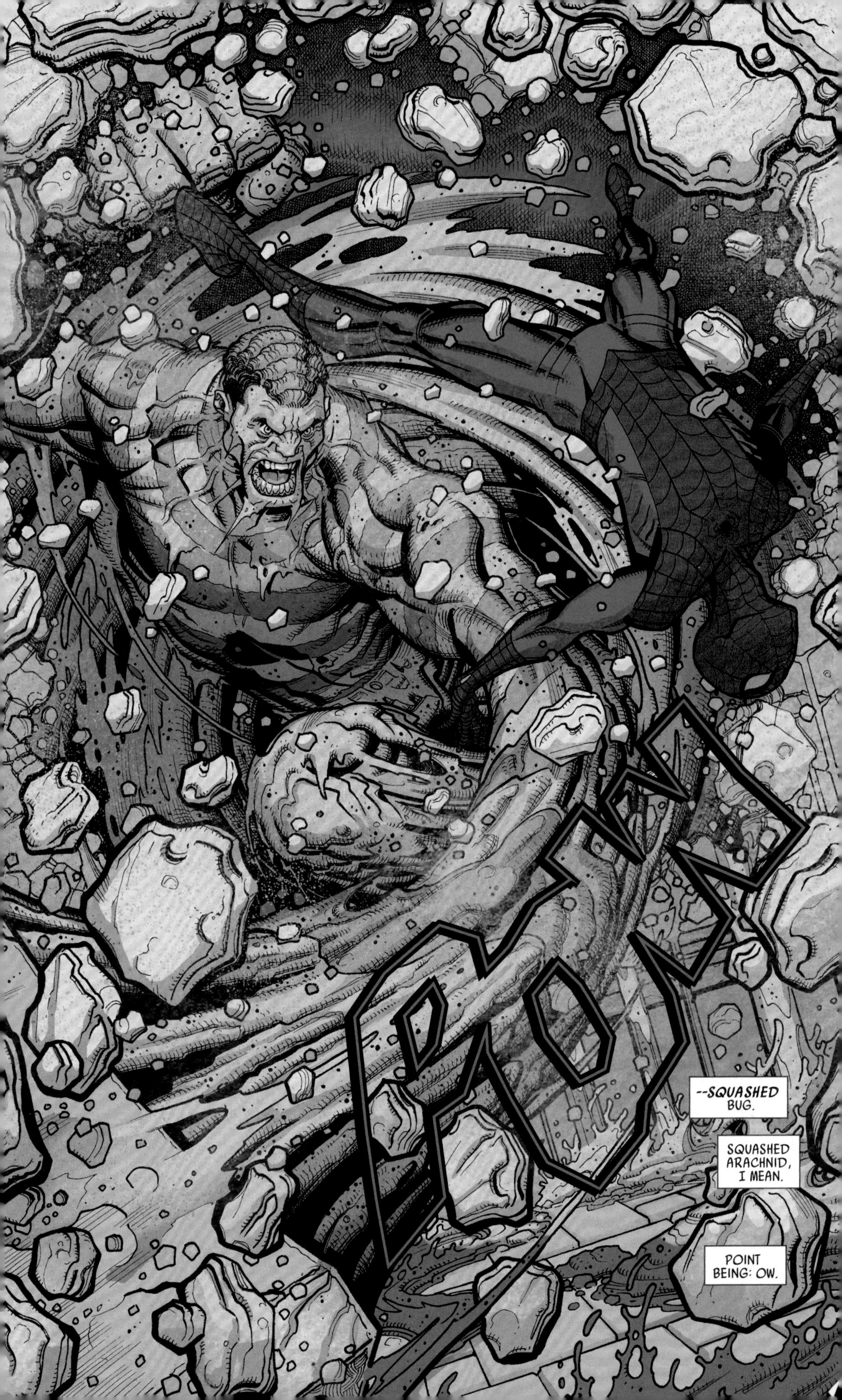

BOOM
--SQUASHED BUG.
SQUASHED ARACHNID, I MEAN.
POINT BEING: OW.

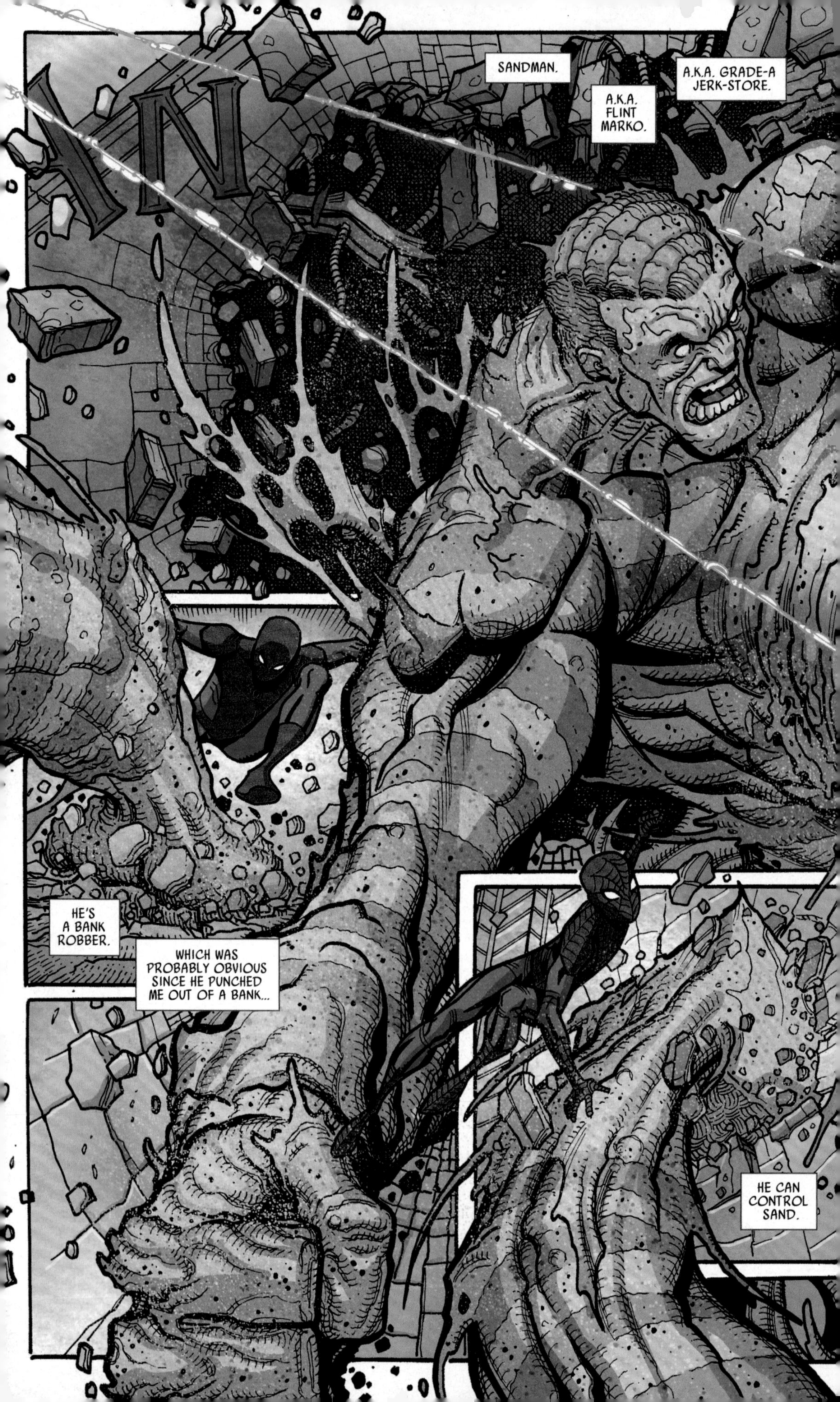
SANDMAN.
A.K.A. FLINT MARKO.
A.K.A. GRADE-A JERK-STORE.
HE'S A BANK ROBBER.
WHICH WAS PROBABLY OBVIOUS SINCE HE PUNCHED ME OUT OF A BANK...
HE CAN CONTROL SAND.

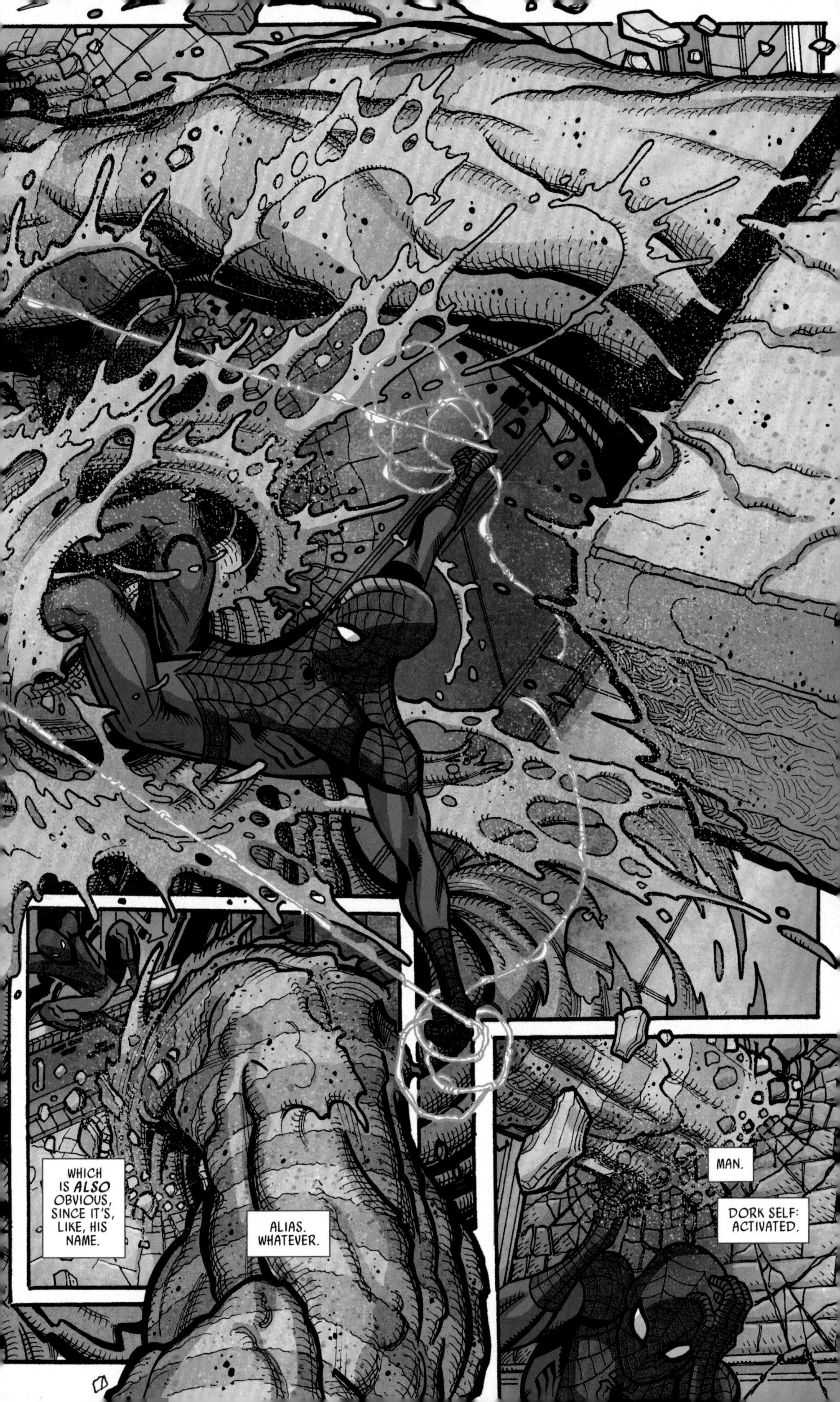
WHICH IS *ALSO* OBVIOUS, SINCE IT'S, LIKE, HIS NAME.
ALIAS. WHATEVER.
MAN.
DORK SELF: ACTIVATED.

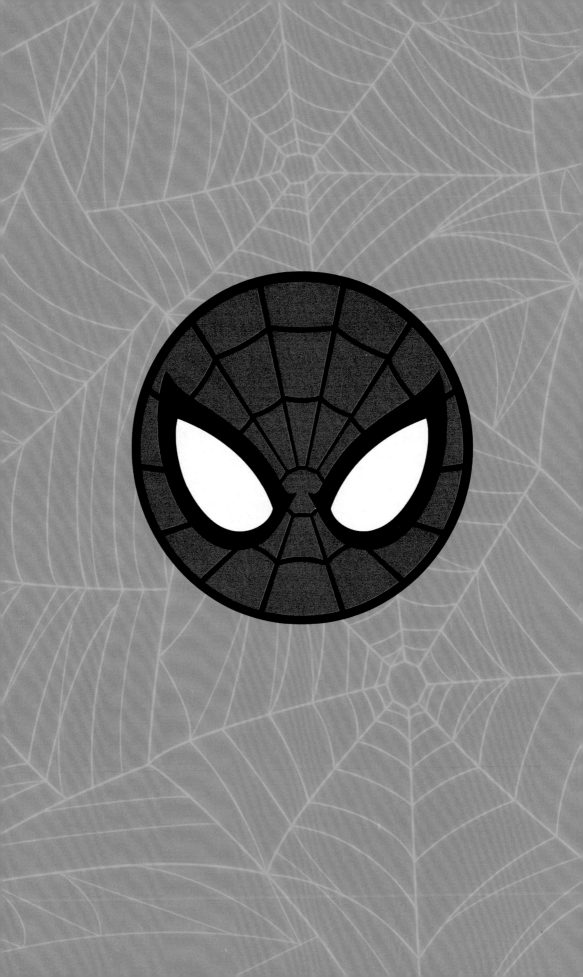

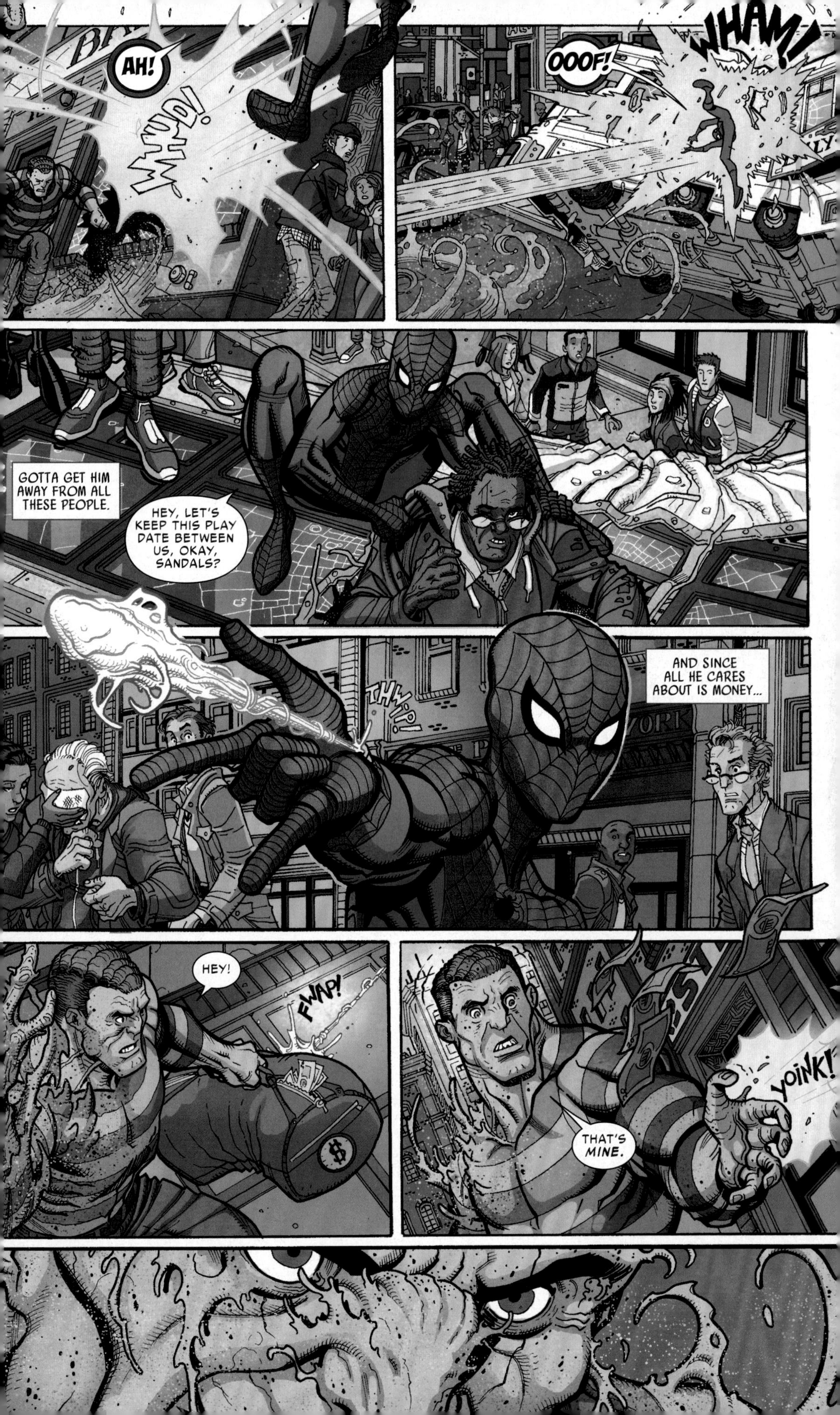
AH!
WHUD!
OOOF!
WHAM!
GOTTA GET HIM AWAY FROM ALL THESE PEOPLE.
HEY, LET'S KEEP THIS PLAY DATE BETWEEN US, OKAY, SANDALS?
THWIP!
AND SINCE ALL HE CARES ABOUT IS MONEY...
HEY!
FWAP!
THAT'S MINE.
YOINK!

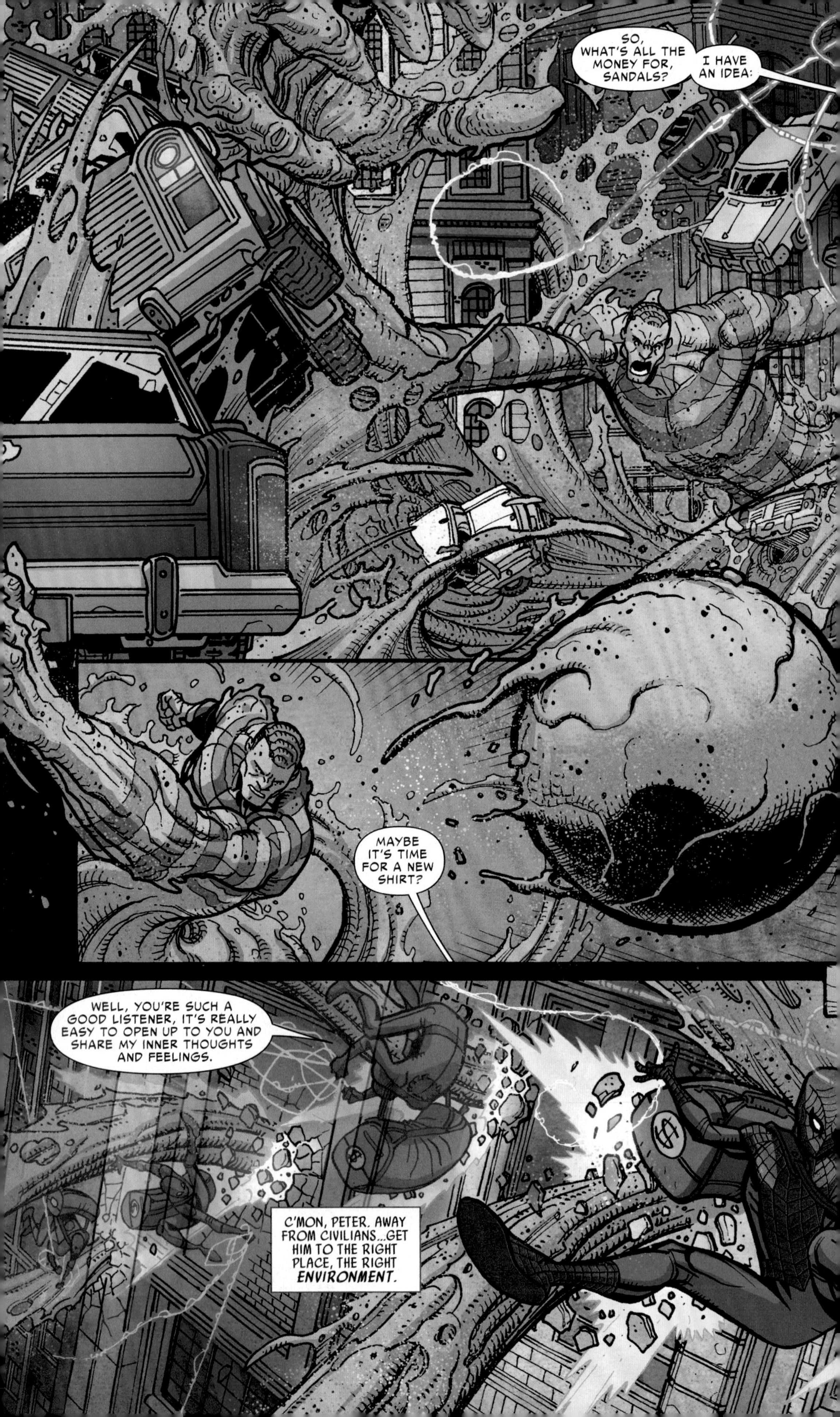

SO, WHAT'S ALL THE MONEY FOR, SANDALS?
I HAVE AN IDEA:
MAYBE IT'S TIME FOR A NEW SHIRT?
WELL, YOU'RE SUCH A GOOD LISTENER, IT'S REALLY EASY TO OPEN UP TO YOU AND SHARE MY INNER THOUGHTS AND FEELINGS.
C'MON, PETER. AWAY FROM CIVILIANS...GET HIM TO THE RIGHT PLACE, THE RIGHT ENVIRONMENT.

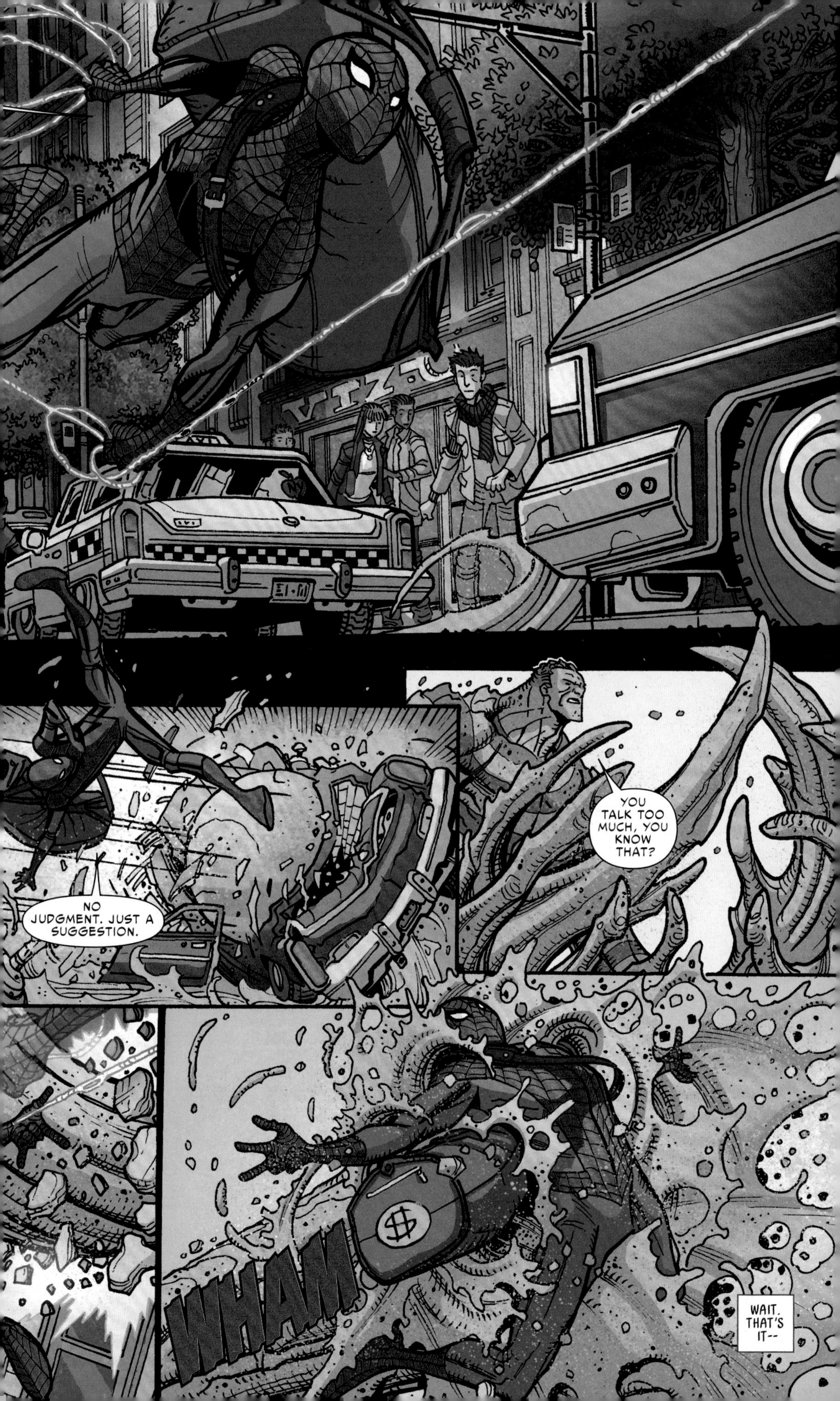
YOU TALK TOO MUCH, YOU KNOW THAT?
NO JUDGMENT. JUST A SUGGESTION.
WHAM
WAIT. THAT'S IT--

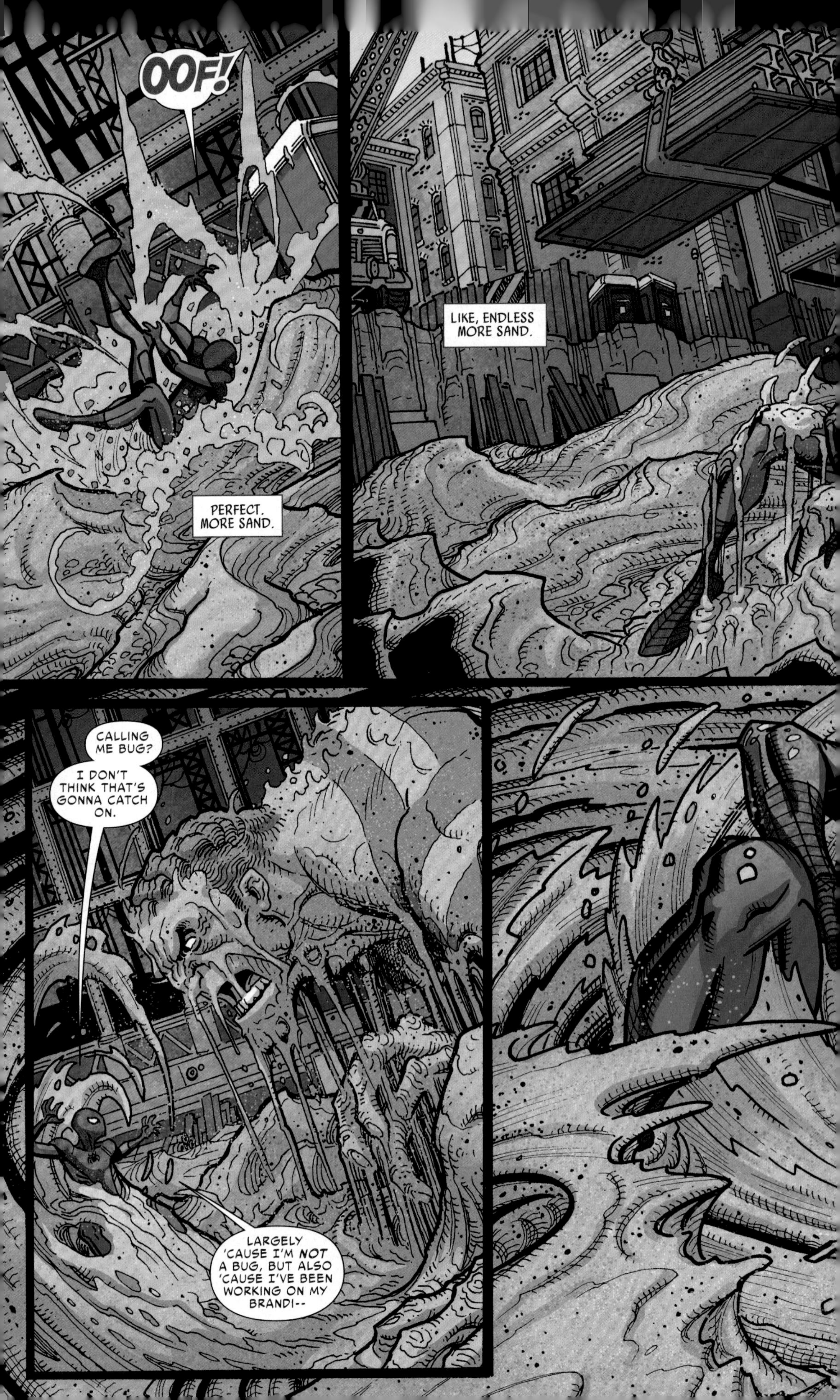
OOF!
PERFECT. MORE SAND.
LIKE, ENDLESS MORE SAND.
CALLING ME BUG?
I DON'T THINK THAT'S GONNA CATCH ON.
LARGELY 'CAUSE I'M NOT A BUG, BUT ALSO 'CAUSE I'VE BEEN WORKING ON MY BRAND!--

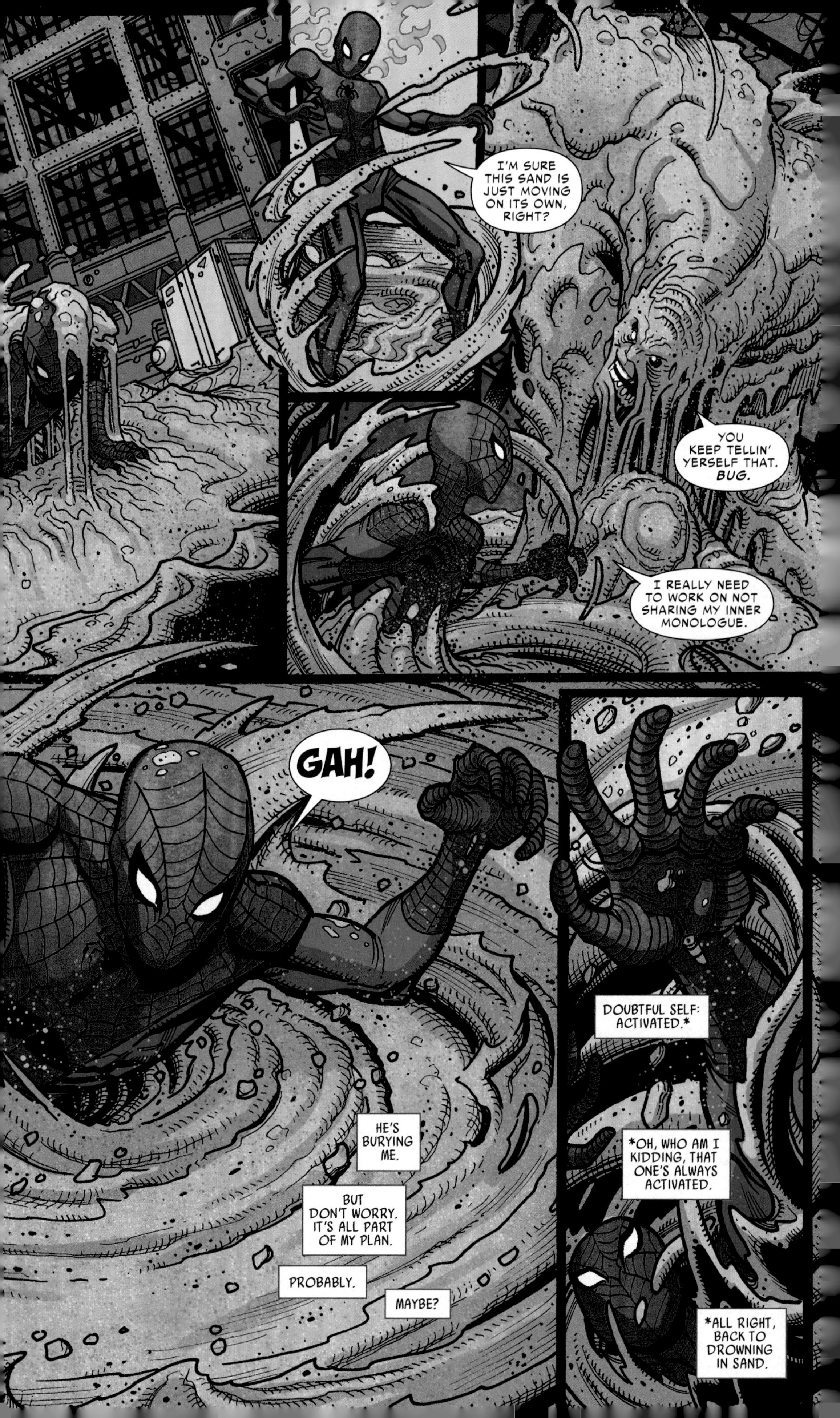
I'M SURE THIS SAND IS JUST MOVING ON ITS OWN, RIGHT?
YOU KEEP TELLIN' YERSELF THAT. BUG.
I REALLY NEED TO WORK ON NOT SHARING MY INNER MONOLOGUE.
GAH!
HE'S BURYING ME.
BUT DON'T WORRY. IT'S ALL PART OF MY PLAN.
PROBABLY.
MAYBE?
DOUBTFUL SELF: ACTIVATED.*
*OH, WHO AM I KIDDING, THAT ONE'S ALWAYS ACTIVATED.
*ALL RIGHT, BACK TO DROWNING IN SAND.

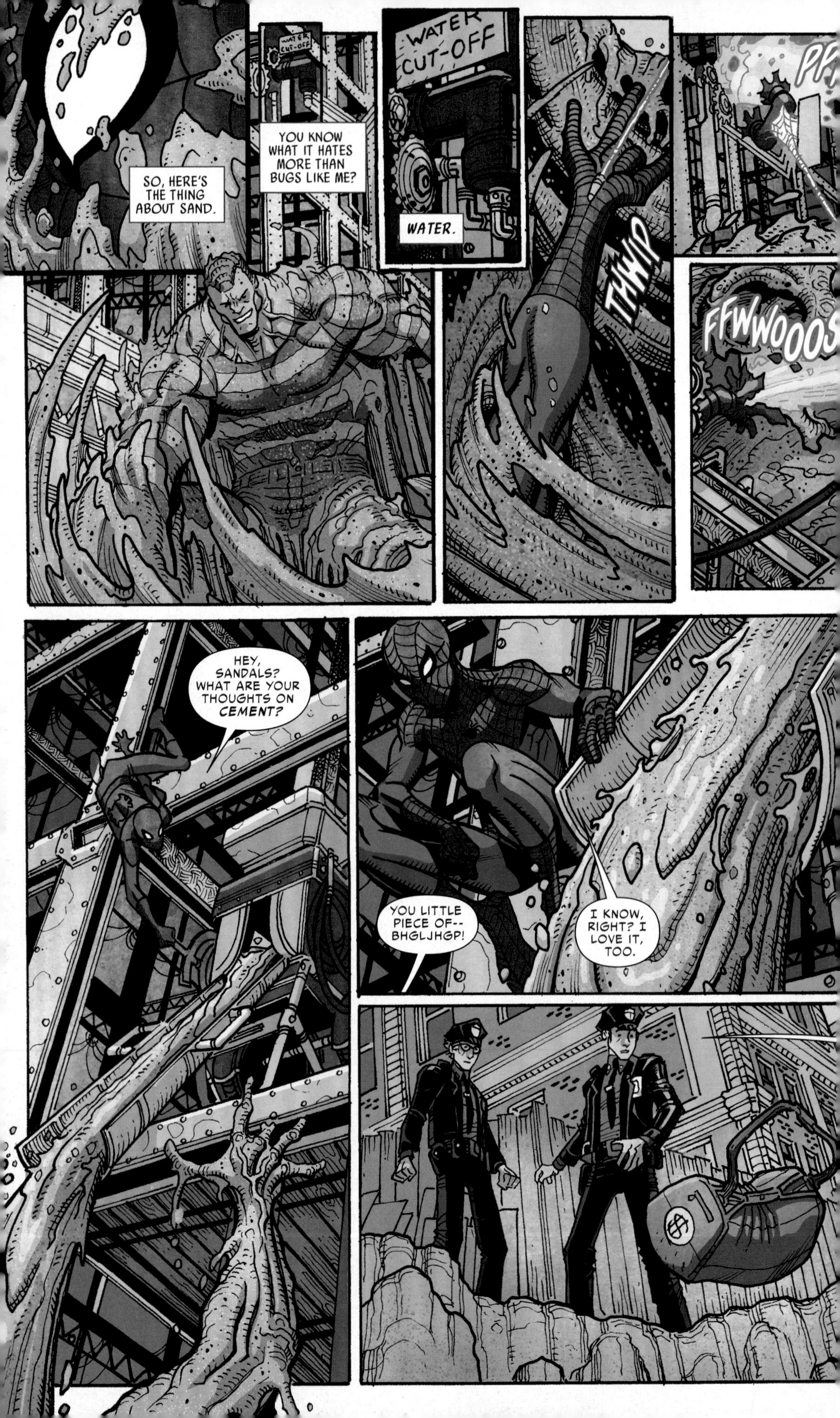
SO, HERE'S THE THING ABOUT SAND.
YOU KNOW WHAT IT HATES MORE THAN BUGS LIKE ME?
WATER CUT-OFF
WATER CUT-OFF
WATER.
THWIP
FFWWOOOS
HEY, SANDALS? WHAT ARE YOUR THOUGHTS ON CEMENT?
YOU LITTLE PIECE OF-- BHGLJHGP!
I KNOW, RIGHT? I LOVE IT, TOO.

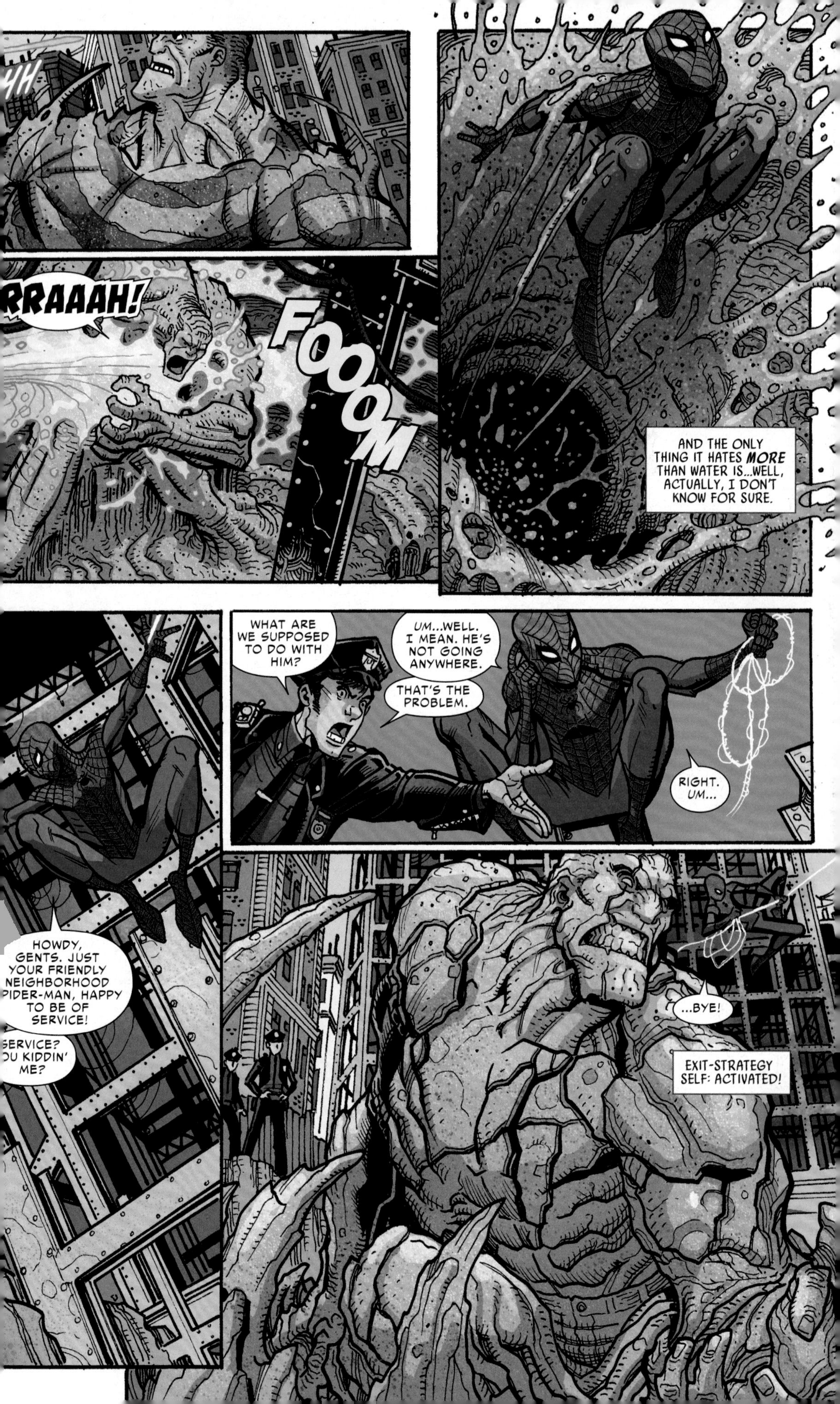

HH
RRAAAH!
FOOOM
AND THE ONLY THING IT HATES MORE THAN WATER IS...WELL, ACTUALLY, I DON'T KNOW FOR SURE.
HOWDY, GENTS. JUST YOUR FRIENDLY NEIGHBORHOOD PIDER-MAN, HAPPY TO BE OF SERVICE!
ERVICE? OU KIDDIN' ME?
WHAT ARE WE SUPPOSED TO DO WITH HIM?
UM...WELL. I MEAN. HE'S NOT GOING ANYWHERE.
THAT'S THE PROBLEM.
RIGHT. UM...
...BYE!
EXIT-STRATEGY SELF: ACTIVATED!

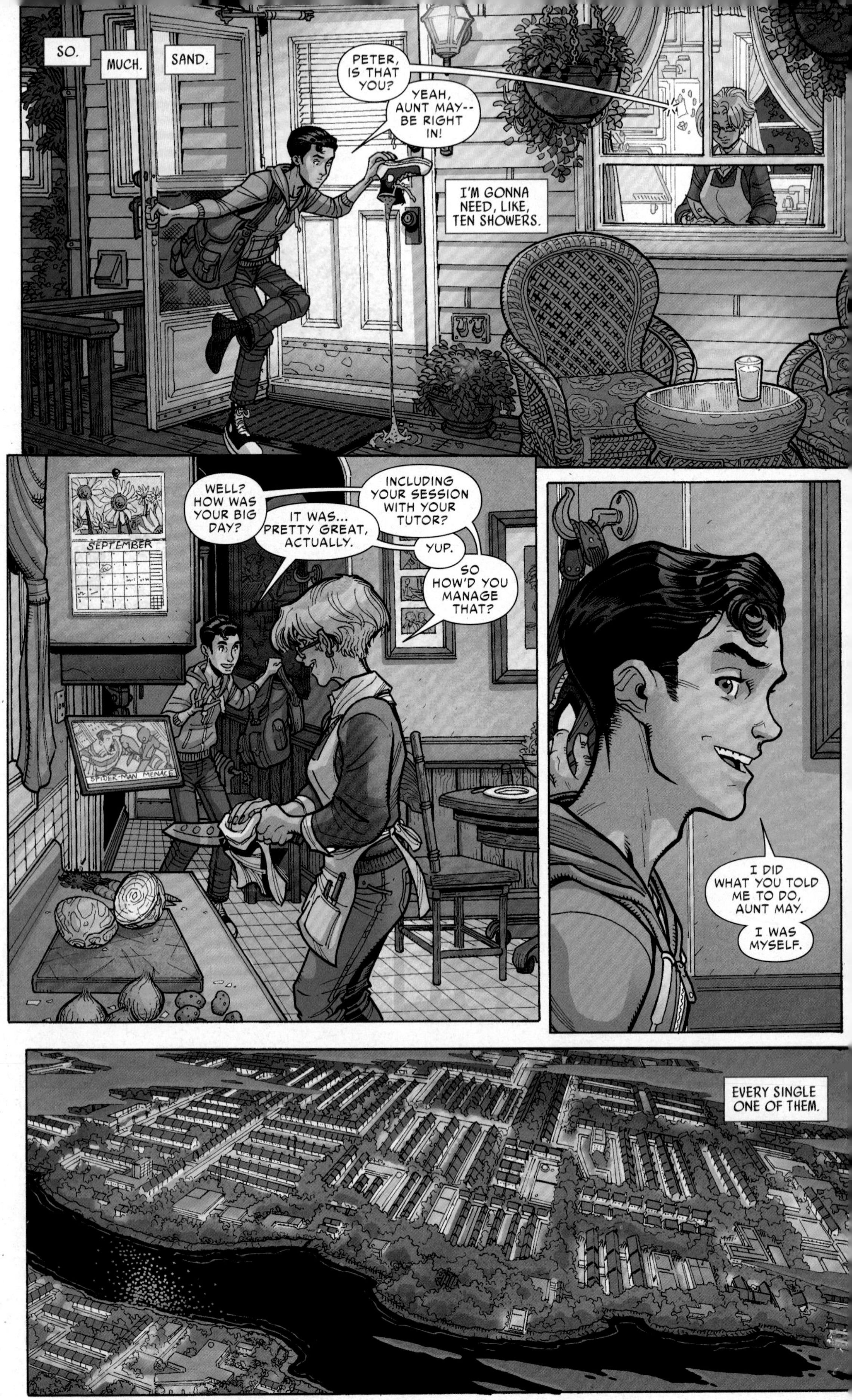
SO.
MUCH.
SAND.
PETER, IS THAT YOU?
YEAH, AUNT MAY-- BE RIGHT IN!
I'M GONNA NEED, LIKE, TEN SHOWERS.
SEPTEMBER
WELL? HOW WAS YOUR BIG DAY?
IT WAS... PRETTY GREAT, ACTUALLY.
INCLUDING YOUR SESSION WITH YOUR TUTOR?
YUP.
SO HOW'D YOU MANAGE THAT?
SPIDER-MAN MENACE
I DID WHAT YOU TOLD ME TO DO, AUNT MAY.
I WAS MYSELF.
EVERY SINGLE ONE OF THEM.

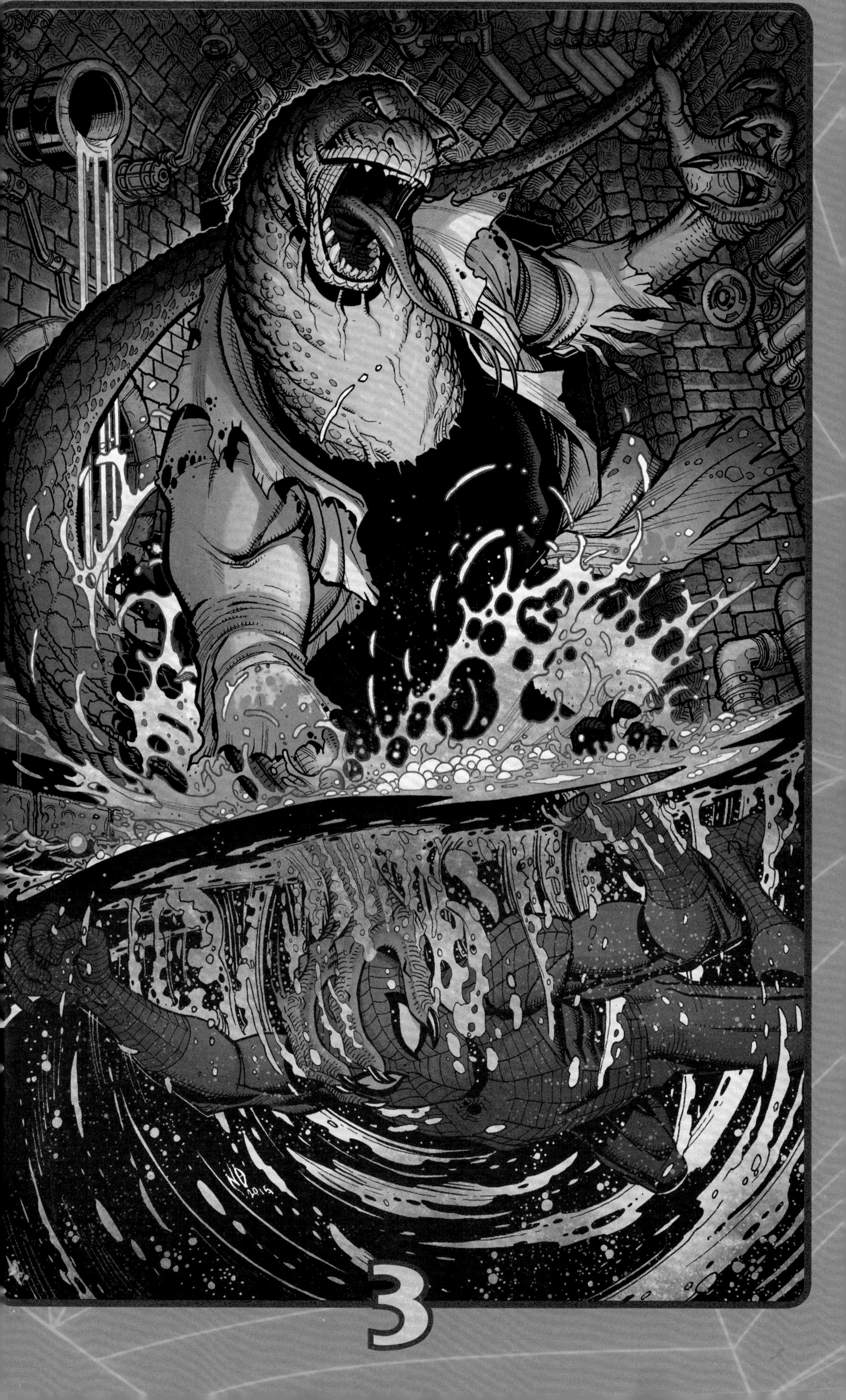

# 3

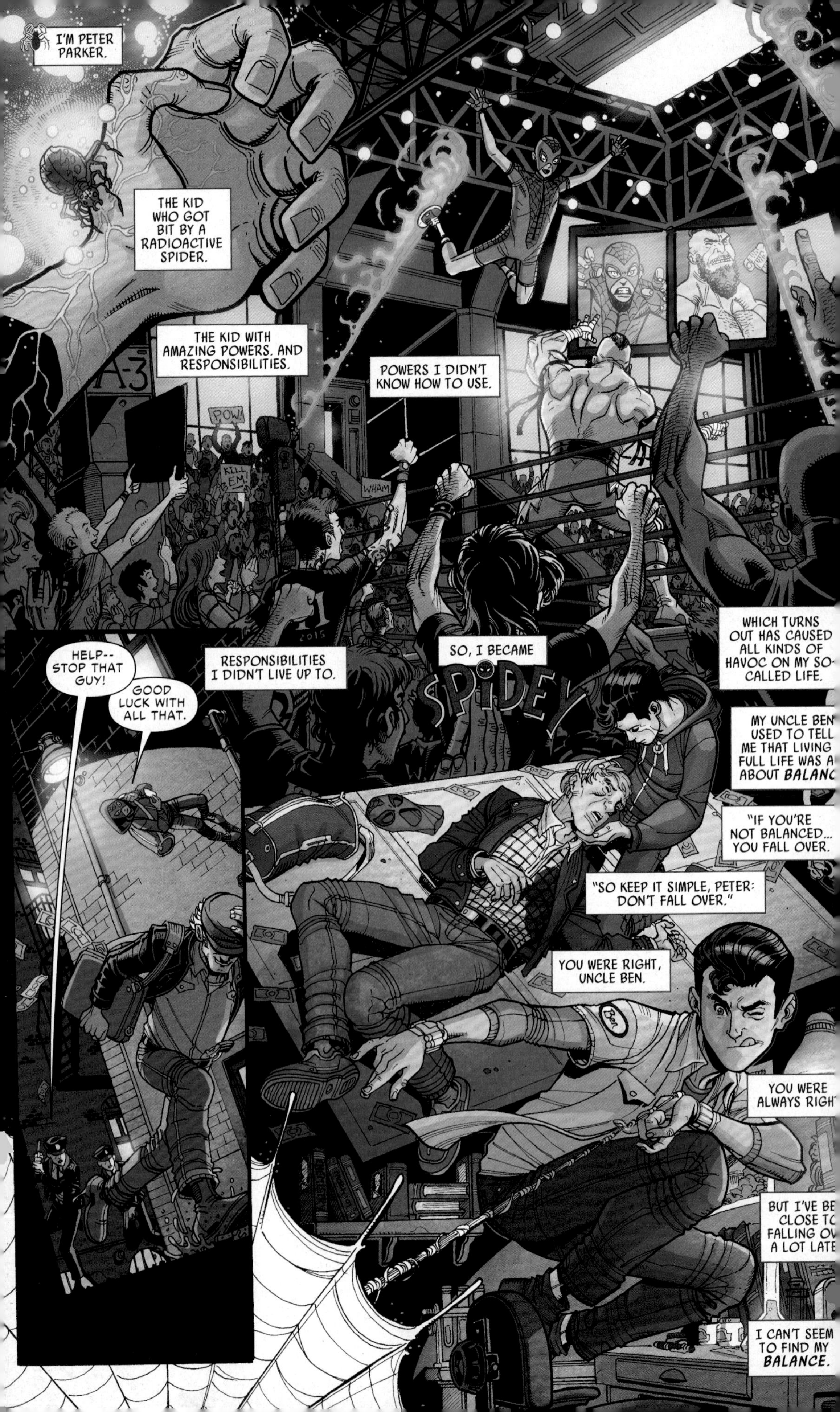
I'M PETER PARKER.
THE KID WHO GOT BIT BY A RADIOACTIVE SPIDER.
THE KID WITH AMAZING POWERS. AND RESPONSIBILITIES.
POWERS I DIDN'T KNOW HOW TO USE.
POW!
KILL 'EM!
WHAM
RESPONSIBILITIES I DIDN'T LIVE UP TO.
SO, I BECAME
SPIDEY
WHICH TURNS OUT HAS CAUSED ALL KINDS OF HAVOC ON MY SO-CALLED LIFE.
HELP-- STOP THAT GUY!
GOOD LUCK WITH ALL THAT.
MY UNCLE BEN USED TO TELL ME THAT LIVING FULL LIFE WAS A ABOUT BALANC
"IF YOU'RE NOT BALANCED... YOU FALL OVER.
"SO KEEP IT SIMPLE, PETER: DON'T FALL OVER."
YOU WERE RIGHT, UNCLE BEN.
YOU WERE ALWAYS RIGHT
BUT I'VE BE CLOSE TO FALLING OV A LOT LATE
I CAN'T SEEM TO FIND MY BALANCE.

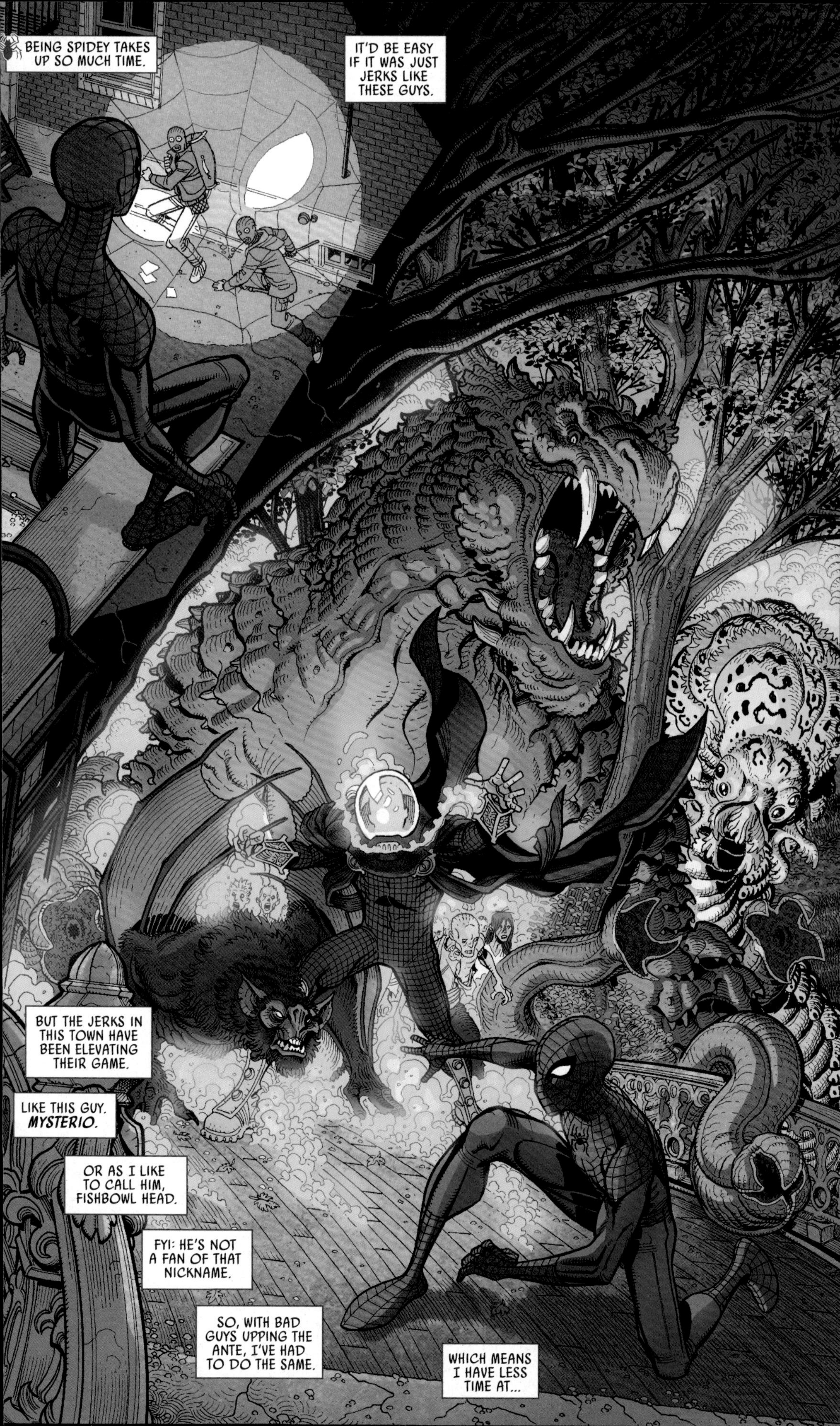
BEING SPIDEY TAKES UP SO MUCH TIME.
IT'D BE EASY IF IT WAS JUST JERKS LIKE THESE GUYS.
BUT THE JERKS IN THIS TOWN HAVE BEEN ELEVATING THEIR GAME.
LIKE THIS GUY. *MYSTERIO.*
OR AS I LIKE TO CALL HIM, FISHBOWL HEAD.
FYI: HE'S NOT A FAN OF THAT NICKNAME.
SO, WITH BAD GUYS UPPING THE ANTE, I'VE HAD TO DO THE SAME.
WHICH MEANS I HAVE LESS TIME AT...

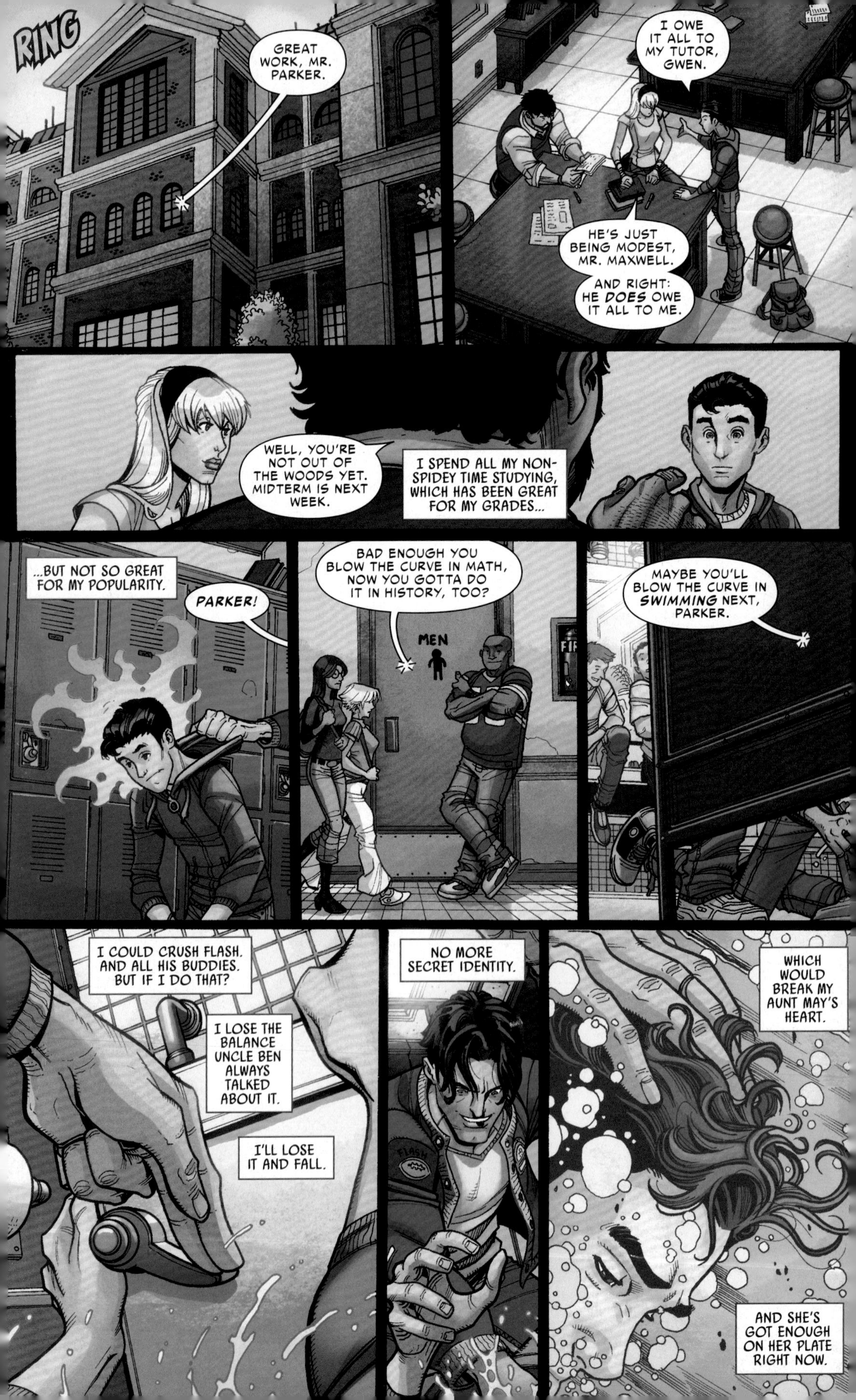
RING
GREAT WORK, MR. PARKER.
I OWE IT ALL TO MY TUTOR, GWEN.
HE'S JUST BEING MODEST, MR. MAXWELL.
AND RIGHT: HE DOES OWE IT ALL TO ME.
WELL, YOU'RE NOT OUT OF THE WOODS YET. MIDTERM IS NEXT WEEK.
I SPEND ALL MY NON-SPIDEY TIME STUDYING, WHICH HAS BEEN GREAT FOR MY GRADES...
...BUT NOT SO GREAT FOR MY POPULARITY.
PARKER!
BAD ENOUGH YOU BLOW THE CURVE IN MATH, NOW YOU GOTTA DO IT IN HISTORY, TOO?
MEN
MAYBE YOU'LL BLOW THE CURVE IN SWIMMING NEXT, PARKER.
I COULD CRUSH FLASH. AND ALL HIS BUDDIES. BUT IF I DO THAT?
I LOSE THE BALANCE UNCLE BEN ALWAYS TALKED ABOUT IT.
I'LL LOSE IT AND FALL.
NO MORE SECRET IDENTITY.
WHICH WOULD BREAK MY AUNT MAY'S HEART.
AND SHE'S GOT ENOUGH ON HER PLATE RIGHT NOW.

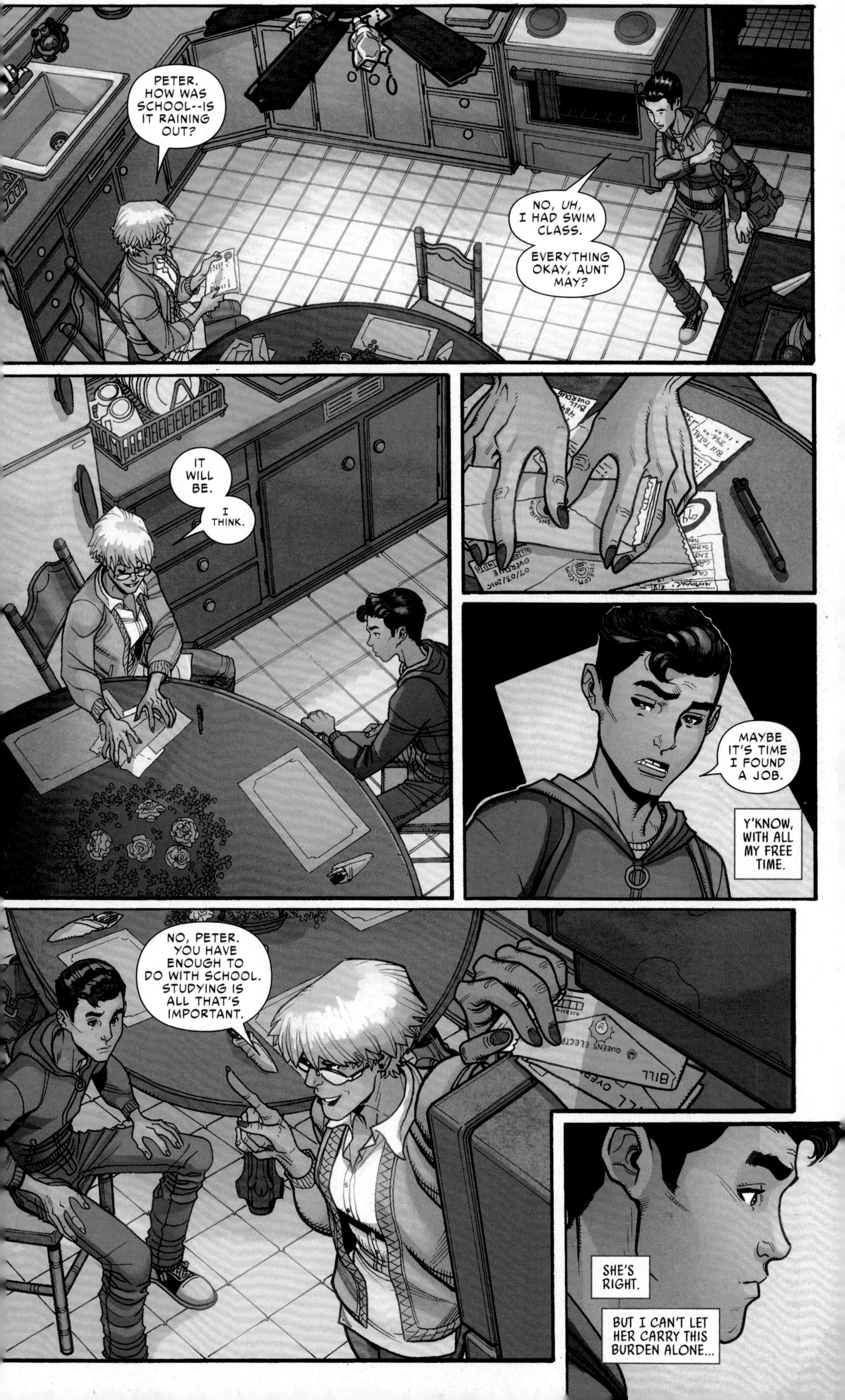
PETER. HOW WAS SCHOOL--IS IT RAINING OUT?
NO, UH, I HAD SWIM CLASS.
EVERYTHING OKAY, AUNT MAY?
IT WILL BE.
I THINK.
MAYBE IT'S TIME I FOUND A JOB.
Y'KNOW, WITH ALL MY FREE TIME.
NO, PETER. YOU HAVE ENOUGH TO DO WITH SCHOOL. STUDYING IS ALL THAT'S IMPORTANT.
SHE'S RIGHT.
BUT I CAN'T LET HER CARRY THIS BURDEN ALONE...

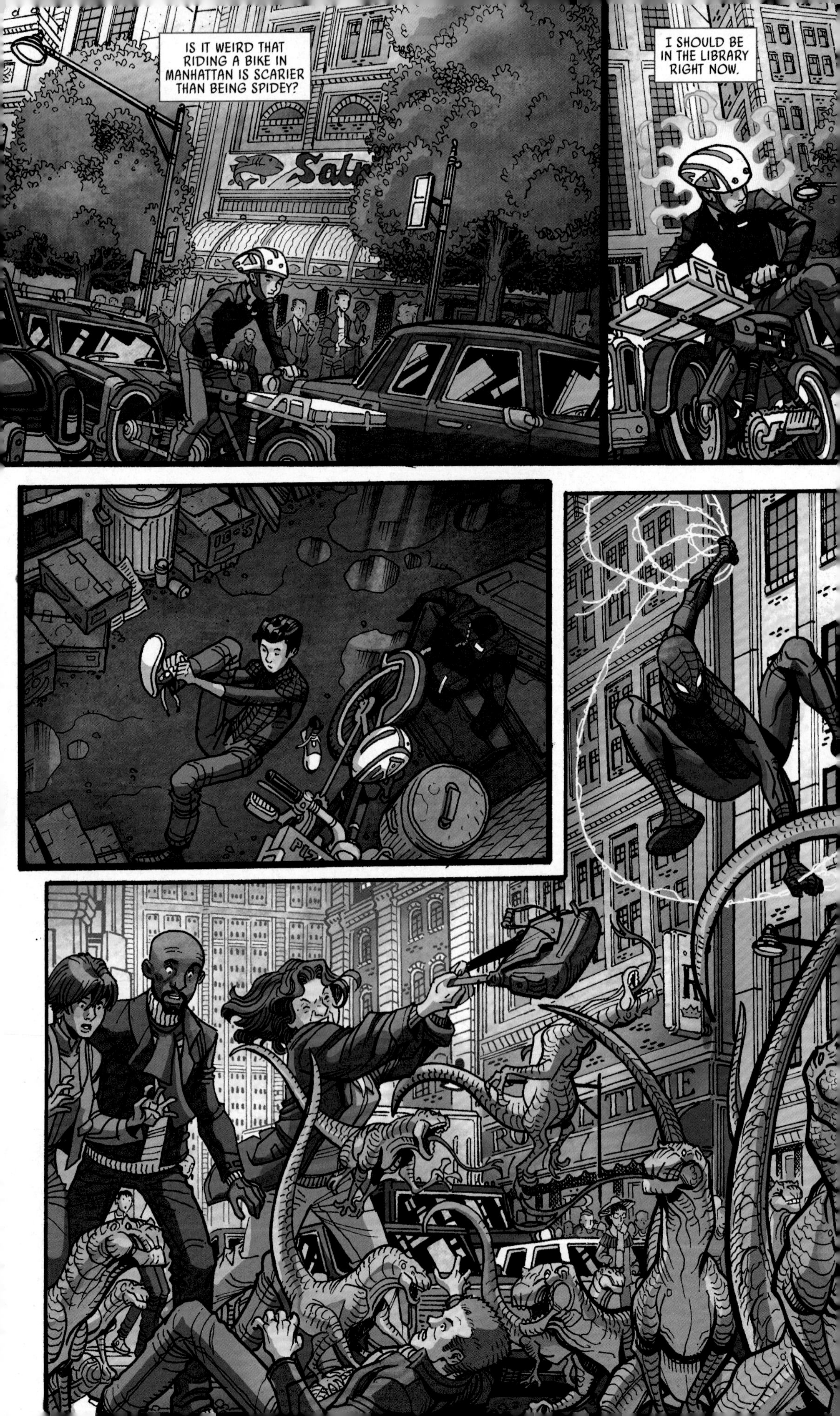
IS IT WEIRD THAT RIDING A BIKE IN MANHATTAN IS SCARIER THAN BEING SPIDEY?
I SHOULD BE IN THE LIBRARY RIGHT NOW.

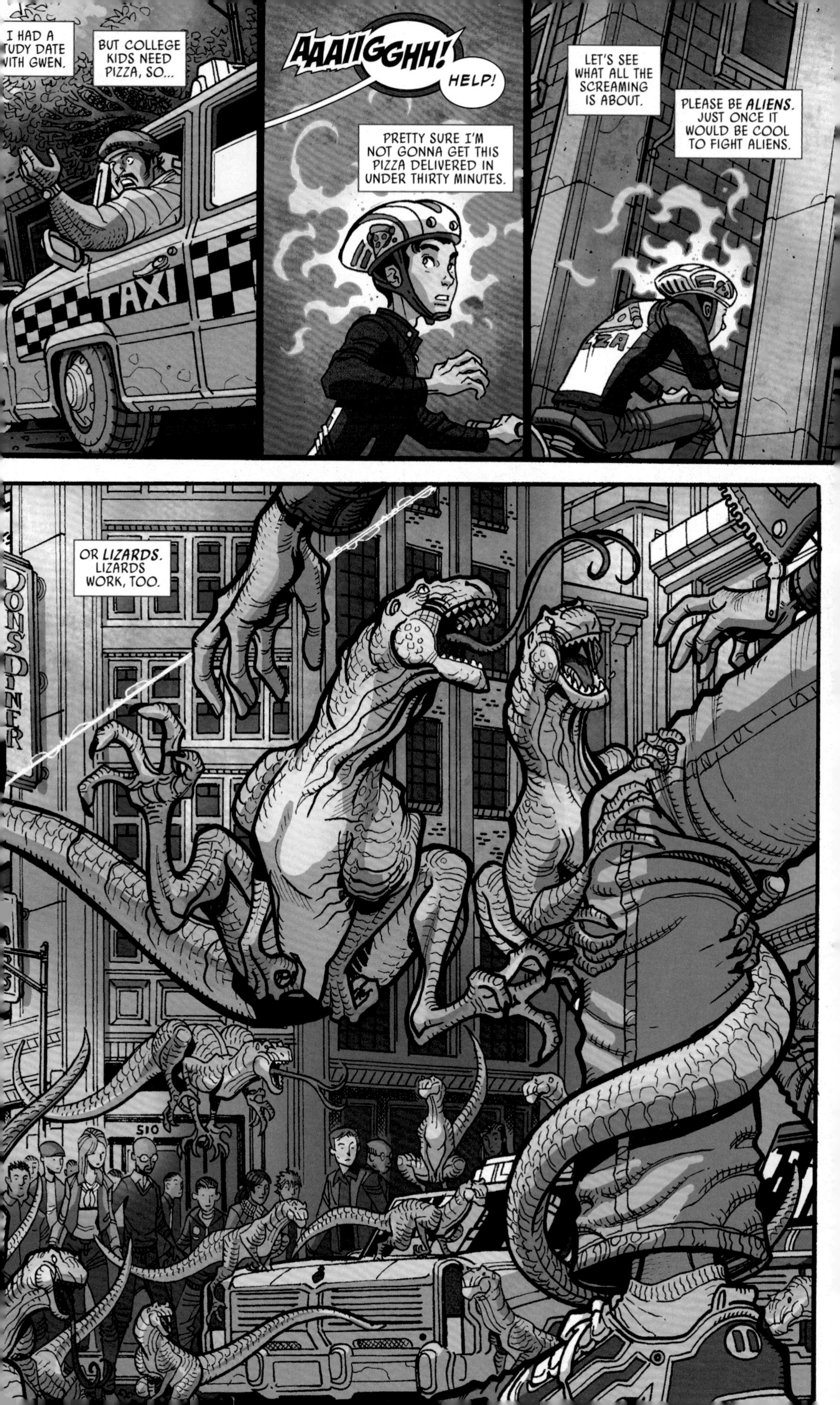
I HAD A
STUDY DATE
WITH GWEN.
BUT COLLEGE
KIDS NEED
PIZZA, SO...
TAXI
AAAIIGGHH!
HELP!
PRETTY SURE I'M
NOT GONNA GET THIS
PIZZA DELIVERED IN
UNDER THIRTY MINUTES.
LET'S SEE
WHAT ALL THE
SCREAMING
IS ABOUT.
PLEASE BE *ALIENS.*
JUST ONCE IT
WOULD BE COOL
TO FIGHT ALIENS.
OR *LIZARDS.*
LIZARDS
WORK, TOO.
DONS DINER
510

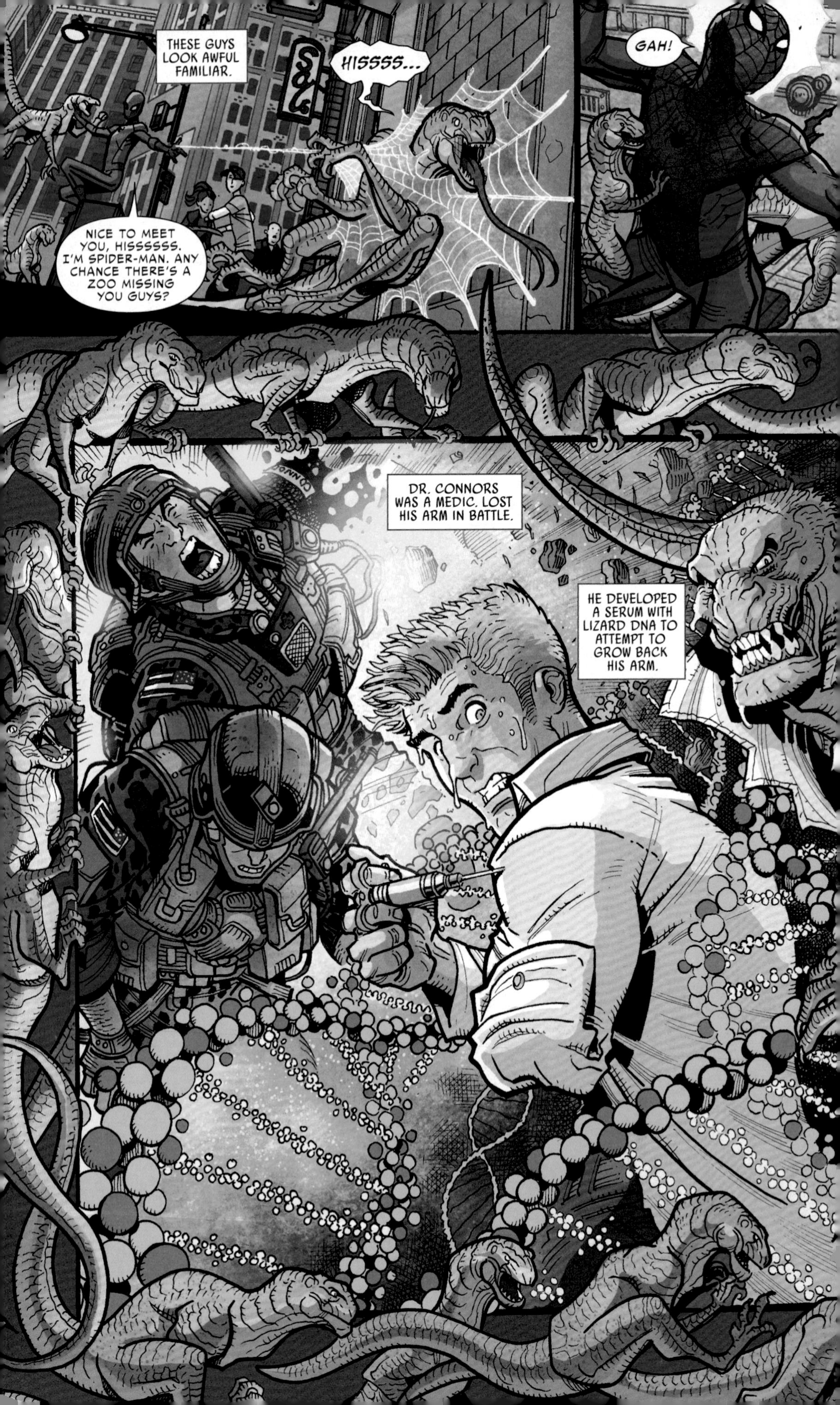
THESE GUYS LOOK AWFUL FAMILIAR.
HISSSS...
NICE TO MEET YOU, HISSSSSS. I'M SPIDER-MAN. ANY CHANCE THERE'S A ZOO MISSING YOU GUYS?
GAH!
DR. CONNORS WAS A MEDIC. LOST HIS ARM IN BATTLE.
HE DEVELOPED A SERUM WITH LIZARD DNA TO ATTEMPT TO GROW BACK HIS ARM.

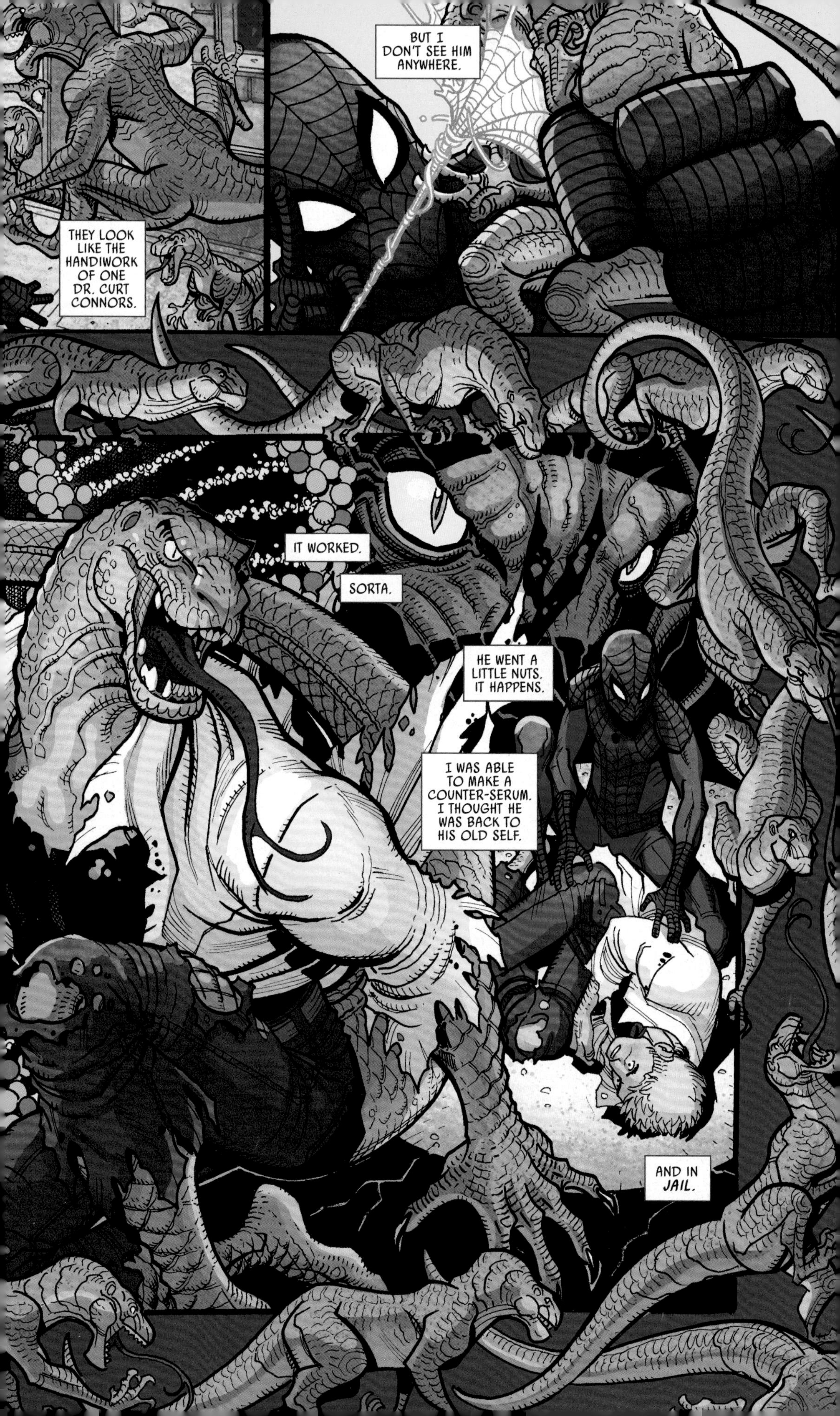
THEY LOOK LIKE THE HANDIWORK OF ONE DR. CURT CONNORS.
BUT I DON'T SEE HIM ANYWHERE.
IT WORKED.
SORTA.
HE WENT A LITTLE NUTS. IT HAPPENS.
I WAS ABLE TO MAKE A COUNTER-SERUM. I THOUGHT HE WAS BACK TO HIS OLD SELF.
AND IN JAIL.

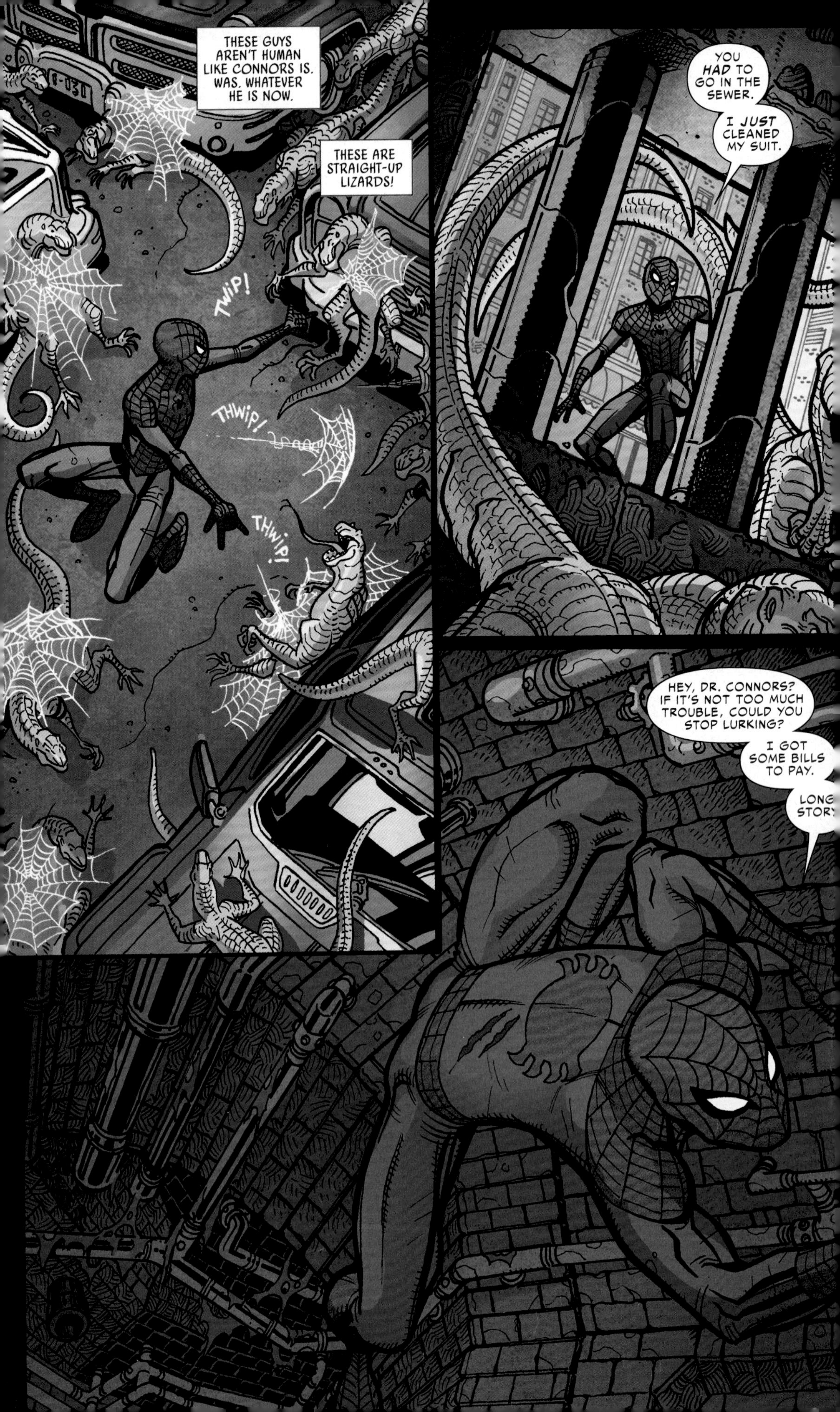
THESE GUYS AREN'T HUMAN LIKE CONNORS IS. WAS. WHATEVER HE IS NOW.
THESE ARE STRAIGHT-UP LIZARDS!
TWIP!
THWIP!
THWIP!
YOU HAD TO GO IN THE SEWER.
I JUST CLEANED MY SUIT.
HEY, DR. CONNORS? IF IT'S NOT TOO MUCH TROUBLE, COULD YOU STOP LURKING?
I GOT SOME BILLS TO PAY.
LONG STORY

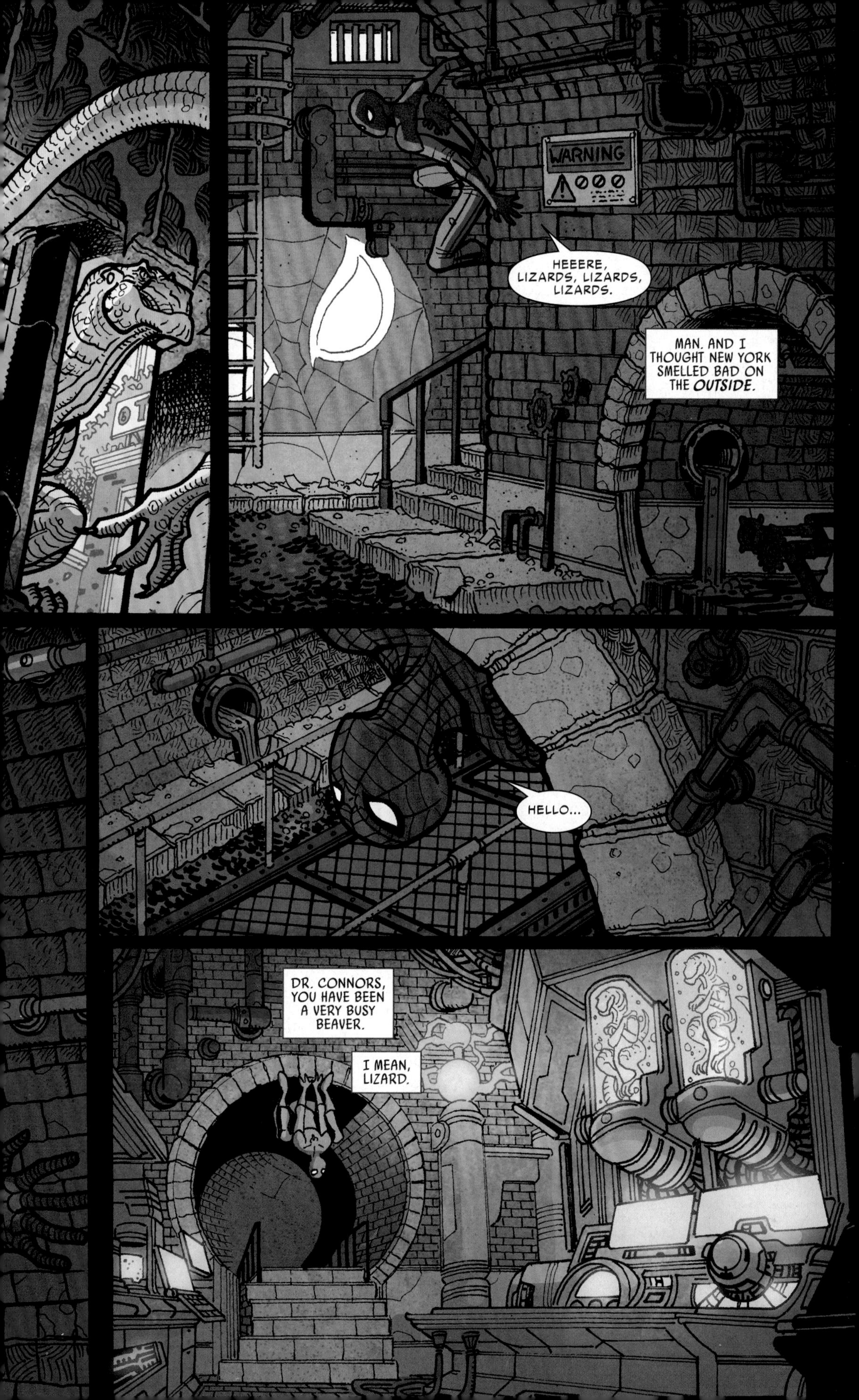
WARNING
HEEERE, LIZARDS, LIZARDS, LIZARDS.
MAN. AND I THOUGHT NEW YORK SMELLED BAD ON THE *OUTSIDE.*
HELLO...
DR. CONNORS, YOU HAVE BEEN A VERY BUSY BEAVER.
I MEAN, LIZARD.

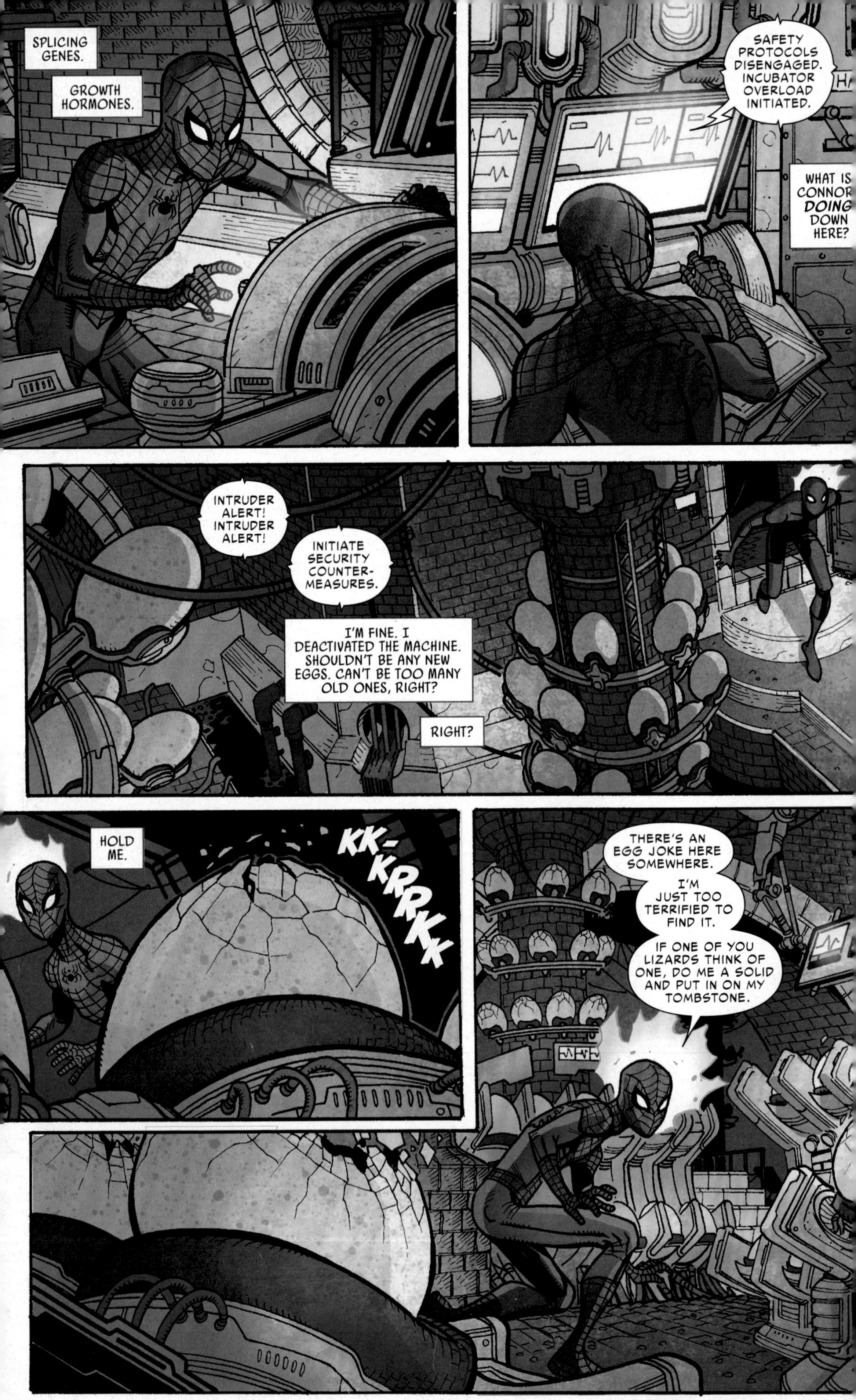

SPLICING GENES.
GROWTH HORMONES.
SAFETY PROTOCOLS DISENGAGED. INCUBATOR OVERLOAD INITIATED.
WHAT IS CONNOR DOING DOWN HERE?
INTRUDER ALERT! INTRUDER ALERT!
INITIATE SECURITY COUNTER-MEASURES.
I'M FINE. I DEACTIVATED THE MACHINE. SHOULDN'T BE ANY NEW EGGS. CAN'T BE TOO MANY OLD ONES, RIGHT?
RIGHT?
HOLD ME.
KK-KRRKKK
THERE'S AN EGG JOKE HERE SOMEWHERE.
I'M JUST TOO TERRIFIED TO FIND IT.
IF ONE OF YOU LIZARDS THINK OF ONE, DO ME A SOLID AND PUT IN ON MY TOMBSTONE.

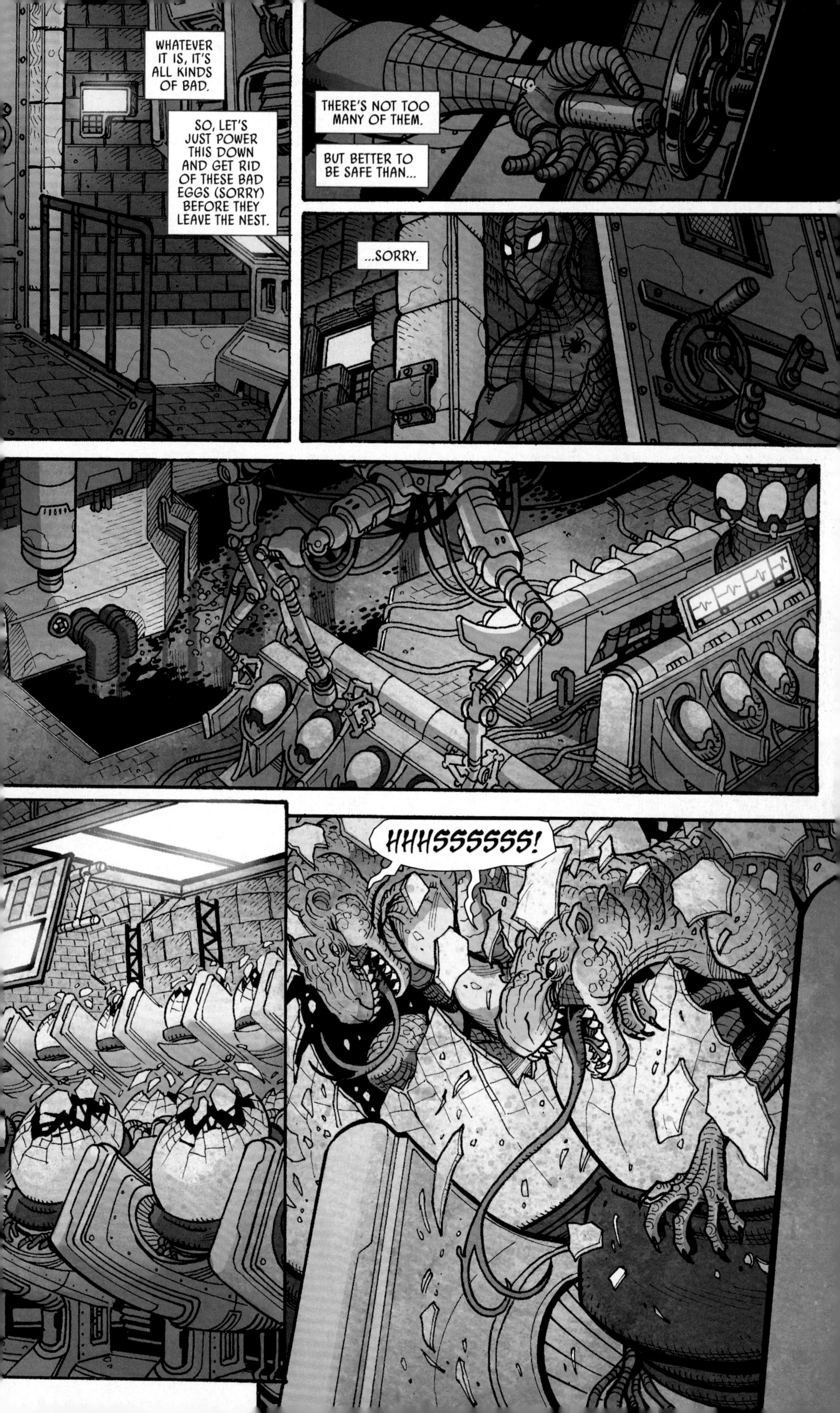
WHATEVER IT IS, IT'S ALL KINDS OF BAD.
SO, LET'S JUST POWER THIS DOWN AND GET RID OF THESE BAD EGGS (SORRY) BEFORE THEY LEAVE THE NEST.
THERE'S NOT TOO MANY OF THEM.
BUT BETTER TO BE SAFE THAN...
...SORRY.
HHHSSSSSSS!

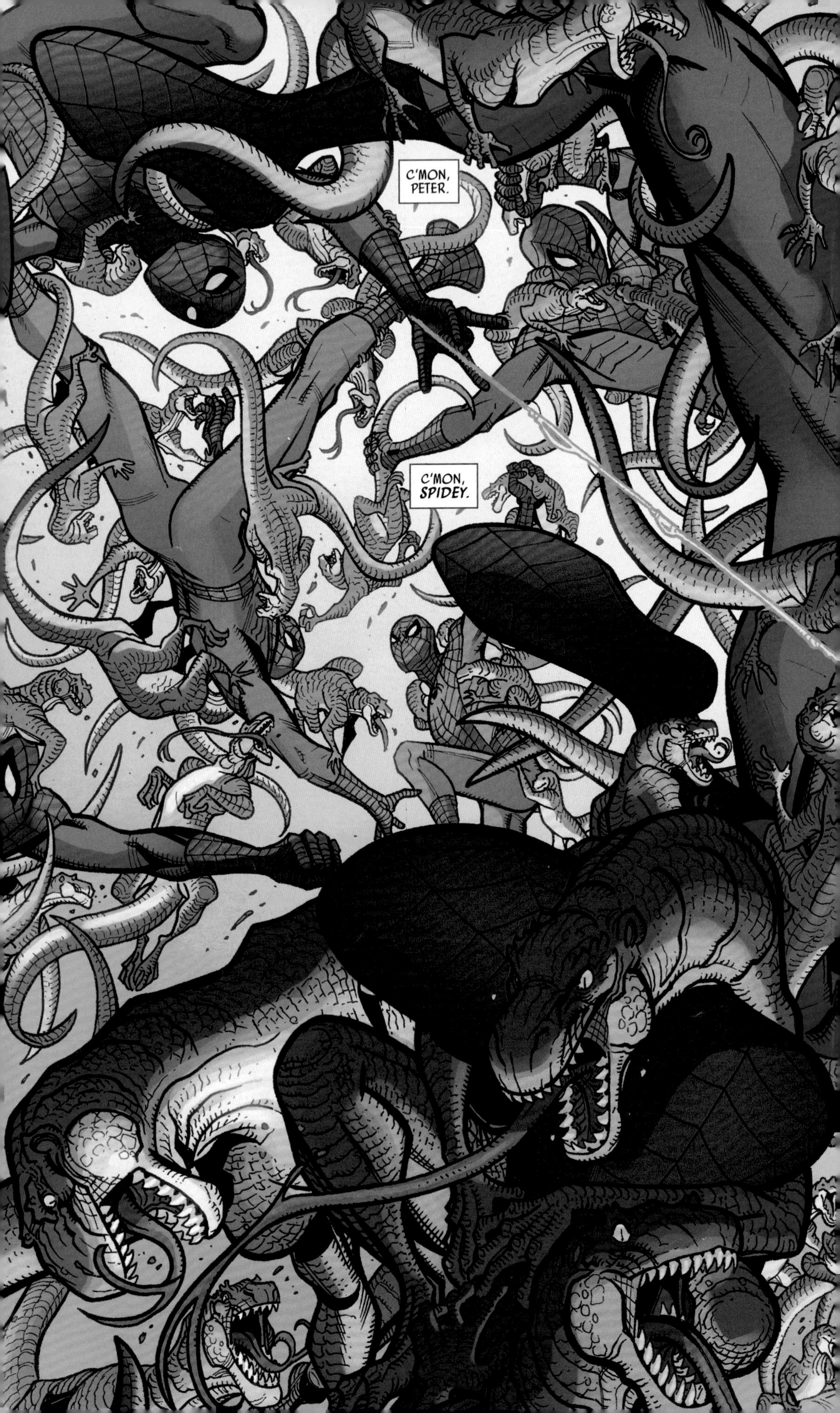
C'MON, PETER.
C'MON, SPIDEY.

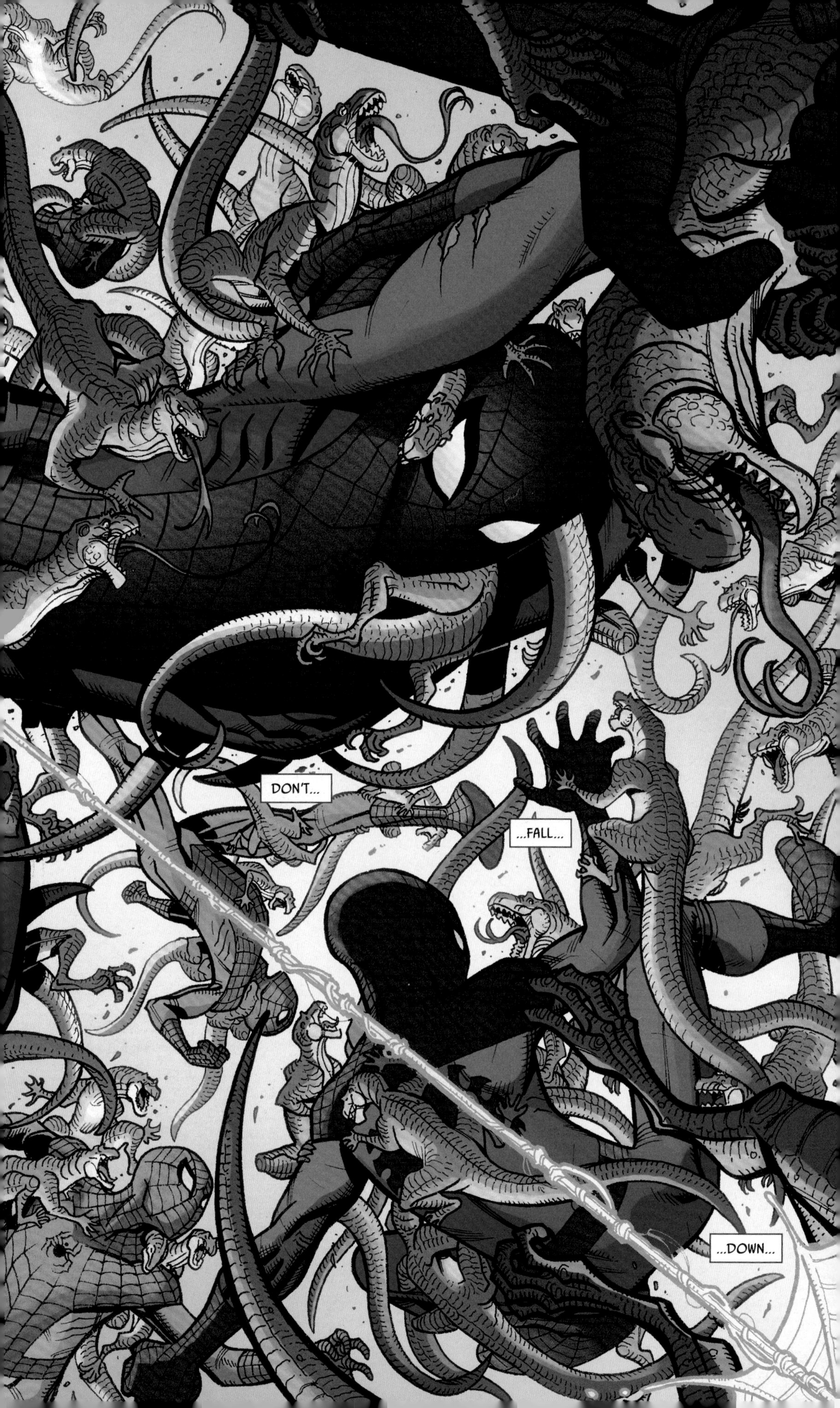
DON'T...
...FALL...
...DOWN...

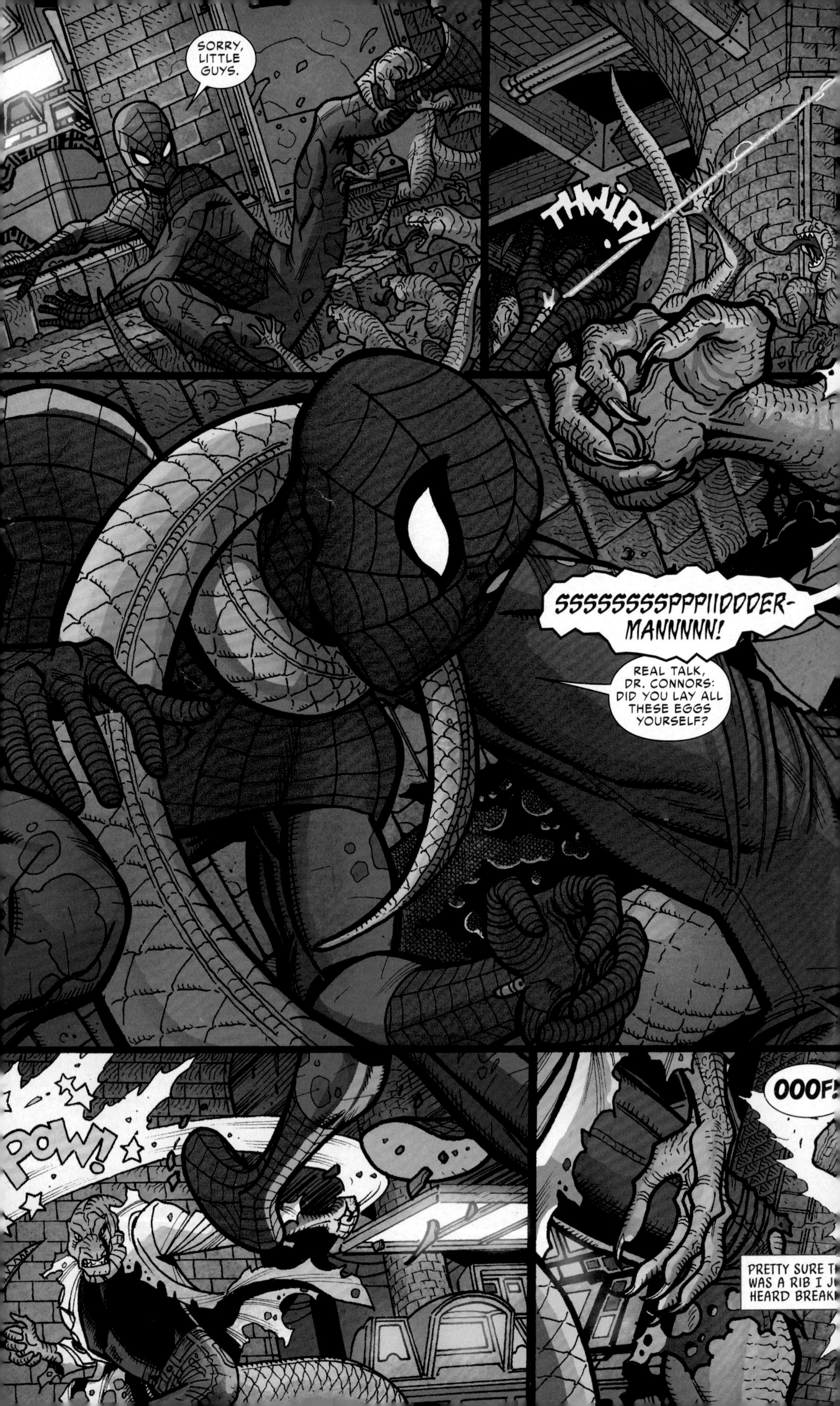
SORRY, LITTLE GUYS.
THWIP!
SSSSSSSSPPPIIDDDER-MANNNNN!
REAL TALK, DR. CONNORS: DID YOU LAY ALL THESE EGGS YOURSELF?
POW!
OOOF!
PRETTY SURE T
WAS A RIB I J
HEARD BREAK

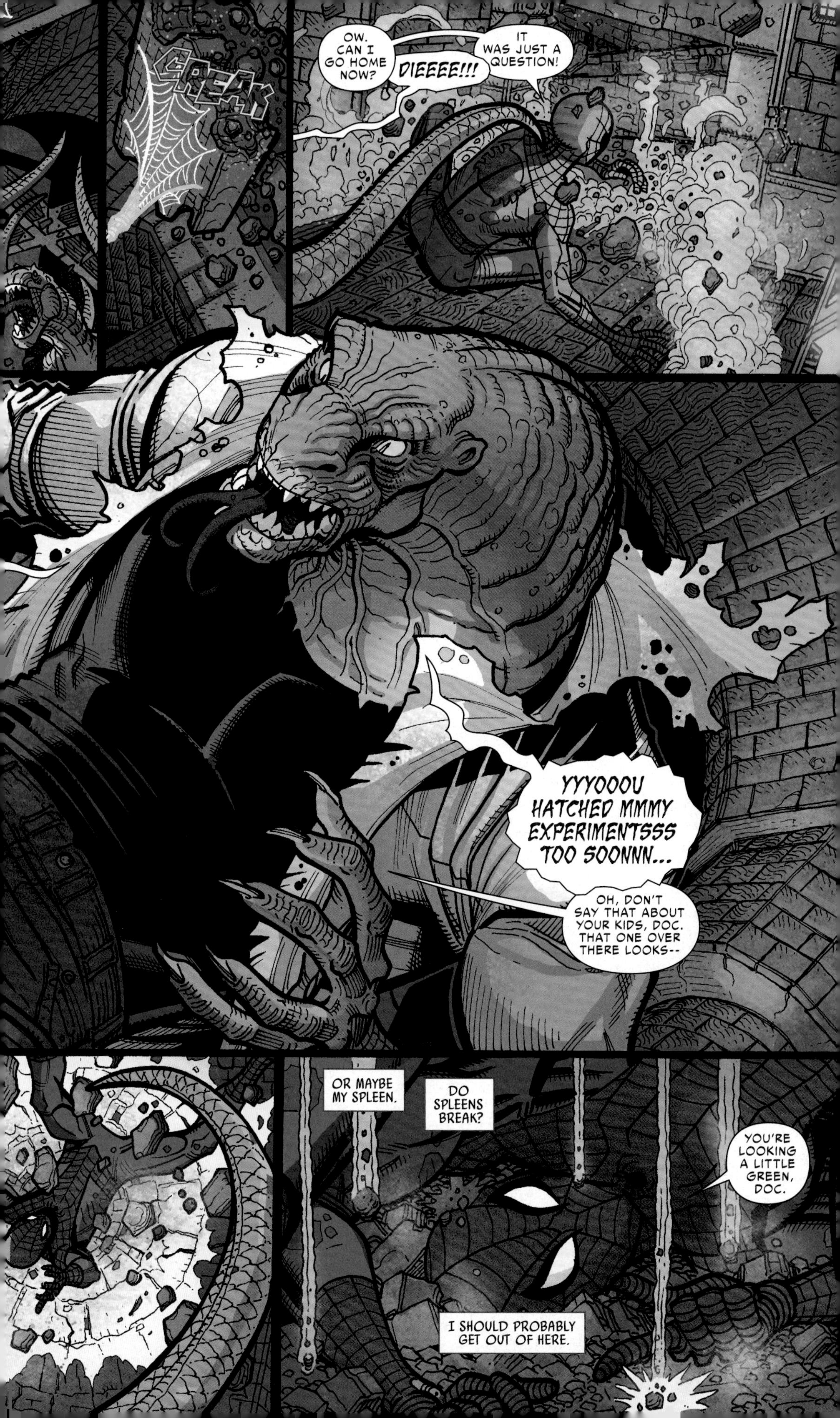
CREAK
OW. CAN I GO HOME NOW?
DIEEEE!!!
IT WAS JUST A QUESTION!
YYYOOOU HATCHED MMMY EXPERIMENTSSS TOO SOONNN...
OH, DON'T SAY THAT ABOUT YOUR KIDS, DOC. THAT ONE OVER THERE LOOKS--
OR MAYBE MY SPLEEN.
DO SPLEENS BREAK?
YOU'RE LOOKING A LITTLE GREEN, DOC.
I SHOULD PROBABLY GET OUT OF HERE.

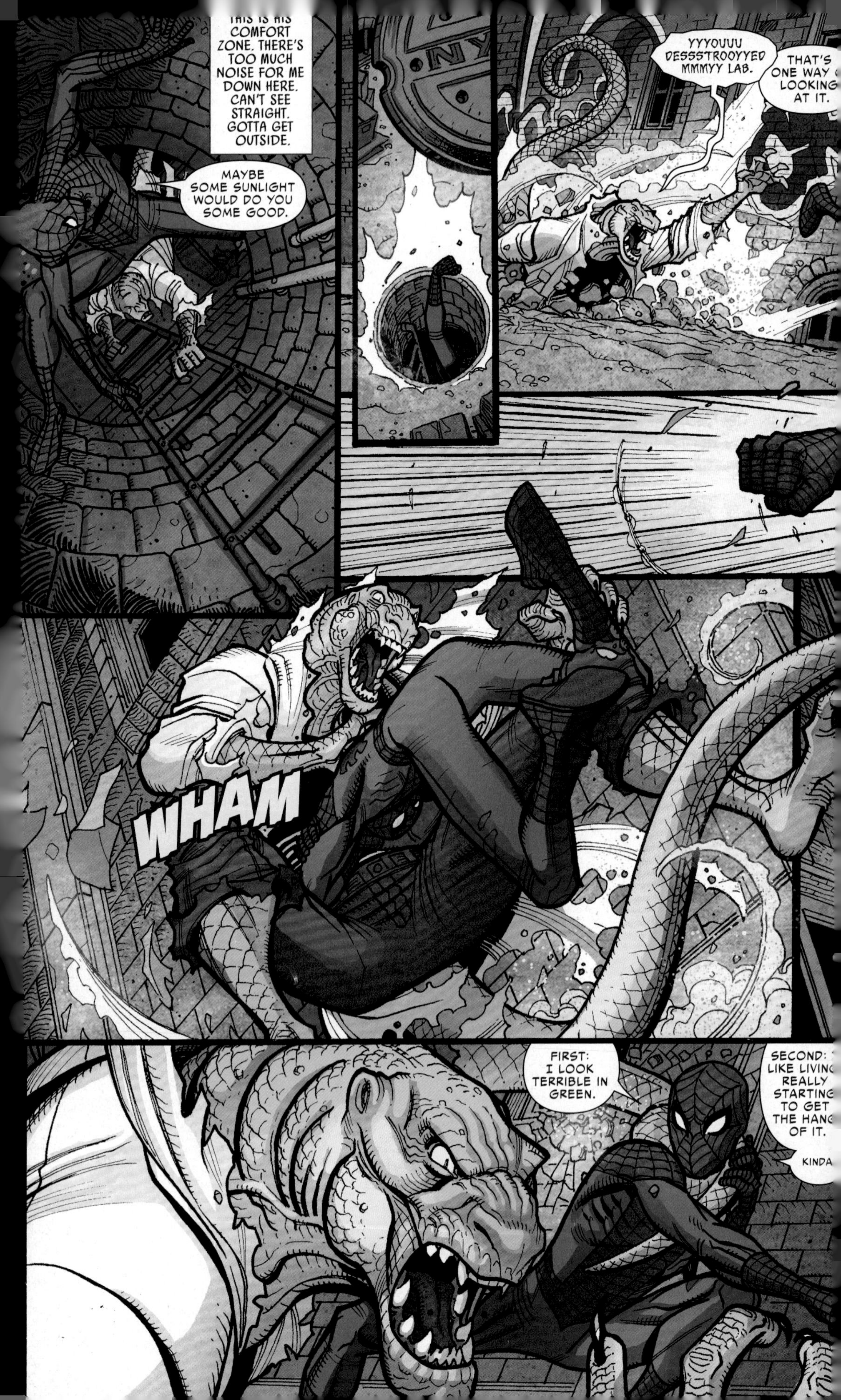
THIS IS HIS COMFORT ZONE. THERE'S TOO MUCH NOISE FOR ME DOWN HERE. CAN'T SEE STRAIGHT. GOTTA GET OUTSIDE.
MAYBE SOME SUNLIGHT WOULD DO YOU SOME GOOD.
YYYOUUU DESSSTROOYYED MMMYY LAB.
THAT'S ONE WAY OF LOOKING AT IT.
WHAM
FIRST: I LOOK TERRIBLE IN GREEN.
SECOND: I LIKE LIVING. REALLY STARTING TO GET THE HANG OF IT.
KINDA.

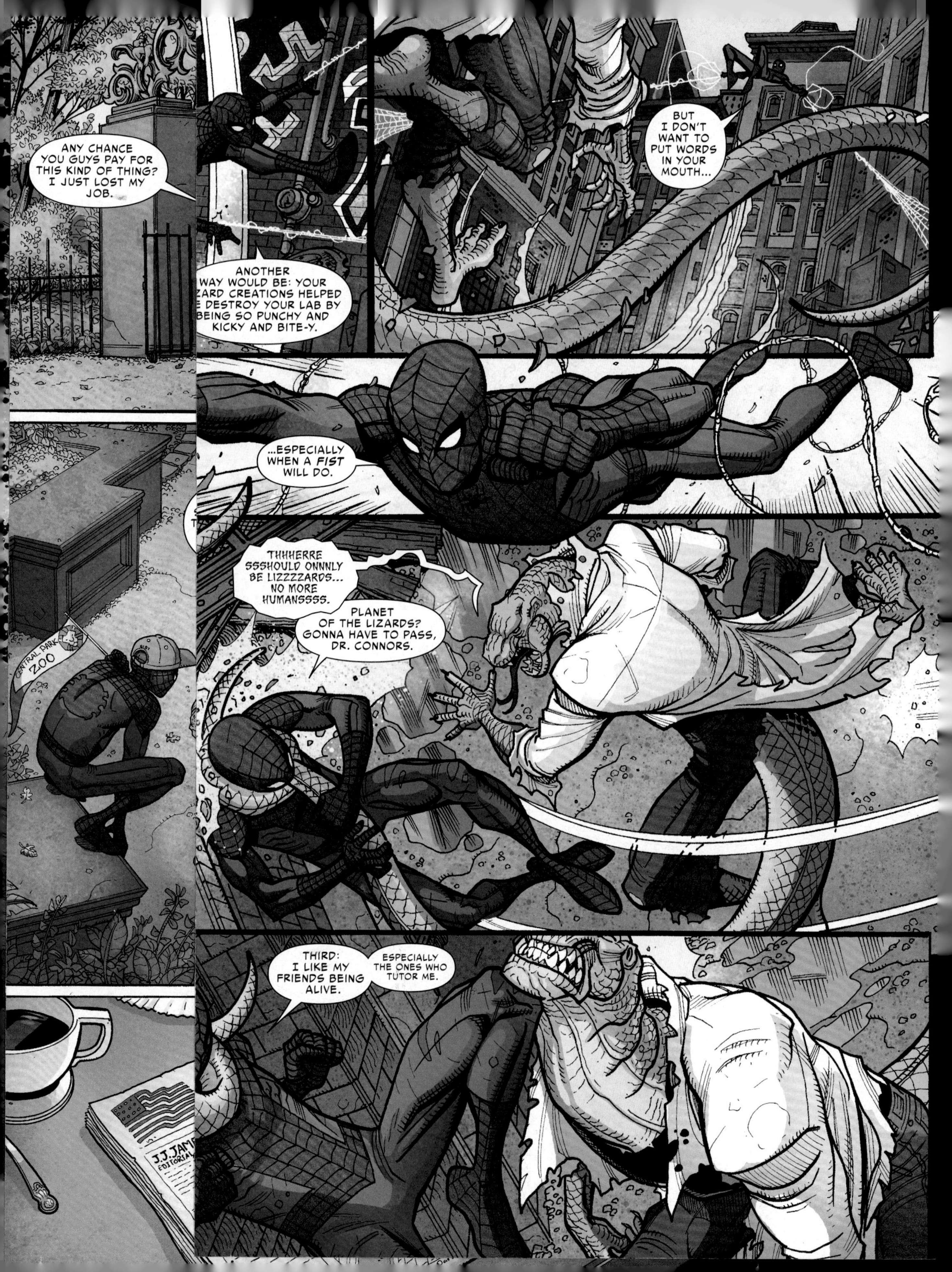
ANY CHANCE YOU GUYS PAY FOR THIS KIND OF THING? I JUST LOST MY JOB.
ANOTHER WAY WOULD BE: YOUR ZARD CREATIONS HELPED E DESTROY YOUR LAB BY BEING SO PUNCHY AND KICKY AND BITE-Y.
BUT I DON'T WANT TO PUT WORDS IN YOUR MOUTH...
...ESPECIALLY WHEN A FIST WILL DO.
THHHERRE SSSHOULD ONNNLY BE LIZZZZARDS... NO MORE HUMANSSSS.
PLANET OF THE LIZARDS? GONNA HAVE TO PASS, DR. CONNORS.
CENTRAL PARK ZOO
THIRD: I LIKE MY FRIENDS BEING ALIVE.
ESPECIALLY THE ONES WHO TUTOR ME.
J.J. JAM
EDITORIAL

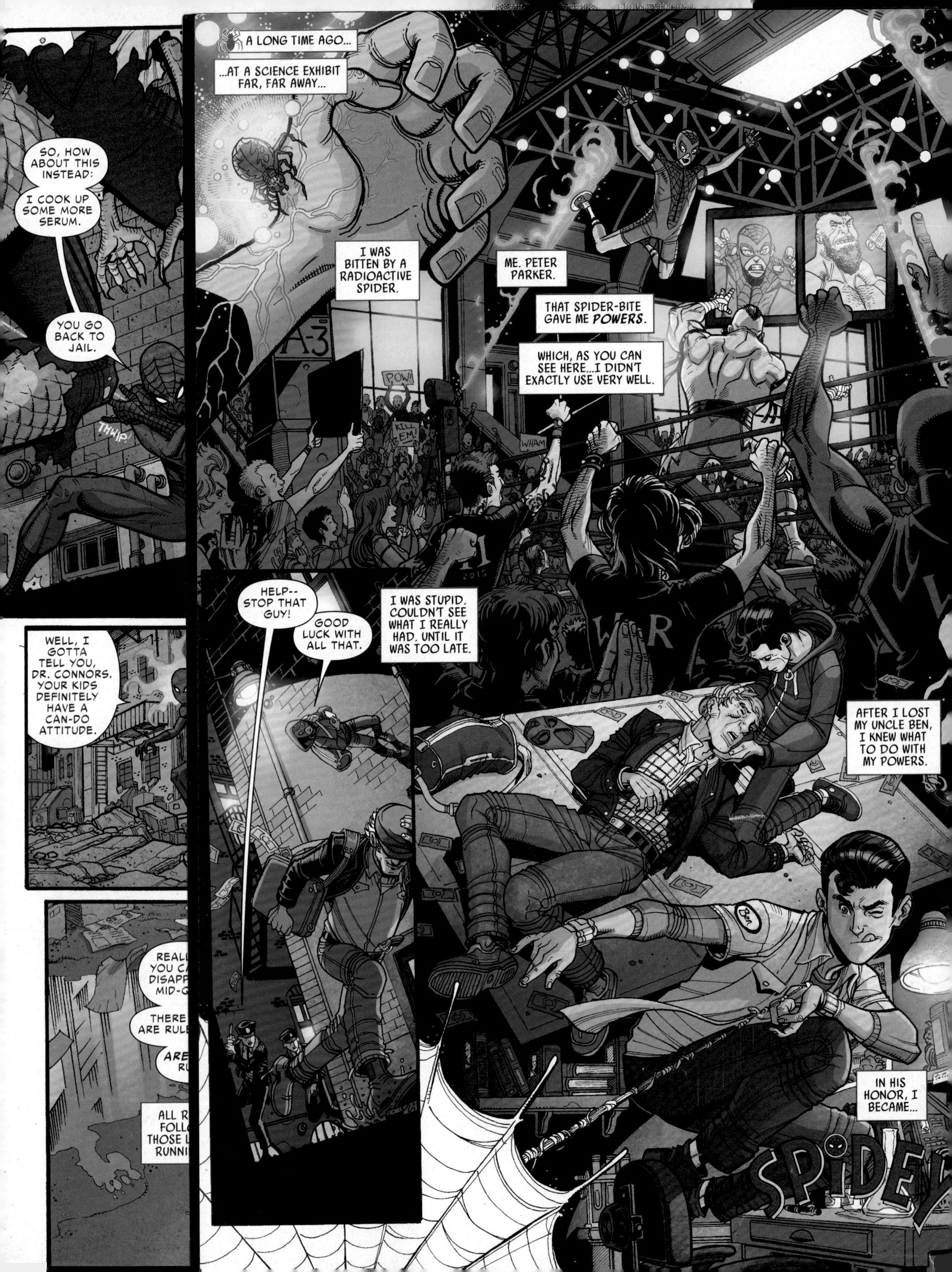

SO, HOW ABOUT THIS INSTEAD:
I COOK UP SOME MORE SERUM.
YOU GO BACK TO JAIL.
THWIP!
WELL, I GOTTA TELL YOU, DR. CONNORS. YOUR KIDS DEFINITELY HAVE A CAN-DO ATTITUDE.
A LONG TIME AGO...
...AT A SCIENCE EXHIBIT FAR, FAR AWAY...
I WAS BITTEN BY A RADIOACTIVE SPIDER.
ME. PETER PARKER.
THAT SPIDER-BITE GAVE ME POWERS.
WHICH, AS YOU CAN SEE HERE...I DIDN'T EXACTLY USE VERY WELL.
POW!
KILL 'EM!
WHAM
HELP-- STOP THAT GUY!
GOOD LUCK WITH ALL THAT.
I WAS STUPID. COULDN'T SEE WHAT I REALLY HAD. UNTIL IT WAS TOO LATE.
AFTER I LOST MY UNCLE BEN, I KNEW WHAT TO DO WITH MY POWERS.
IN HIS HONOR, I BECAME...

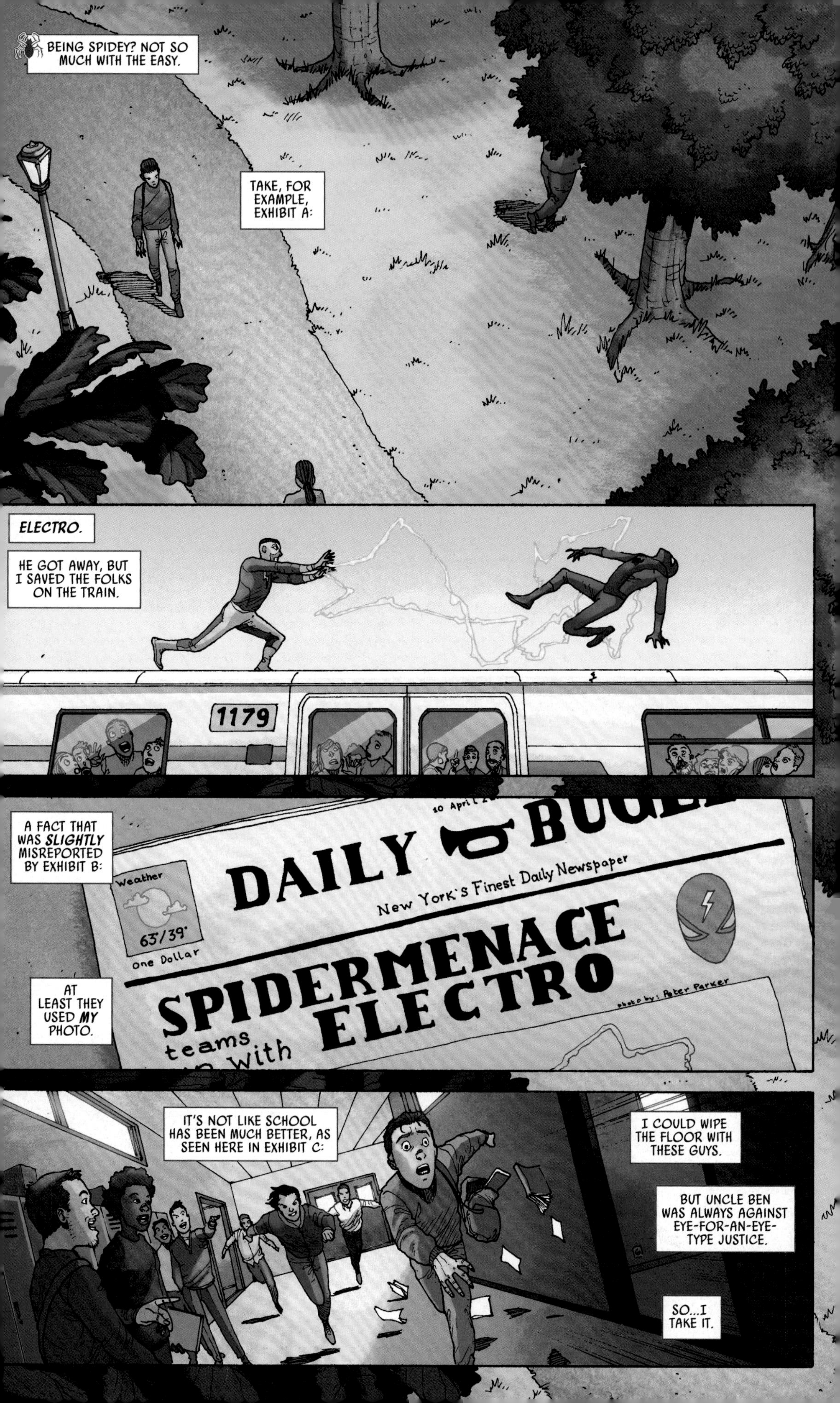
BEING SPIDEY? NOT SO MUCH WITH THE EASY.
TAKE, FOR EXAMPLE, EXHIBIT A:
ELECTRO.
HE GOT AWAY, BUT I SAVED THE FOLKS ON THE TRAIN.
1179
A FACT THAT WAS SLIGHTLY MISREPORTED BY EXHIBIT B:
DAILY BUGLE
New York's Finest Daily Newspaper
Weather
63°/39°
One Dollar
SPIDERMENACE teams with ELECTRO
photo by: Peter Parker
AT LEAST THEY USED MY PHOTO.
IT'S NOT LIKE SCHOOL HAS BEEN MUCH BETTER, AS SEEN HERE IN EXHIBIT C:
I COULD WIPE THE FLOOR WITH THESE GUYS.
BUT UNCLE BEN WAS ALWAYS AGAINST EYE-FOR-AN-EYE-TYPE JUSTICE.
SO...I TAKE IT.

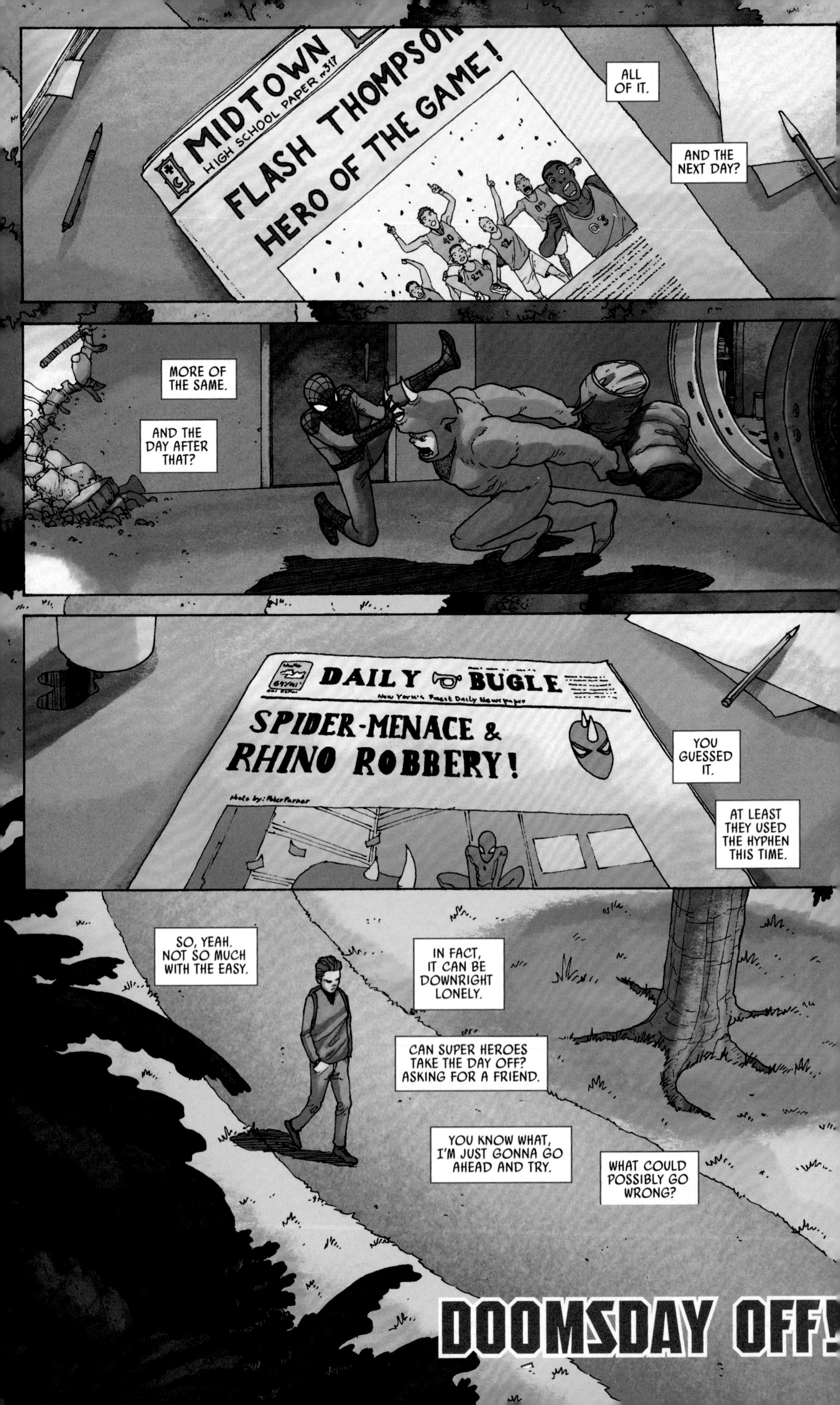

MIDTOWN
HIGH SCHOOL PAPER nr317
FLASH THOMPSON
HERO OF THE GAME!
ALL OF IT.
AND THE NEXT DAY?
MORE OF THE SAME.
AND THE DAY AFTER THAT?
DAILY BUGLE
New York's Finest Daily Newspaper
SPIDER-MENACE & RHINO ROBBERY!
photo by: Peter Parker
YOU GUESSED IT.
AT LEAST THEY USED THE HYPHEN THIS TIME.
SO, YEAH. NOT SO MUCH WITH THE EASY.
IN FACT, IT CAN BE DOWNRIGHT LONELY.
CAN SUPER HEROES TAKE THE DAY OFF? ASKING FOR A FRIEND.
YOU KNOW WHAT, I'M JUST GONNA GO AHEAD AND TRY.
WHAT COULD POSSIBLY GO WRONG?
DOOMSDAY OFF!

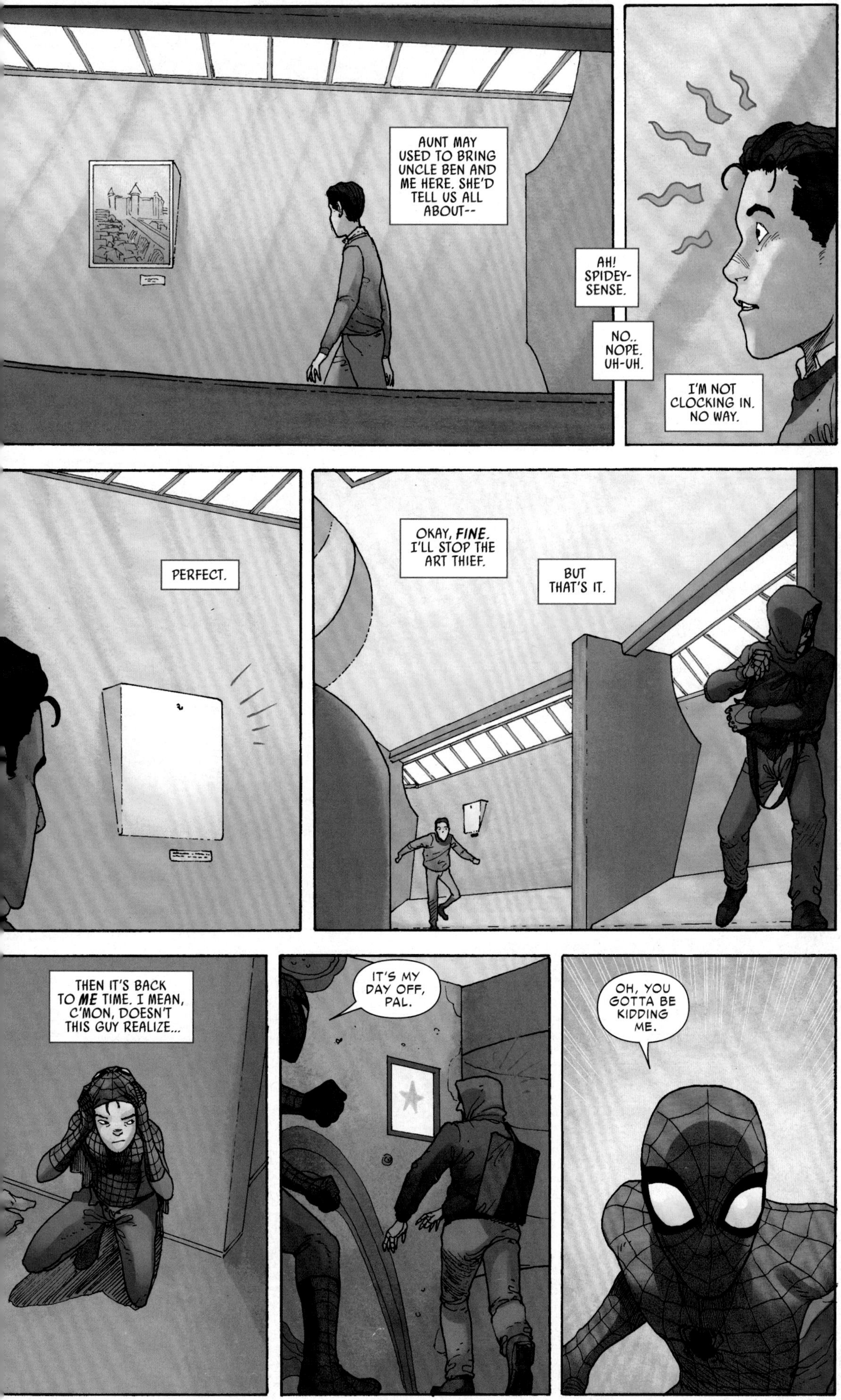
AUNT MAY USED TO BRING UNCLE BEN AND ME HERE. SHE'D TELL US ALL ABOUT--
AH! SPIDEY-SENSE.
NO.. NOPE. UH-UH.
I'M NOT CLOCKING IN. NO WAY.
PERFECT.
OKAY, FINE. I'LL STOP THE ART THIEF.
BUT THAT'S IT.
THEN IT'S BACK TO ME TIME. I MEAN, C'MON, DOESN'T THIS GUY REALIZE...
IT'S MY DAY OFF, PAL.
OH, YOU GOTTA BE KIDDING ME.

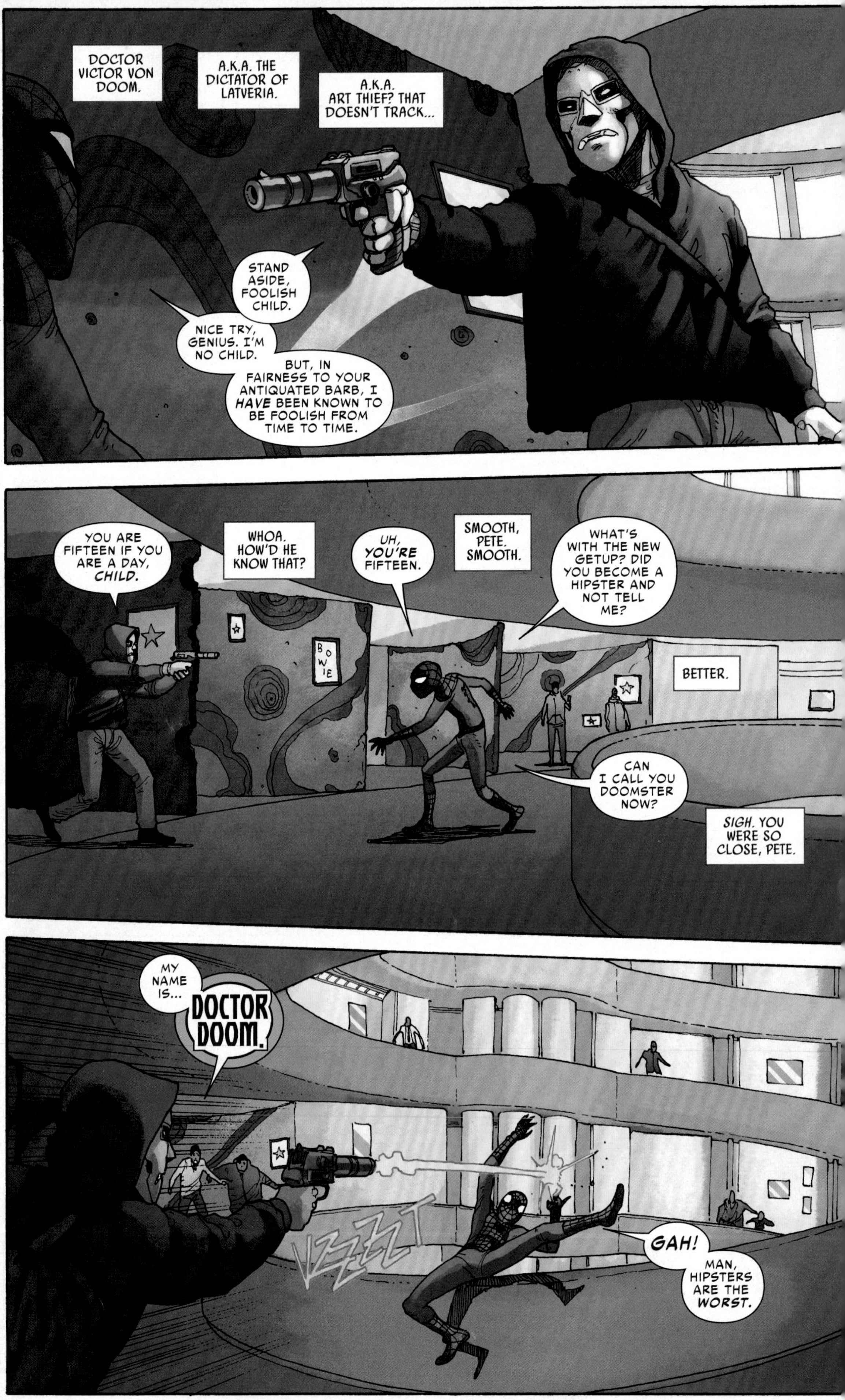
DOCTOR VICTOR VON DOOM.
A.K.A. THE DICTATOR OF LATVERIA.
A.K.A. ART THIEF? THAT DOESN'T TRACK...
STAND ASIDE, FOOLISH CHILD.
NICE TRY, GENIUS. I'M NO CHILD.
BUT, IN FAIRNESS TO YOUR ANTIQUATED BARB, I *HAVE* BEEN KNOWN TO BE FOOLISH FROM TIME TO TIME.
YOU ARE FIFTEEN IF YOU ARE A DAY, *CHILD.*
WHOA. HOW'D HE KNOW THAT?
UH, *YOU'RE* FIFTEEN.
SMOOTH, PETE. SMOOTH.
WHAT'S WITH THE NEW GETUP? DID YOU BECOME A HIPSTER AND NOT TELL ME?
BOWIE
BETTER.
CAN I CALL YOU DOOMSTER NOW?
*SIGH.* YOU WERE SO CLOSE, PETE.
MY NAME IS... **DOCTOR DOOM.**
VZZZZT
**GAH!**
MAN, HIPSTERS ARE THE *WORST.*

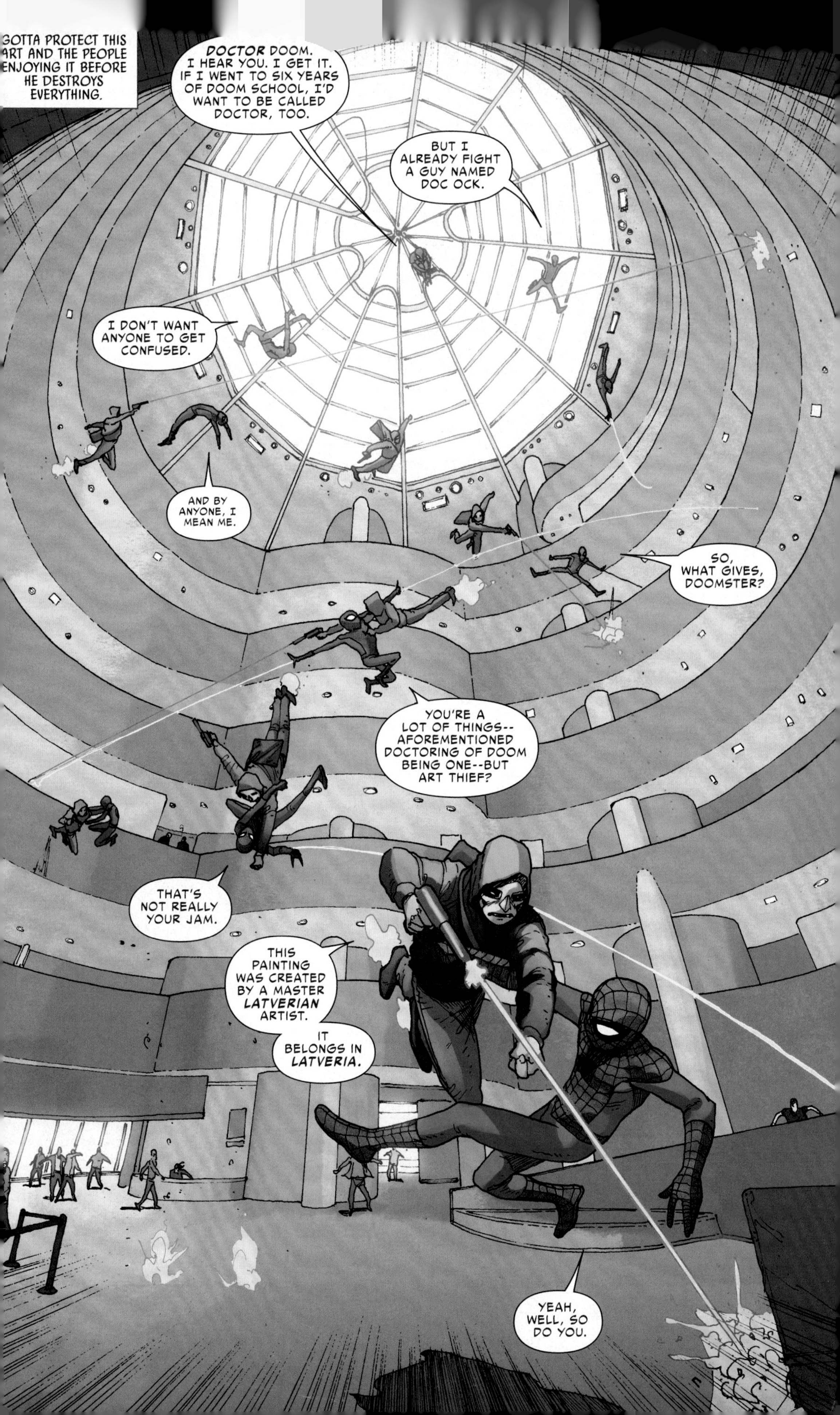
GOTTA PROTECT THIS ART AND THE PEOPLE ENJOYING IT BEFORE HE DESTROYS EVERYTHING.
DOCTOR DOOM. I HEAR YOU. I GET IT. IF I WENT TO SIX YEARS OF DOOM SCHOOL, I'D WANT TO BE CALLED DOCTOR, TOO.
BUT I ALREADY FIGHT A GUY NAMED DOC OCK.
I DON'T WANT ANYONE TO GET CONFUSED.
AND BY ANYONE, I MEAN ME.
SO, WHAT GIVES, DOOMSTER?
YOU'RE A LOT OF THINGS-- AFOREMENTIONED DOCTORING OF DOOM BEING ONE--BUT ART THIEF?
THAT'S NOT REALLY YOUR JAM.
THIS PAINTING WAS CREATED BY A MASTER LATVERIAN ARTIST.
IT BELONGS IN LATVERIA.
YEAH, WELL, SO DO YOU.

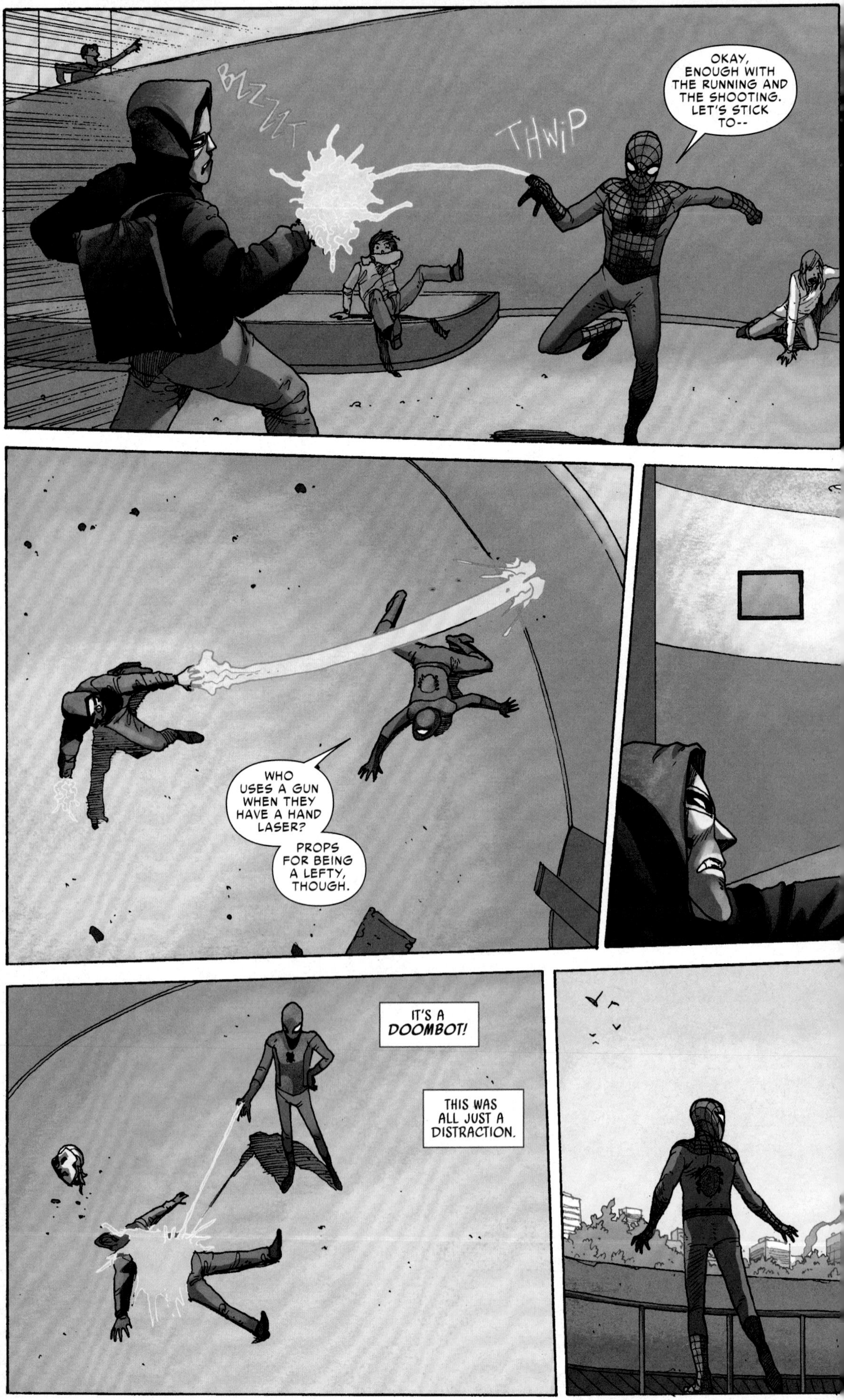
BZZZZT
THWIP
OKAY, ENOUGH WITH THE RUNNING AND THE SHOOTING. LET'S STICK TO--
WHO USES A GUN WHEN THEY HAVE A HAND LASER?
PROPS FOR BEING A LEFTY, THOUGH.
IT'S A *DOOMBOT!*
THIS WAS ALL JUST A DISTRACTION.

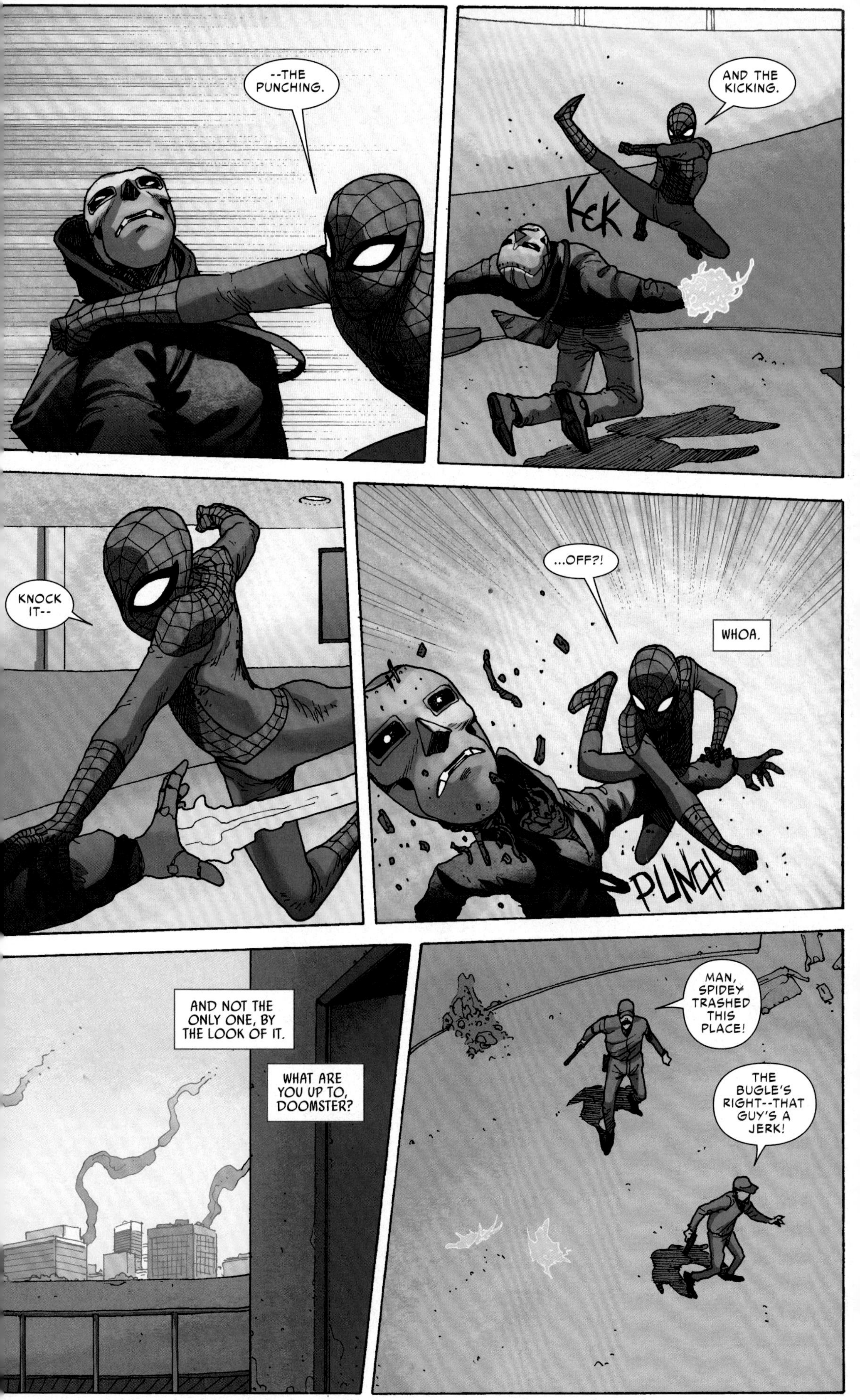
--THE PUNCHING.
AND THE KICKING.
KICK
KNOCK IT--
...OFF?!
WHOA.
PUNCH
AND NOT THE ONLY ONE, BY THE LOOK OF IT.
WHAT ARE YOU UP TO, DOOMSTER?
MAN, SPIDEY TRASHED THIS PLACE!
THE BUGLE'S RIGHT--THAT GUY'S A JERK!

I NEED EYES. LIKE... EVERYWHERE. HERE WE GO.

CEBULSKI'S TVs
THE BEST TVS IN AMERICA

COMICS

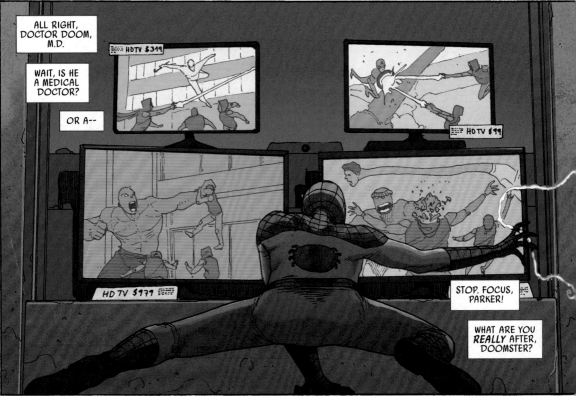

ALL RIGHT, DOCTOR DOOM, M.D.

WAIT, IS HE A MEDICAL DOCTOR?

OR A--

HDTV $319

HDTV $99

HD TV $979

STOP. FOCUS, PARKER!

WHAT ARE YOU *REALLY* AFTER, DOOMSTER?

POWER.

NEWS UPDATE: POWER OUTAGE IN BROOKLYN. NEWS U

I'M BETTING IT'S LESS "POWER OUTAGE" AND MORE POWER THEFT-AGE.

THAT'S MORE DOOM'S STYLE.

AND YES, I KNOW THEFT-AGE ISN'T A THING. NEITHER IS DOOMSTER. WORK WITH ME, PEOPLE!

HDTV $979

SO DOOM IS STEALING POWER. WHY?

ONE WAY TO FIND OUT...

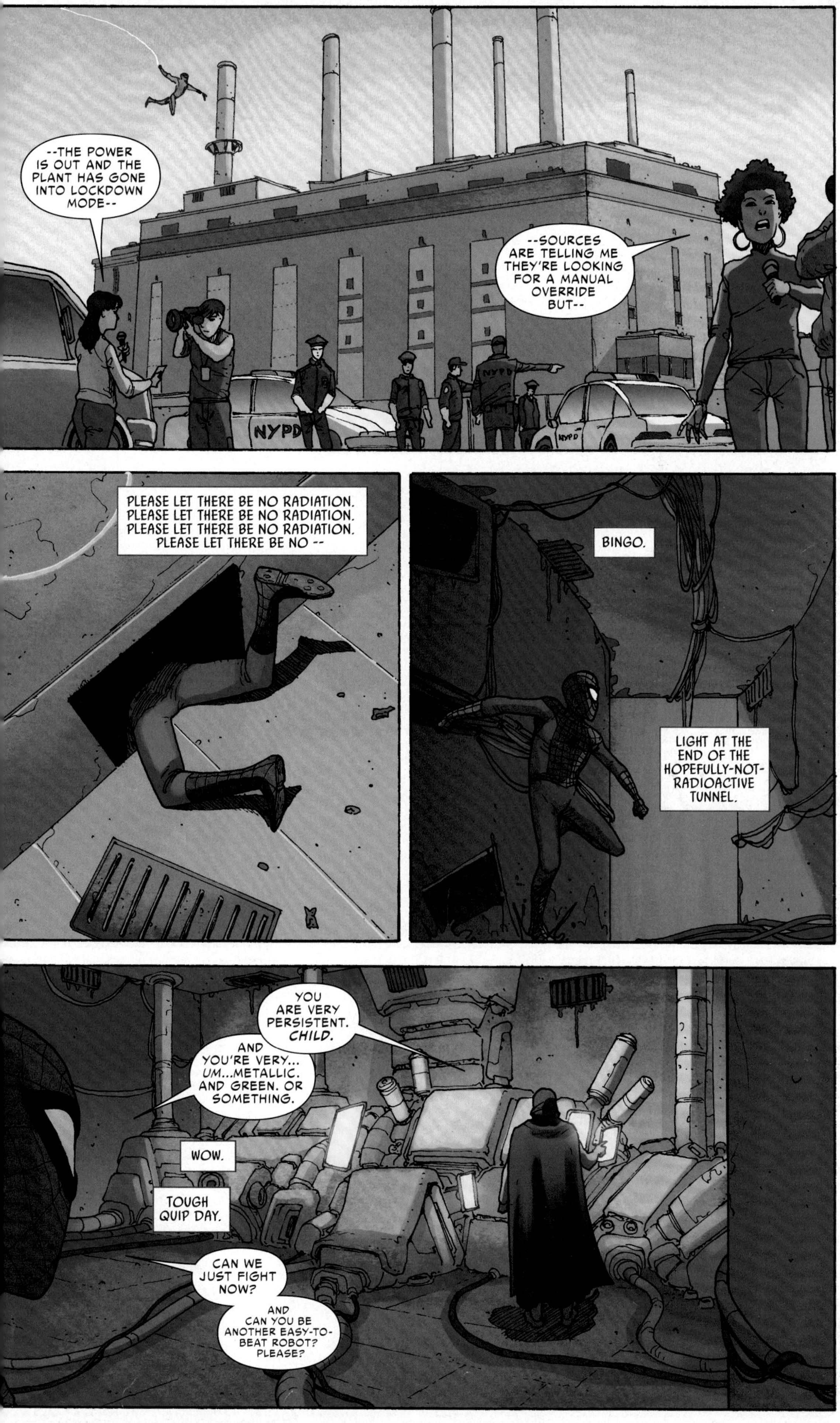
--THE POWER IS OUT AND THE PLANT HAS GONE INTO LOCKDOWN MODE--
--SOURCES ARE TELLING ME THEY'RE LOOKING FOR A MANUAL OVERRIDE BUT--
NYPD
NYPD
NYPD
PLEASE LET THERE BE NO RADIATION. PLEASE LET THERE BE NO RADIATION. PLEASE LET THERE BE NO RADIATION. PLEASE LET THERE BE NO --
BINGO.
LIGHT AT THE END OF THE HOPEFULLY-NOT-RADIOACTIVE TUNNEL.
YOU ARE VERY PERSISTENT. *CHILD.*
AND YOU'RE VERY... *UM*...METALLIC. AND GREEN. OR SOMETHING.
WOW.
TOUGH QUIP DAY.
CAN WE JUST FIGHT NOW?
AND CAN YOU BE ANOTHER EASY-TO-BEAT ROBOT? PLEASE?

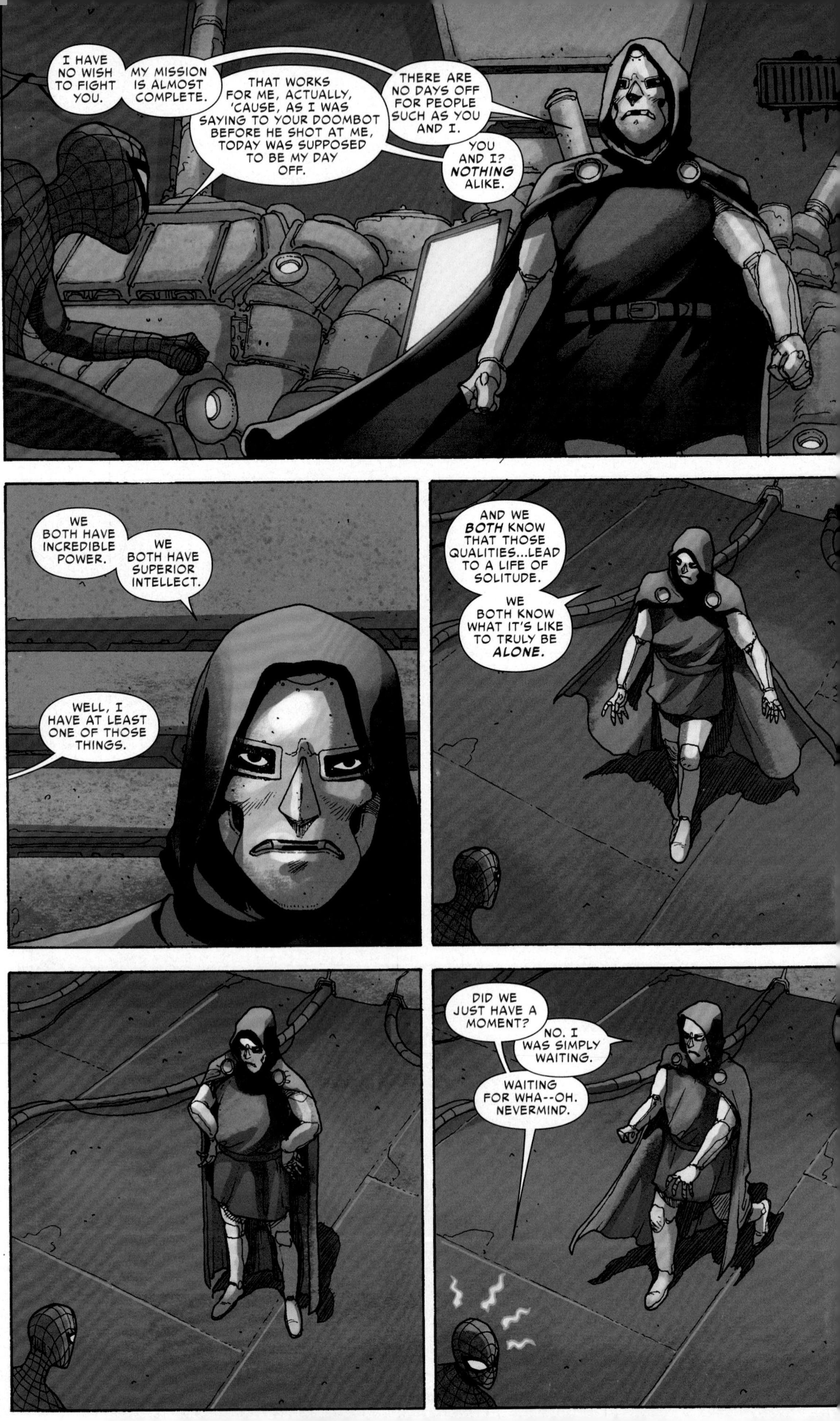
I HAVE NO WISH TO FIGHT YOU.
MY MISSION IS ALMOST COMPLETE.
THAT WORKS FOR ME, ACTUALLY, 'CAUSE, AS I WAS SAYING TO YOUR DOOMBOT BEFORE HE SHOT AT ME, TODAY WAS SUPPOSED TO BE MY DAY OFF.
THERE ARE NO DAYS OFF FOR PEOPLE SUCH AS YOU AND I.
YOU AND I? NOTHING ALIKE.
WE BOTH HAVE INCREDIBLE POWER.
WE BOTH HAVE SUPERIOR INTELLECT.
WELL, I HAVE AT LEAST ONE OF THOSE THINGS.
AND WE BOTH KNOW THAT THOSE QUALITIES...LEAD TO A LIFE OF SOLITUDE.
WE BOTH KNOW WHAT IT'S LIKE TO TRULY BE ALONE.
DID WE JUST HAVE A MOMENT?
NO. I WAS SIMPLY WAITING.
WAITING FOR WHA--OH. NEVERMIND.

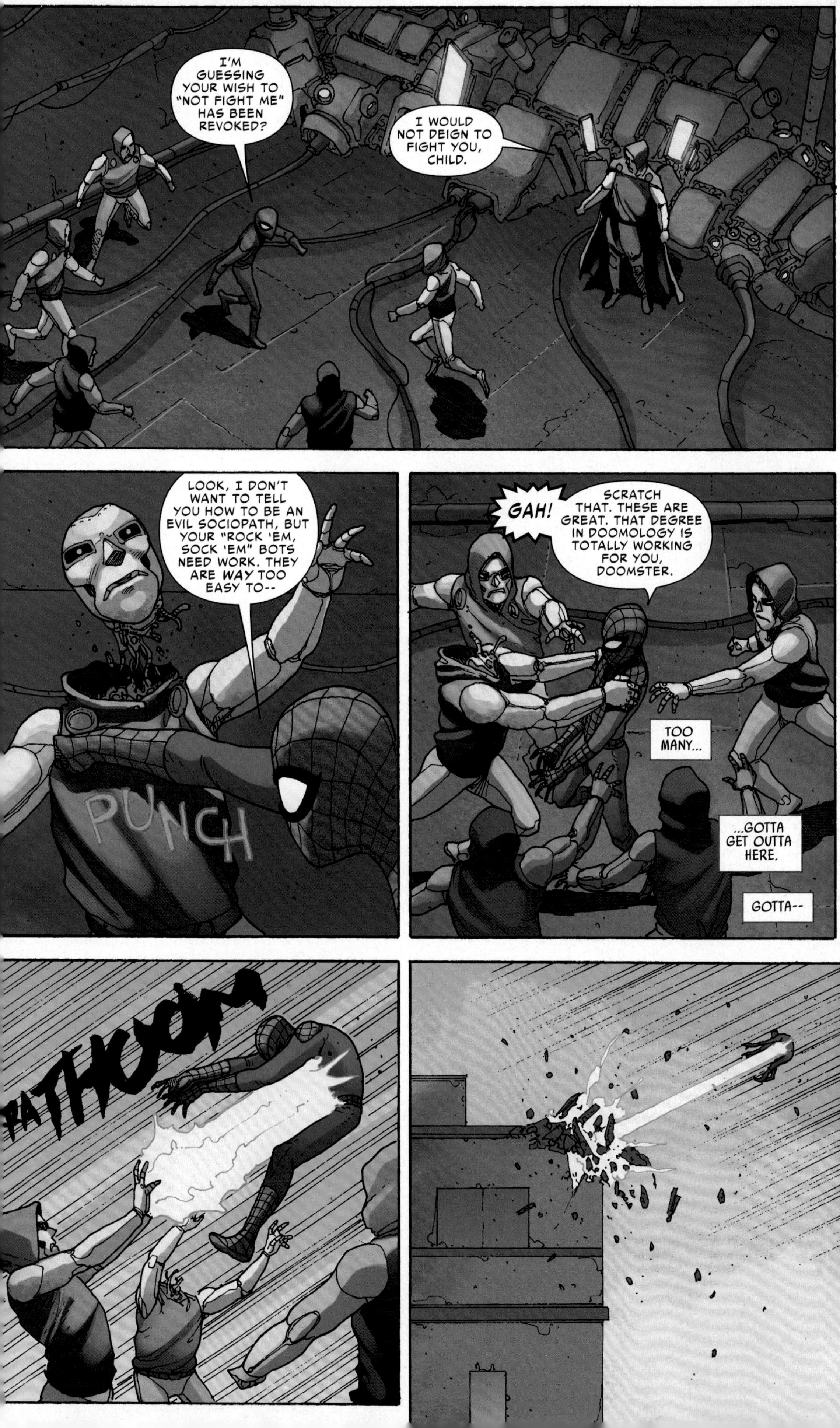

I'M GUESSING YOUR WISH TO "NOT FIGHT ME" HAS BEEN REVOKED?
I WOULD NOT DEIGN TO FIGHT YOU, CHILD.
LOOK, I DON'T WANT TO TELL YOU HOW TO BE AN EVIL SOCIOPATH, BUT YOUR "ROCK 'EM, SOCK 'EM" BOTS NEED WORK. THEY ARE WAY TOO EASY TO--
PUNCH
GAH!
SCRATCH THAT. THESE ARE GREAT. THAT DEGREE IN DOOMOLOGY IS TOTALLY WORKING FOR YOU, DOOMSTER.
TOO MANY...
...GOTTA GET OUTTA HERE.
GOTTA--
RATHOOM

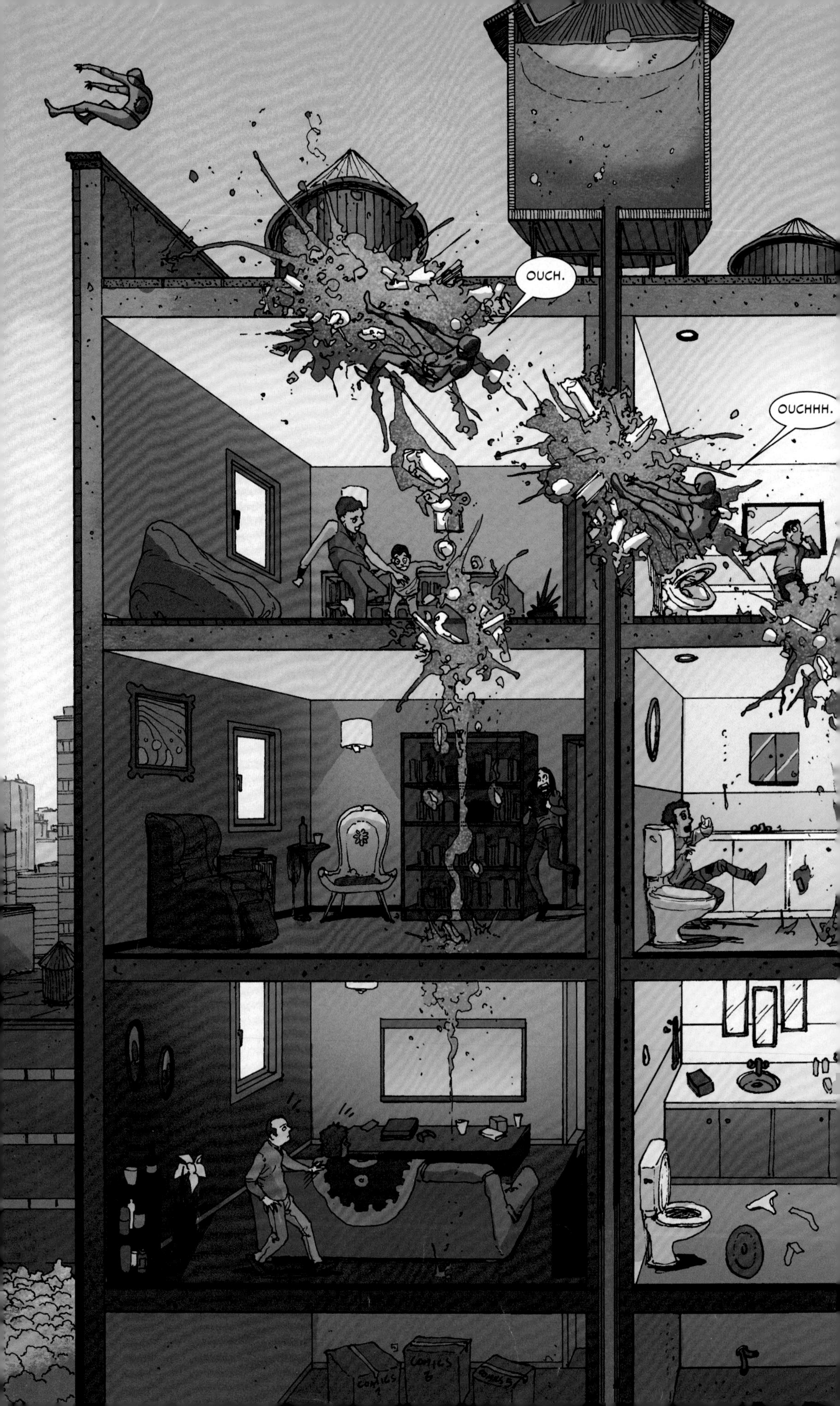
OUCH.
OUCHHH.

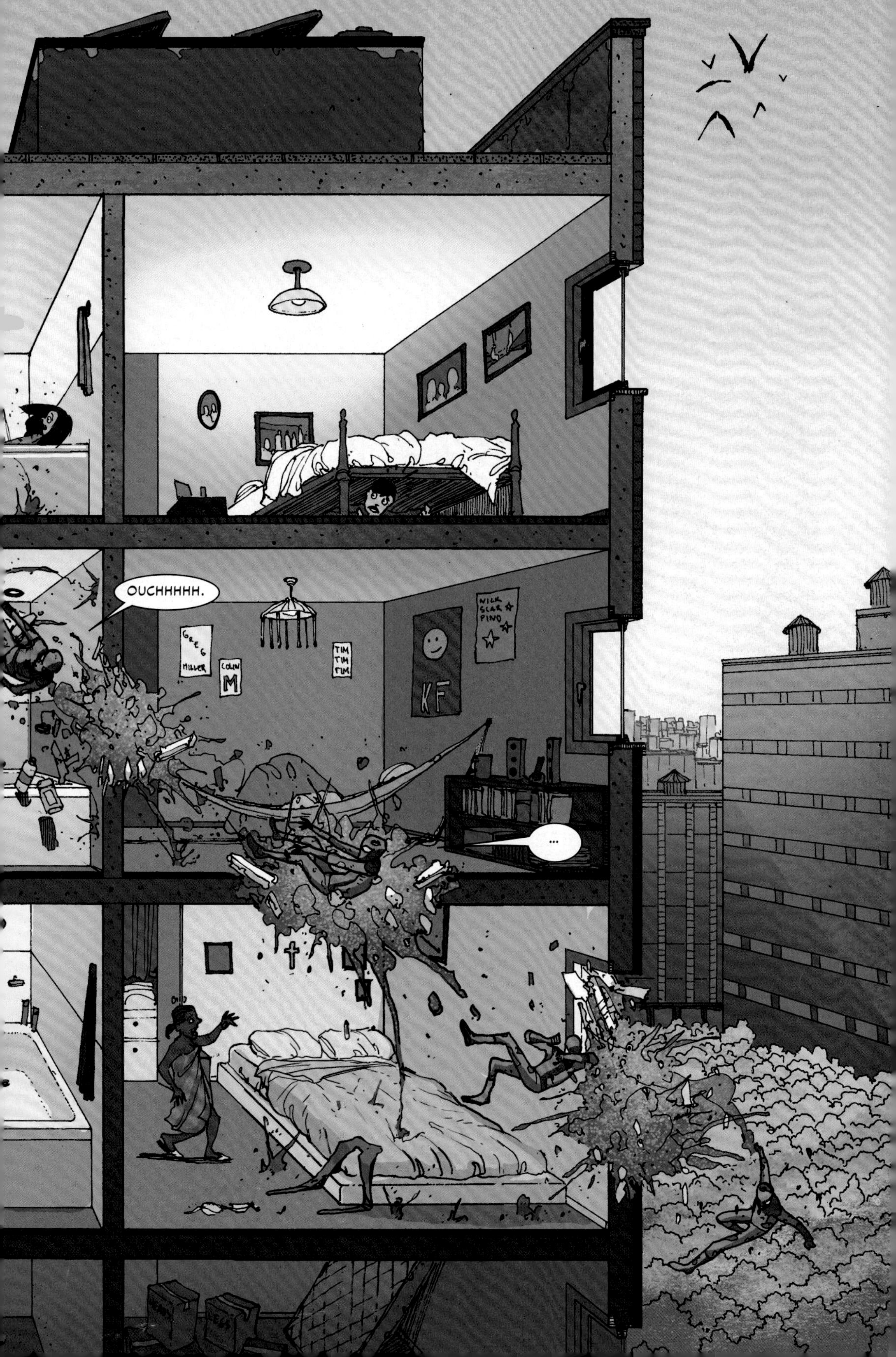

OUCHHHHH.
...
GREG MILLER
COLIN M
TIM TIM TIM
KF
NICK SCAR PINO

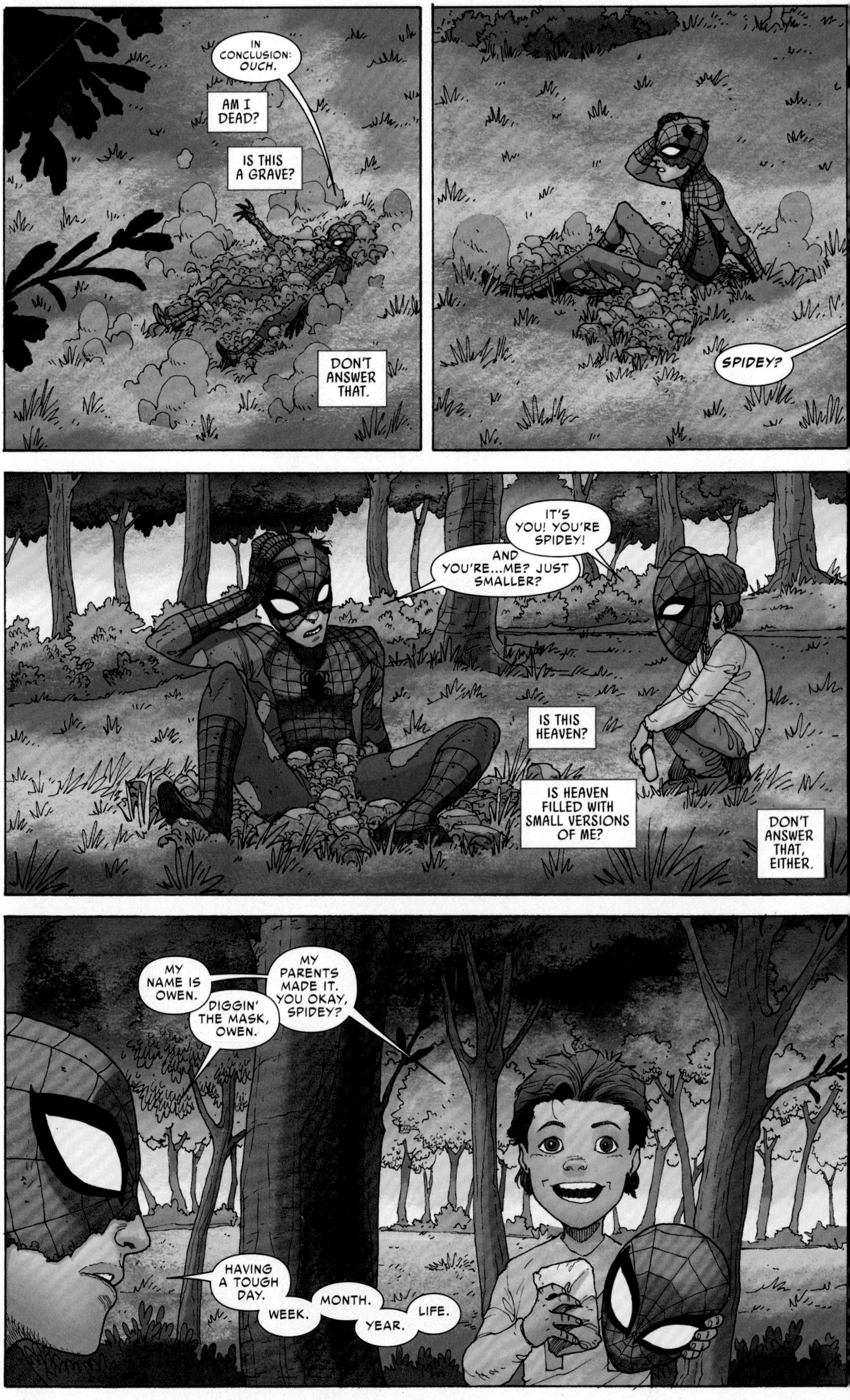

AM I DEAD?
IS THIS A GRAVE?
IN CONCLUSION: OUCH.
DON'T ANSWER THAT.
SPIDEY?
IT'S YOU! YOU'RE SPIDEY!
AND YOU'RE...ME? JUST SMALLER?
IS THIS HEAVEN?
IS HEAVEN FILLED WITH SMALL VERSIONS OF ME?
DON'T ANSWER THAT, EITHER.
MY NAME IS OWEN.
DIGGIN' THE MASK, OWEN.
MY PARENTS MADE IT. YOU OKAY, SPIDEY?
HAVING A TOUGH DAY.
WEEK.
MONTH.
YEAR.
LIFE.

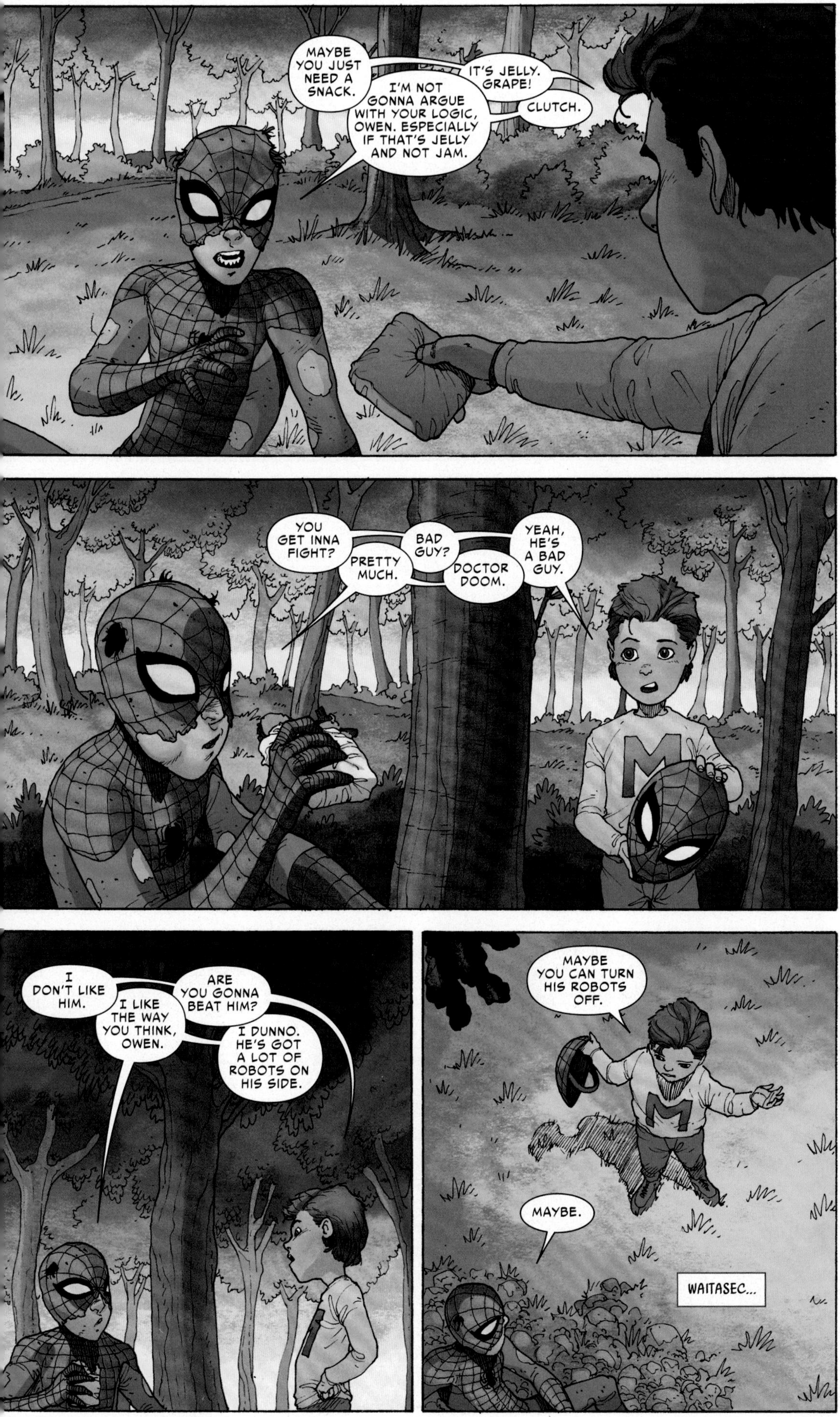
MAYBE YOU JUST NEED A SNACK.
I'M NOT GONNA ARGUE WITH YOUR LOGIC, OWEN. ESPECIALLY IF THAT'S JELLY AND NOT JAM.
IT'S JELLY. GRAPE!
CLUTCH.
YOU GET INNA FIGHT?
PRETTY MUCH.
BAD GUY?
DOCTOR DOOM.
YEAH, HE'S A BAD GUY.
I DON'T LIKE HIM.
I LIKE THE WAY YOU THINK, OWEN.
ARE YOU GONNA BEAT HIM?
I DUNNO. HE'S GOT A LOT OF ROBOTS ON HIS SIDE.
MAYBE YOU CAN TURN HIS ROBOTS OFF.
MAYBE.
WAITASEC...

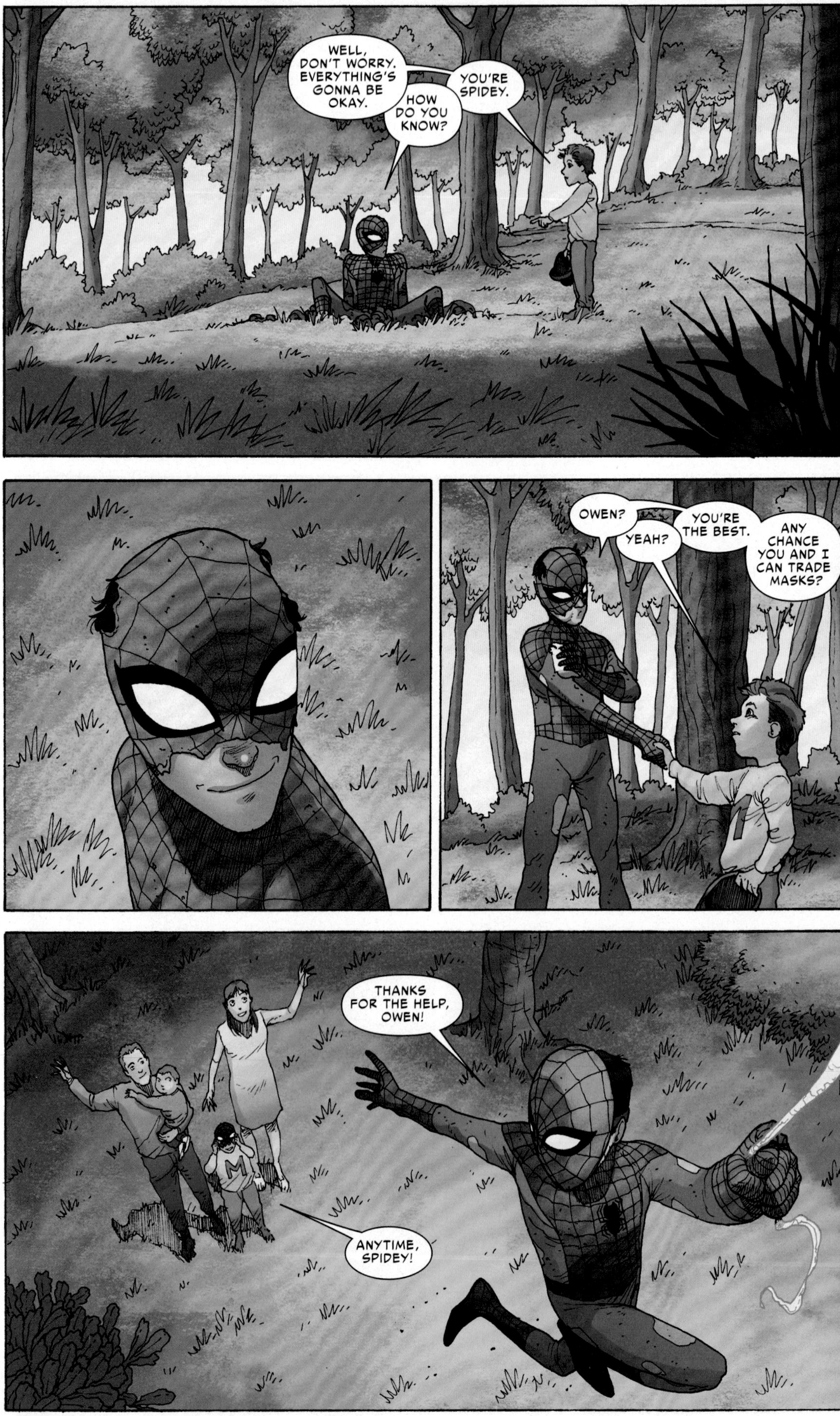
WELL, DON'T WORRY. EVERYTHING'S GONNA BE OKAY.
HOW DO YOU KNOW?
YOU'RE SPIDEY.
OWEN?
YEAH?
YOU'RE THE BEST.
ANY CHANCE YOU AND I CAN TRADE MASKS?
THANKS FOR THE HELP, OWEN!
ANYTIME, SPIDEY!

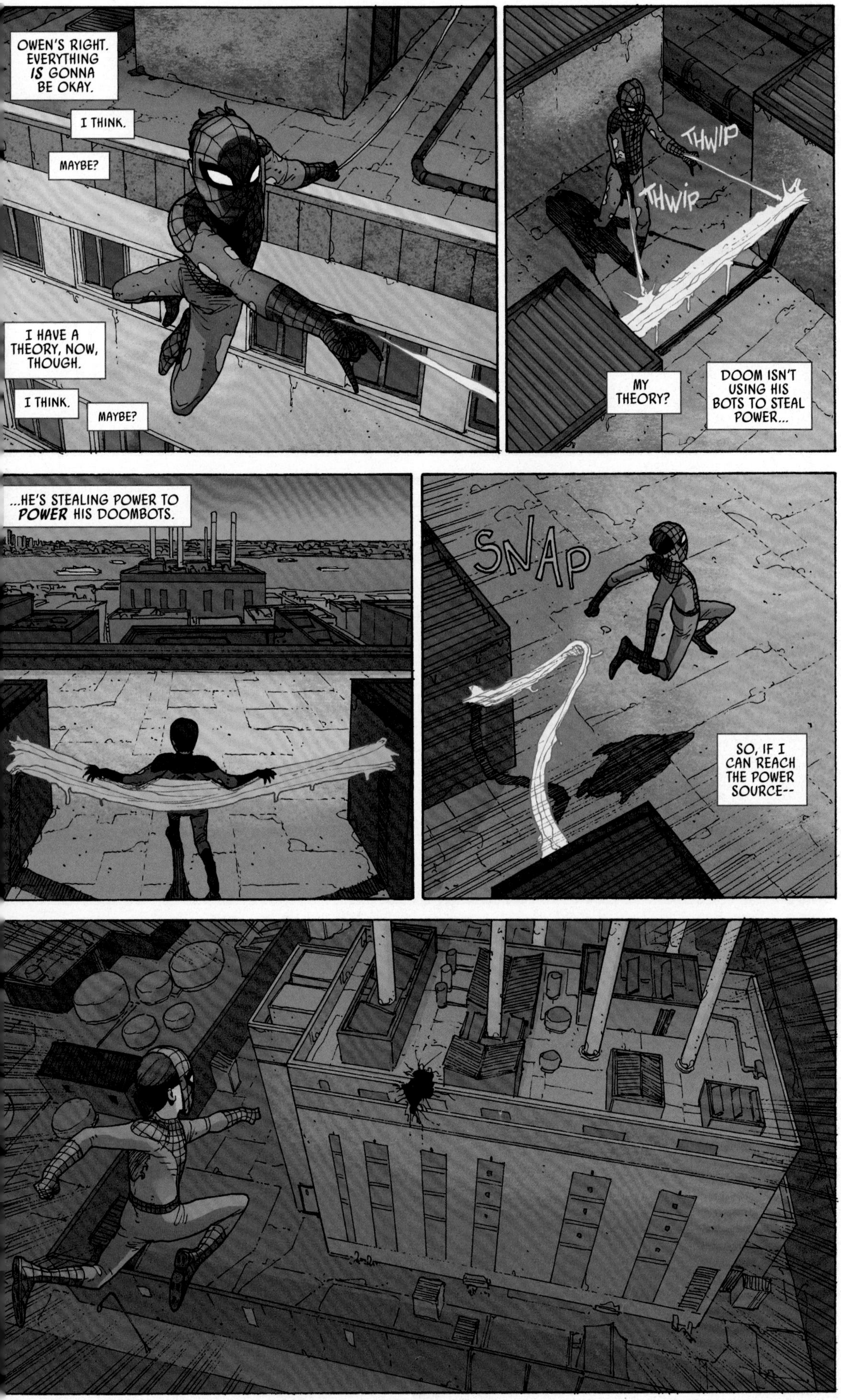
OWEN'S RIGHT. EVERYTHING IS GONNA BE OKAY.
I THINK.
MAYBE?
I HAVE A THEORY, NOW, THOUGH.
I THINK.
MAYBE?
THWIP
THWIP
MY THEORY?
DOOM ISN'T USING HIS BOTS TO STEAL POWER...
...HE'S STEALING POWER TO POWER HIS DOOMBOTS.
SNAP
SO, IF I CAN REACH THE POWER SOURCE--

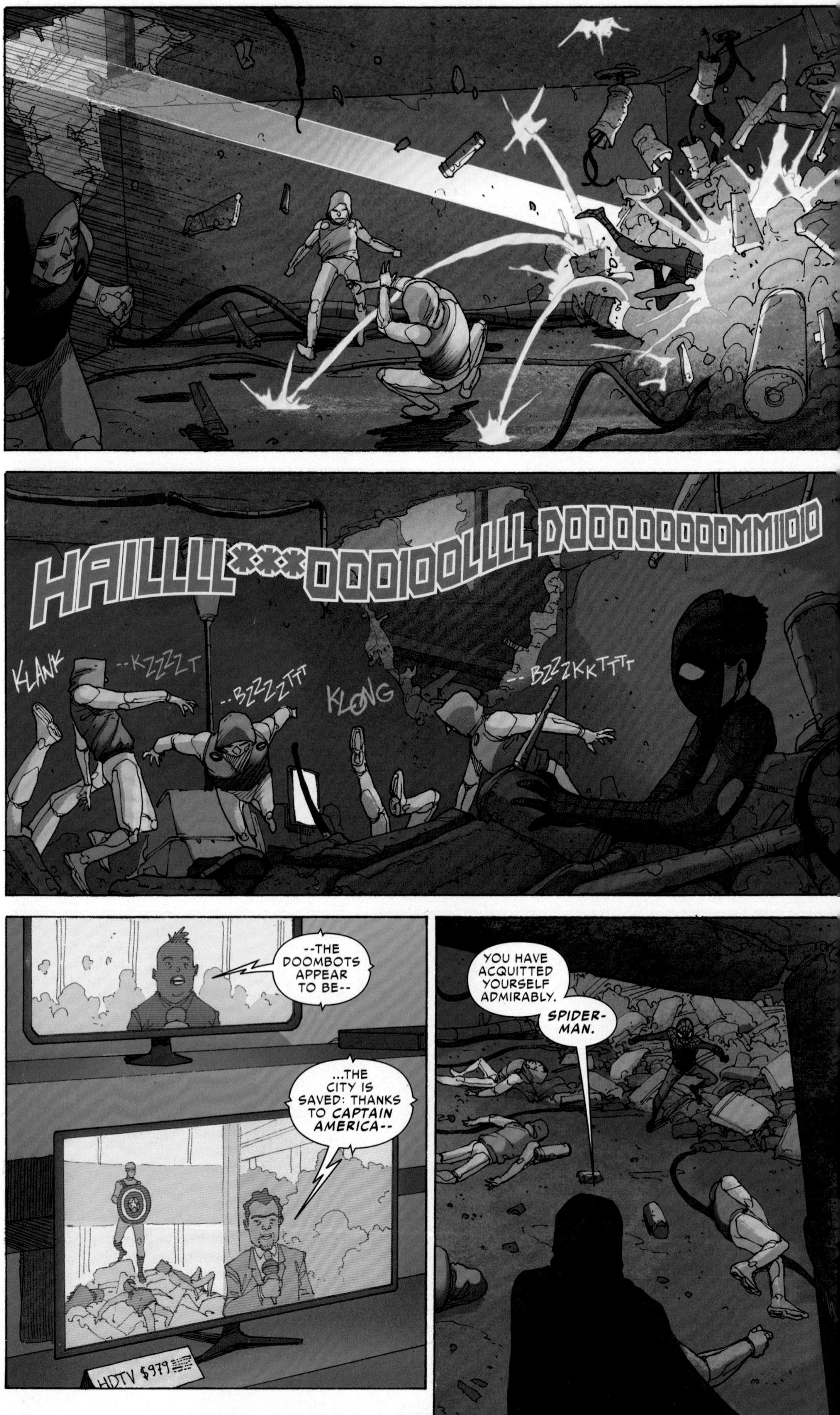

HAILLLL***OOO1OOLLLL DOOOOOOOOMM1O1O
KLANK
--KZZZZT
--BZZZZTTT
KLONG
--BZZZKKTTTT
--THE DOOMBOTS APPEAR TO BE--
...THE CITY IS SAVED: THANKS TO CAPTAIN AMERICA--
HDTV $979
YOU HAVE ACQUITTED YOURSELF ADMIRABLY.
SPIDER-MAN.

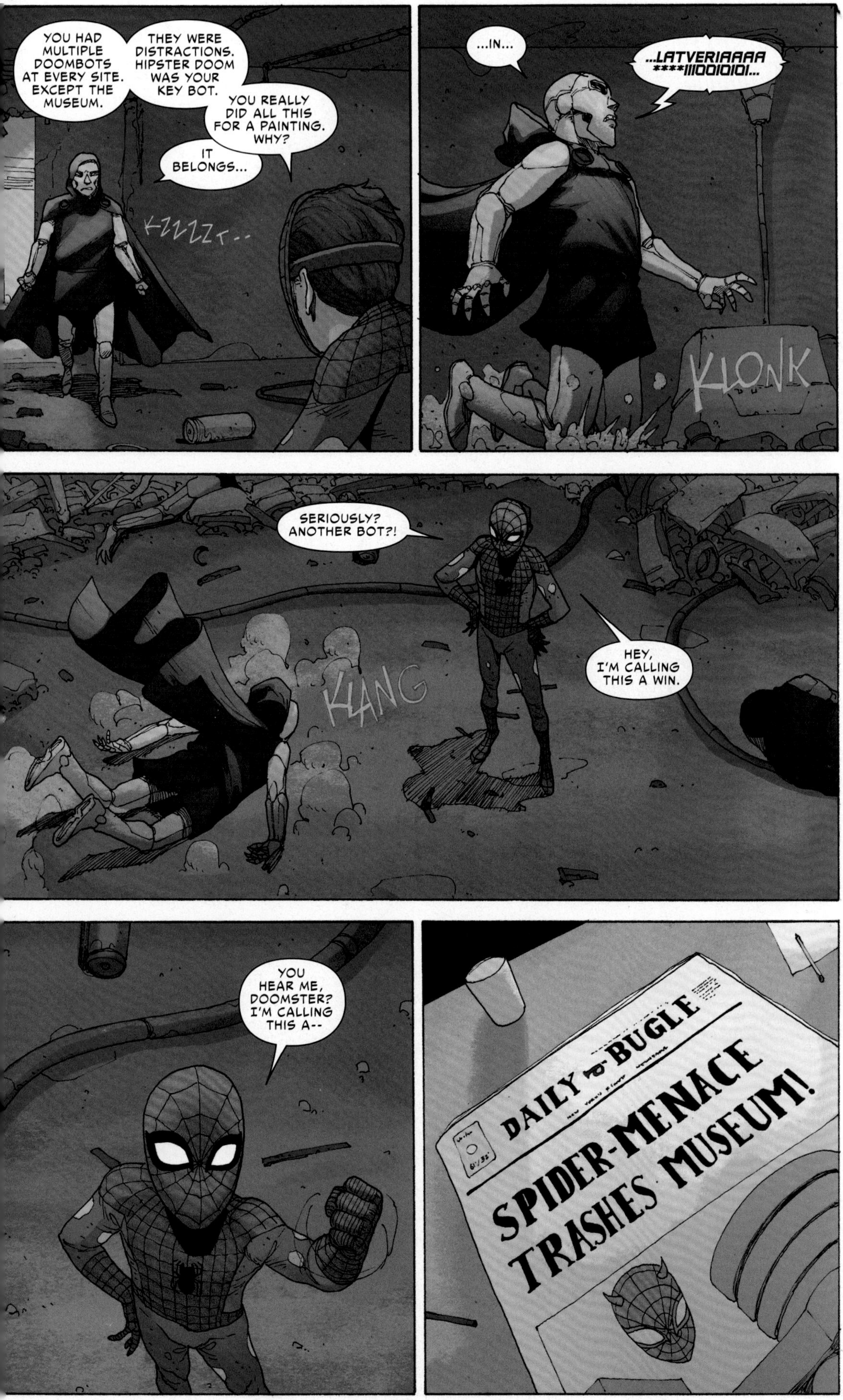
YOU HAD MULTIPLE DOOMBOTS AT EVERY SITE. EXCEPT THE MUSEUM.
THEY WERE DISTRACTIONS. HIPSTER DOOM WAS YOUR KEY BOT.
YOU REALLY DID ALL THIS FOR A PAINTING. WHY?
IT BELONGS...
KZZZZT...
...IN...
...LATVERIAAAA ****1110010101...
KLONK
SERIOUSLY? ANOTHER BOT?!
KLANG
HEY, I'M CALLING THIS A WIN.
YOU HEAR ME, DOOMSTER? I'M CALLING THIS A--
DAILY BUGLE
SPIDER-MENACE TRASHES MUSEUM!

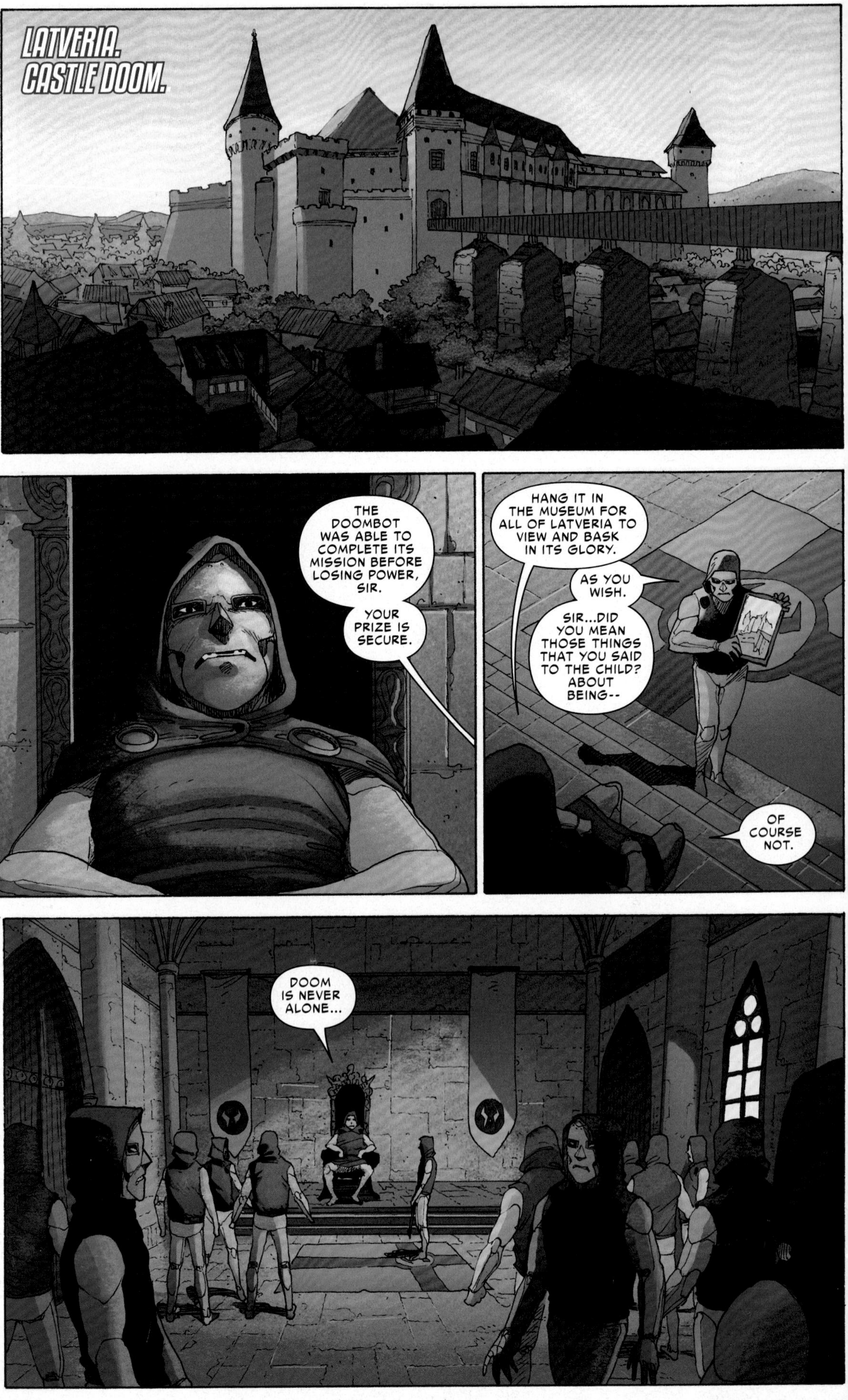
LATVERIA.
CASTLE DOOM.
THE DOOMBOT WAS ABLE TO COMPLETE ITS MISSION BEFORE LOSING POWER, SIR.
YOUR PRIZE IS SECURE.
HANG IT IN THE MUSEUM FOR ALL OF LATVERIA TO VIEW AND BASK IN ITS GLORY.
AS YOU WISH.
SIR...DID YOU MEAN THOSE THINGS THAT YOU SAID TO THE CHILD? ABOUT BEING--
OF COURSE NOT.
DOOM IS NEVER ALONE...

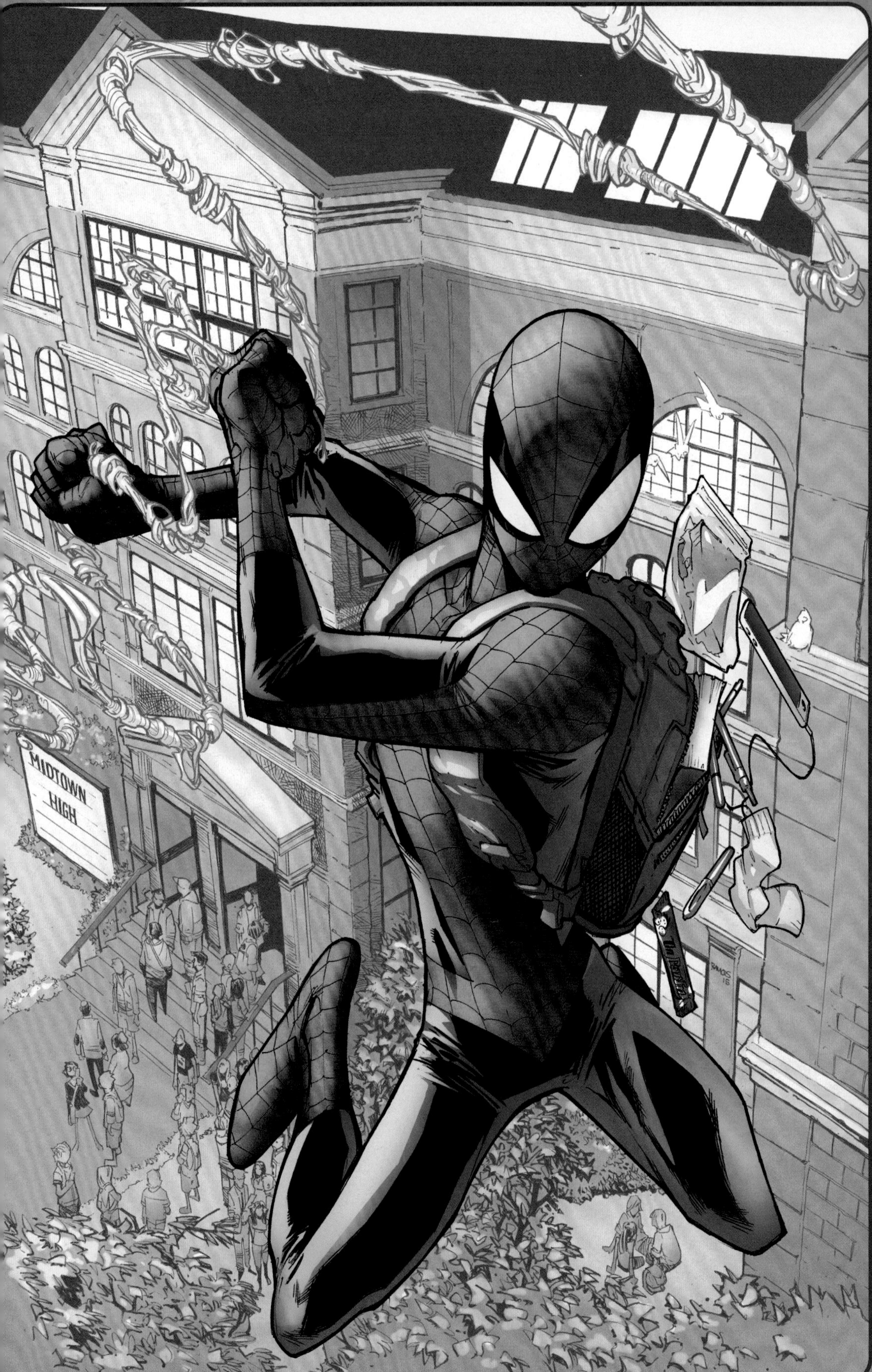
MIDTOWN HIGH

**HUMBERTO RAMOS & EDGAR DELGADO**
**1 VARIANT**

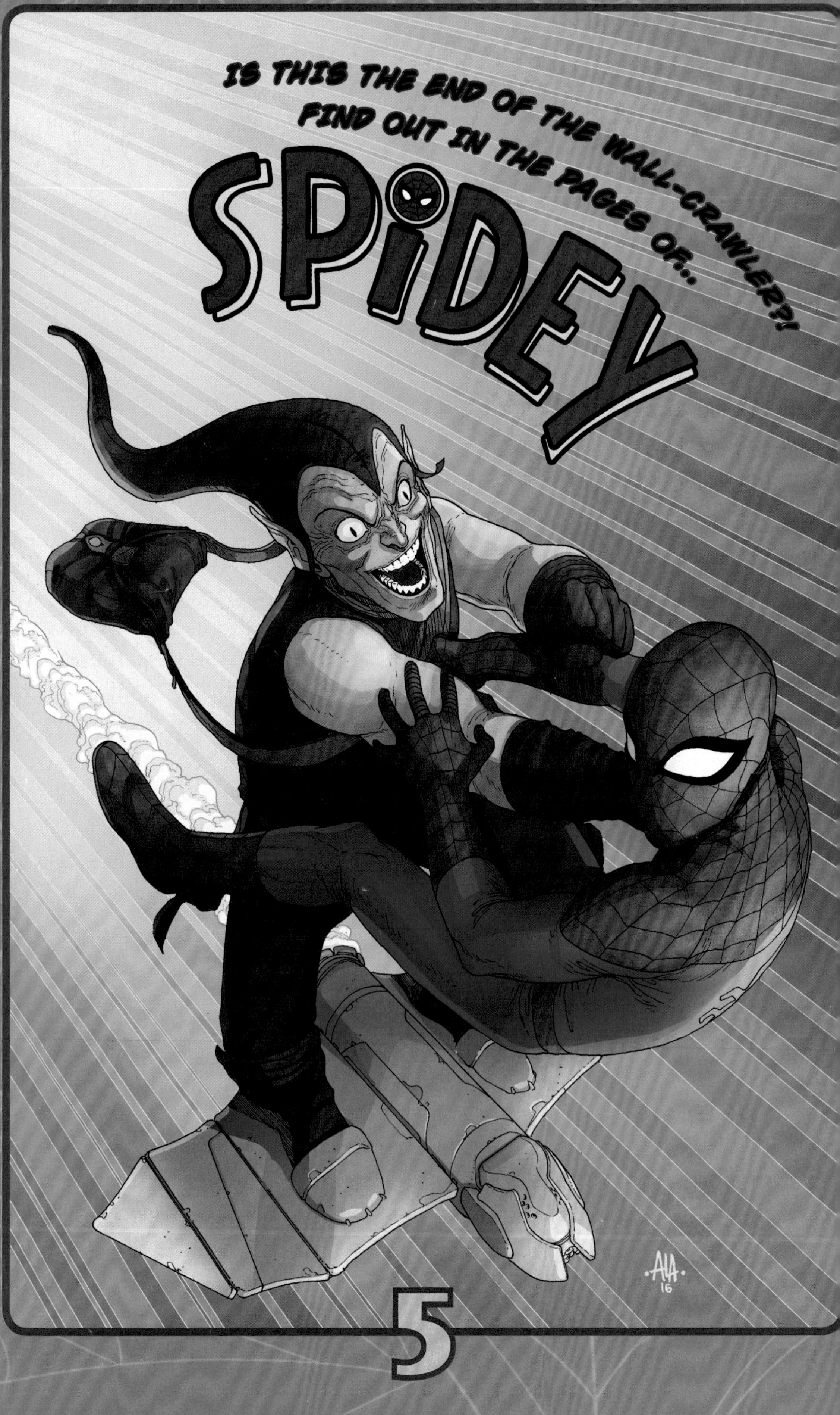
IS THIS THE END OF THE WALL-CRAWLER?!
FIND OUT IN THE PAGES OF...
SPIDEY
5

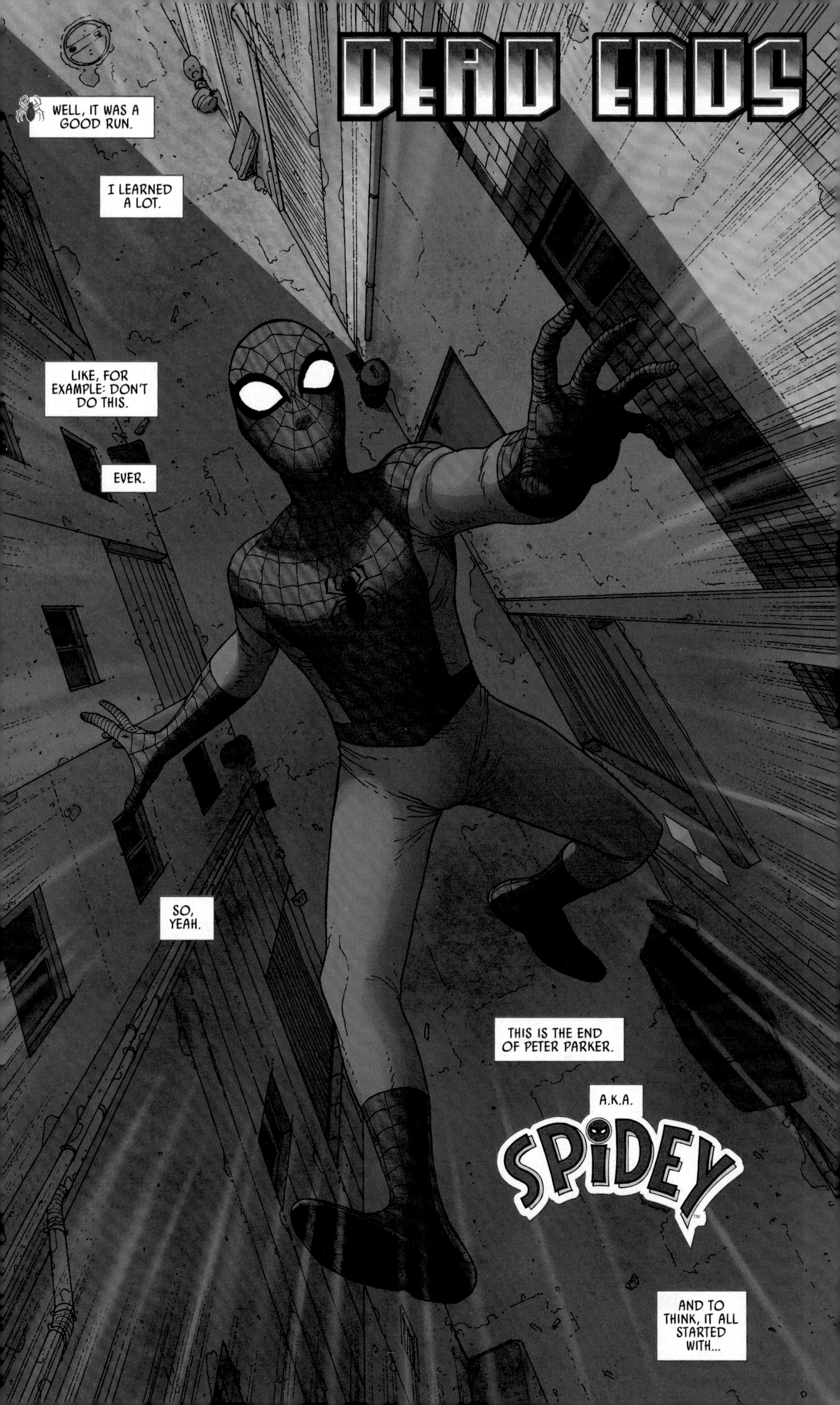

DEAD ENDS
WELL, IT WAS A GOOD RUN.
I LEARNED A LOT.
LIKE, FOR EXAMPLE: DON'T DO THIS.
EVER.
SO, YEAH.
THIS IS THE END OF PETER PARKER.
A.K.A.
SPIDEY
AND TO THINK, IT ALL STARTED WITH...

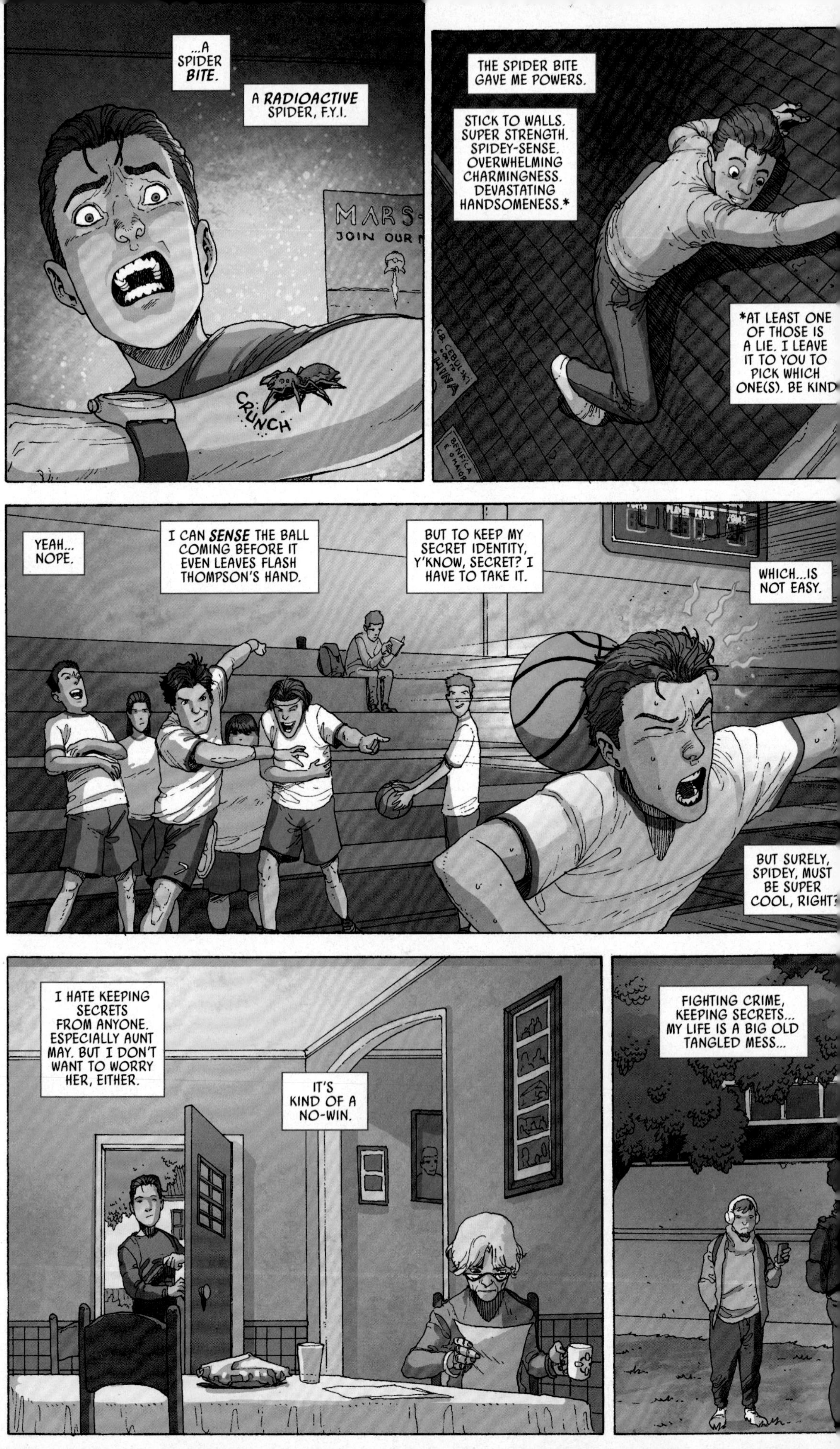
...A SPIDER BITE.
A RADIOACTIVE SPIDER, F.Y.I.
CRUNCH
MARS-
JOIN OUR
THE SPIDER BITE GAVE ME POWERS.
STICK TO WALLS. SUPER STRENGTH. SPIDEY-SENSE. OVERWHELMING CHARMINGNESS. DEVASTATING HANDSOMENESS.*
*AT LEAST ONE OF THOSE IS A LIE. I LEAVE IT TO YOU TO PICK WHICH ONE(S). BE KIND
YEAH... NOPE.
I CAN SENSE THE BALL COMING BEFORE IT EVEN LEAVES FLASH THOMPSON'S HAND.
BUT TO KEEP MY SECRET IDENTITY, Y'KNOW, SECRET? I HAVE TO TAKE IT.
WHICH...IS NOT EASY.
BUT SURELY, SPIDEY, MUST BE SUPER COOL, RIGHT?
I HATE KEEPING SECRETS FROM ANYONE. ESPECIALLY AUNT MAY. BUT I DON'T WANT TO WORRY HER, EITHER.
IT'S KIND OF A NO-WIN.
FIGHTING CRIME, KEEPING SECRETS... MY LIFE IS A BIG OLD TANGLED MESS...

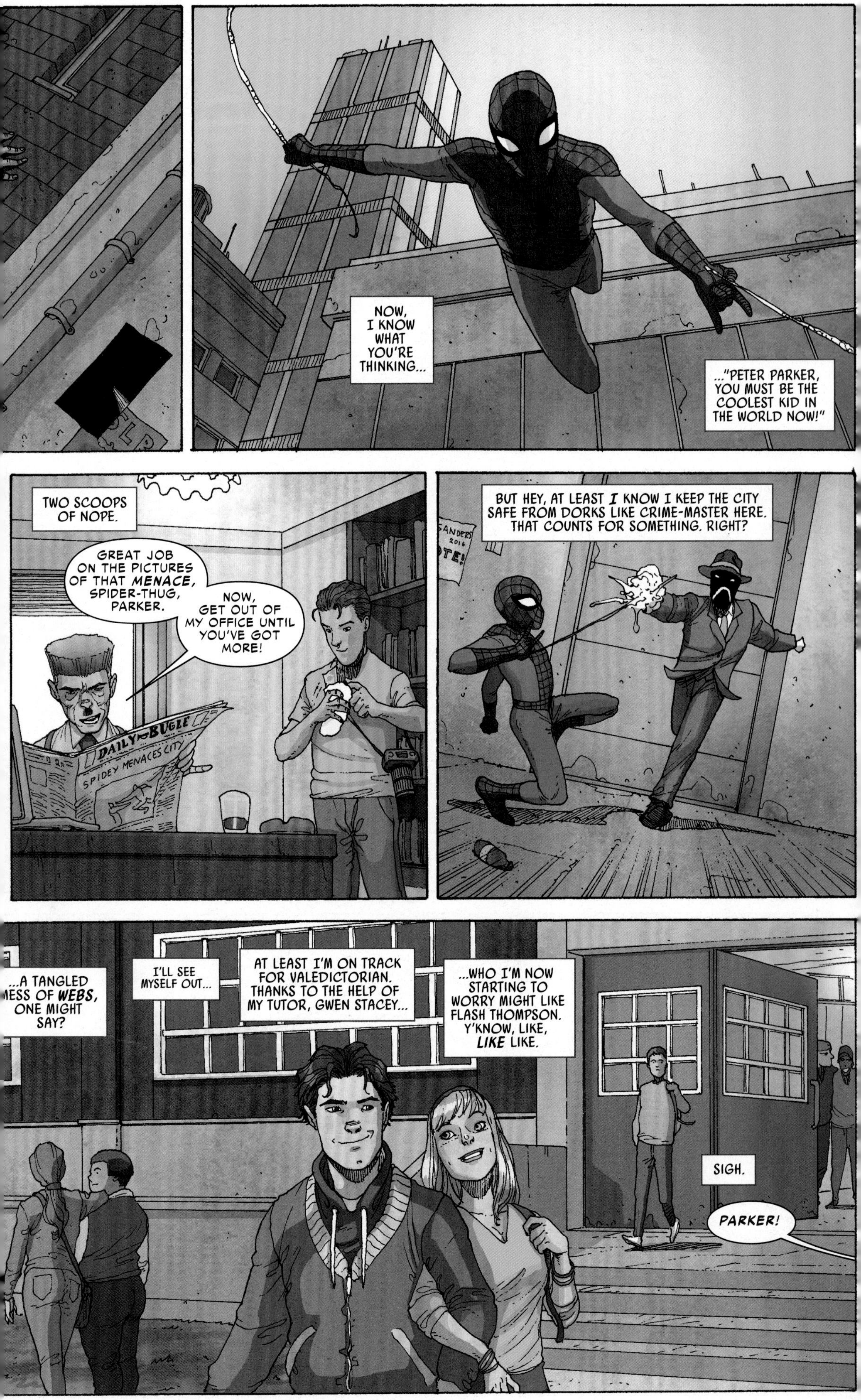
NOW, I KNOW WHAT YOU'RE THINKING...
..."PETER PARKER, YOU MUST BE THE COOLEST KID IN THE WORLD NOW!"
TWO SCOOPS OF NOPE.
GREAT JOB ON THE PICTURES OF THAT *MENACE,* SPIDER-THUG, PARKER.
NOW, GET OUT OF MY OFFICE UNTIL YOU'VE GOT MORE!
DAILY BUGLE
SPIDEY MENACES CITY
BUT HEY, AT LEAST *I* KNOW I KEEP THE CITY SAFE FROM DORKS LIKE CRIME-MASTER HERE. THAT COUNTS FOR SOMETHING. RIGHT?
SANDERS 2016
...A TANGLED MESS OF *WEBS,* ONE MIGHT SAY?
I'LL SEE MYSELF OUT...
AT LEAST I'M ON TRACK FOR VALEDICTORIAN. THANKS TO THE HELP OF MY TUTOR, GWEN STACEY...
...WHO I'M NOW STARTING TO WORRY MIGHT LIKE FLASH THOMPSON. Y'KNOW, LIKE, ***LIKE*** LIKE.
SIGH.
*PARKER!*

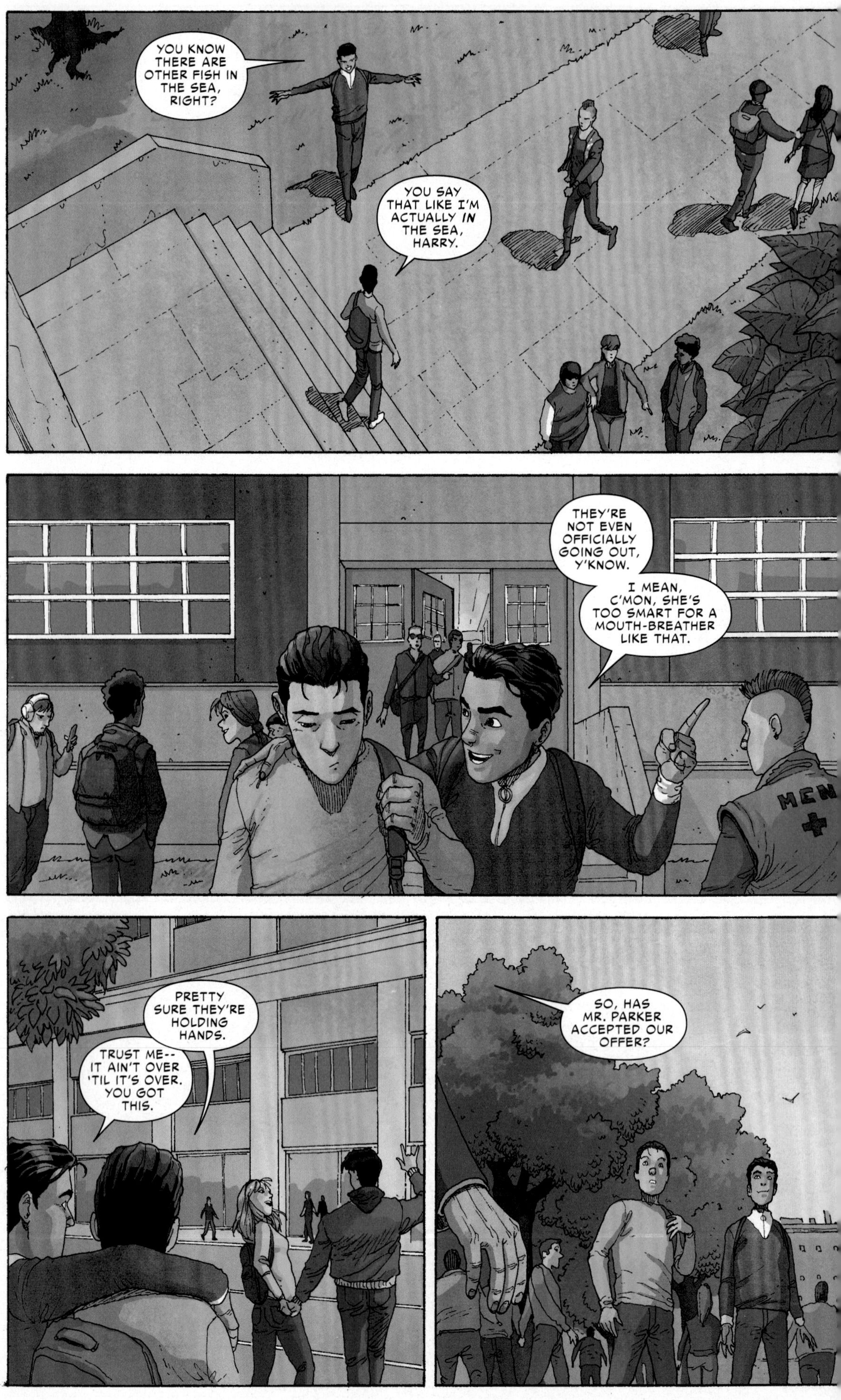

YOU KNOW THERE ARE OTHER FISH IN THE SEA, RIGHT?
YOU SAY THAT LIKE I'M ACTUALLY *IN* THE SEA, HARRY.
THEY'RE NOT EVEN OFFICIALLY GOING OUT, Y'KNOW.
I MEAN, C'MON, SHE'S TOO SMART FOR A MOUTH-BREATHER LIKE THAT.
MEN
PRETTY SURE THEY'RE HOLDING HANDS.
TRUST ME-- IT AIN'T OVER 'TIL IT'S OVER. YOU GOT THIS.
SO, HAS MR. PARKER ACCEPTED OUR OFFER?

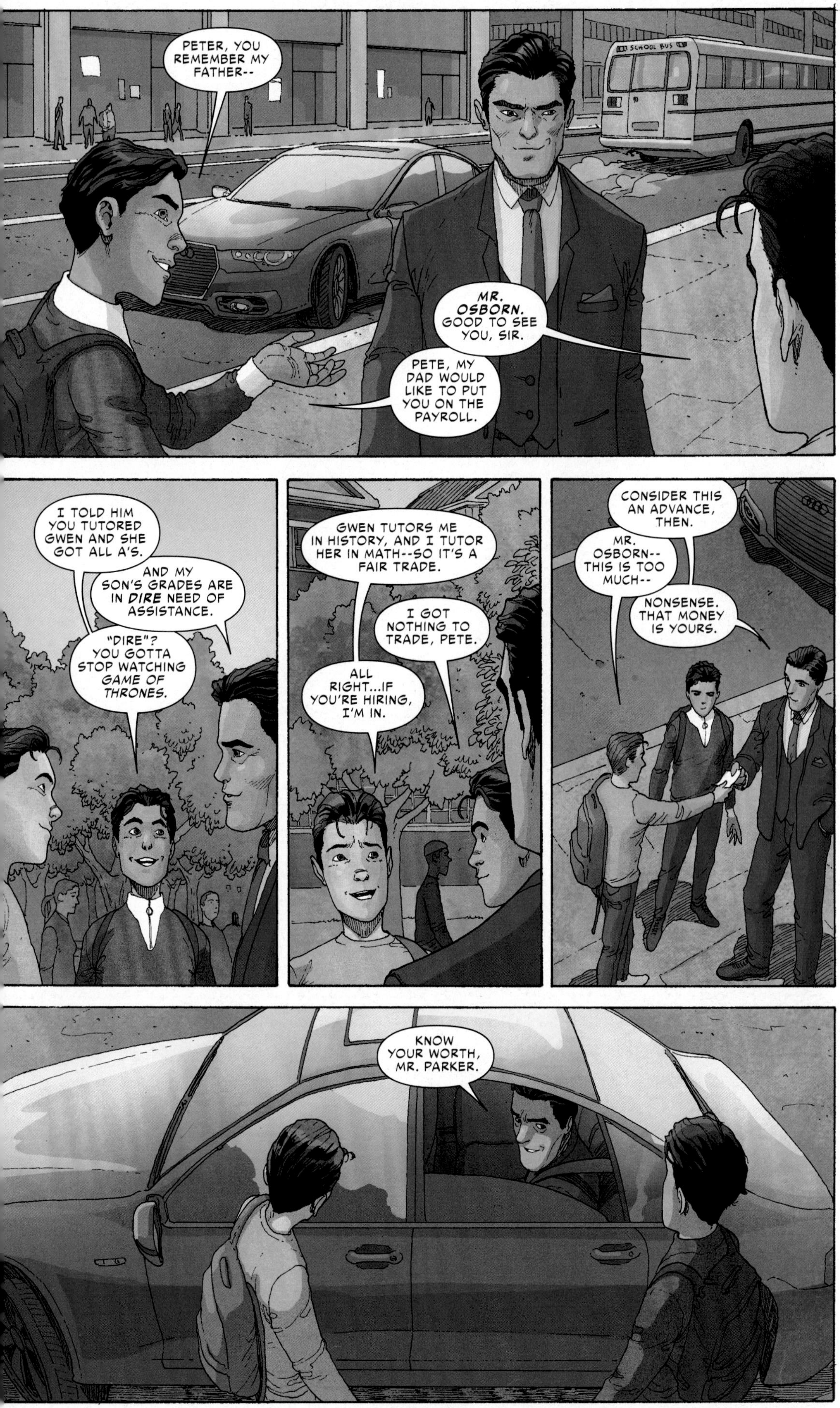
PETER, YOU REMEMBER MY FATHER--
MR. OSBORN. GOOD TO SEE YOU, SIR.
PETE, MY DAD WOULD LIKE TO PUT YOU ON THE PAYROLL.
I TOLD HIM YOU TUTORED GWEN AND SHE GOT ALL A'S.
AND MY SON'S GRADES ARE IN DIRE NEED OF ASSISTANCE.
"DIRE"? YOU GOTTA STOP WATCHING GAME OF THRONES.
GWEN TUTORS ME IN HISTORY, AND I TUTOR HER IN MATH--SO IT'S A FAIR TRADE.
I GOT NOTHING TO TRADE, PETE.
ALL RIGHT...IF YOU'RE HIRING, I'M IN.
CONSIDER THIS AN ADVANCE, THEN.
MR. OSBORN-- THIS IS TOO MUCH--
NONSENSE. THAT MONEY IS YOURS.
KNOW YOUR WORTH, MR. PARKER.

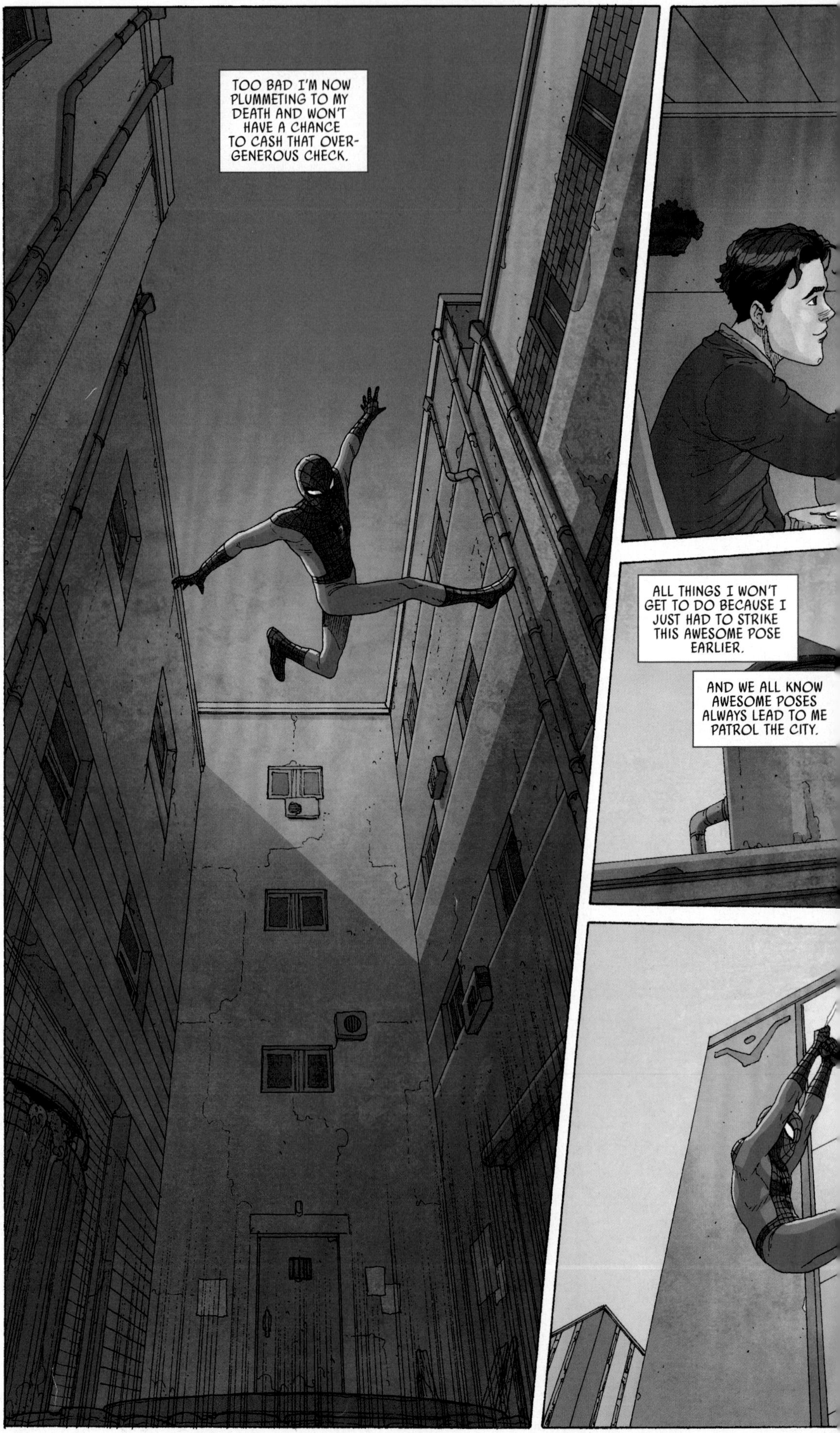
TOO BAD I'M NOW PLUMMETING TO MY DEATH AND WON'T HAVE A CHANCE TO CASH THAT OVER-GENEROUS CHECK.
ALL THINGS I WON'T GET TO DO BECAUSE I JUST HAD TO STRIKE THIS AWESOME POSE EARLIER.
AND WE ALL KNOW AWESOME POSES ALWAYS LEAD TO ME PATROL THE CITY.

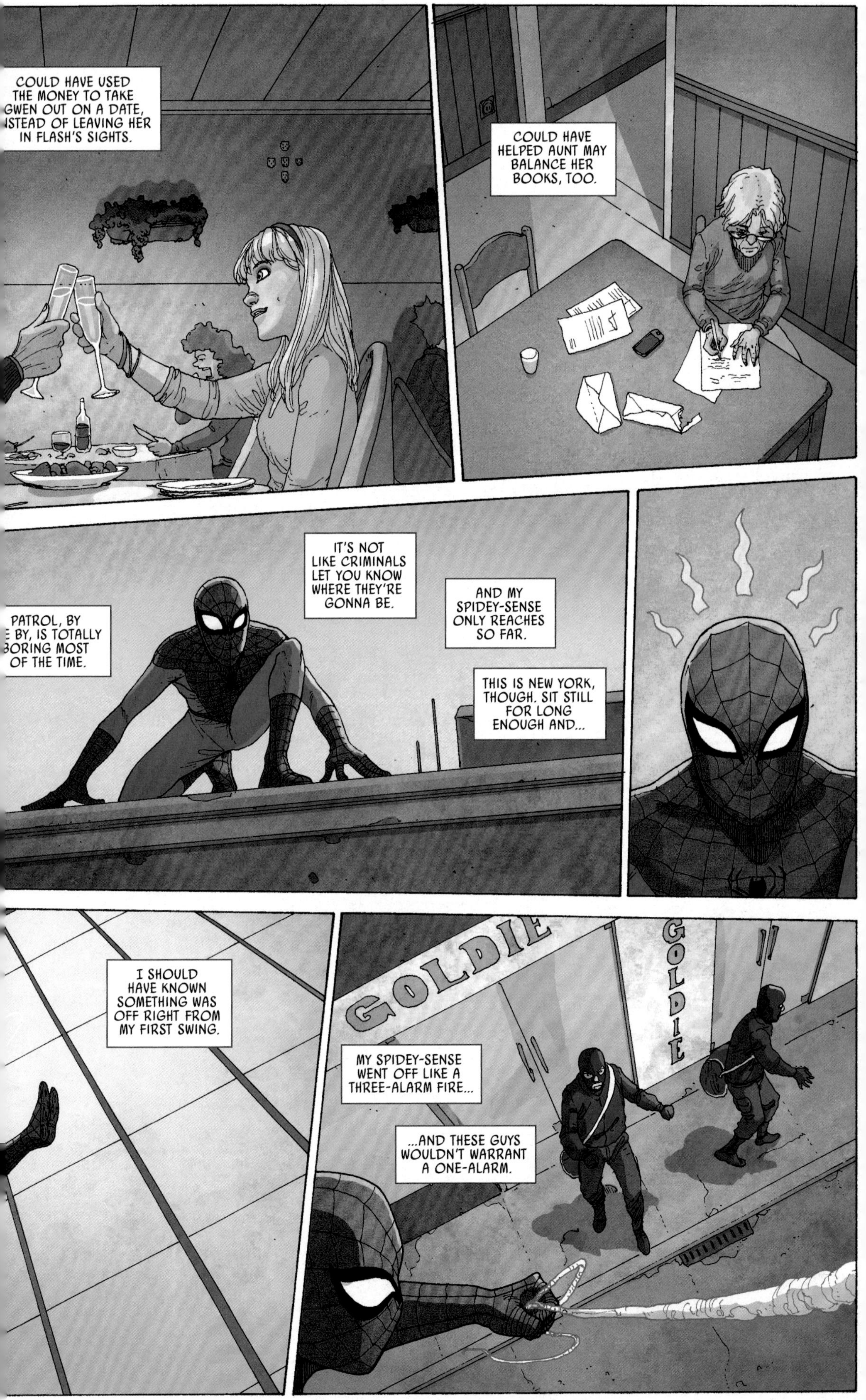

COULD HAVE USED THE MONEY TO TAKE GWEN OUT ON A DATE, INSTEAD OF LEAVING HER IN FLASH'S SIGHTS.
COULD HAVE HELPED AUNT MAY BALANCE HER BOOKS, TOO.
PATROL, BY THE BY, IS TOTALLY BORING MOST OF THE TIME.
IT'S NOT LIKE CRIMINALS LET YOU KNOW WHERE THEY'RE GONNA BE.
AND MY SPIDEY-SENSE ONLY REACHES SO FAR.
THIS IS NEW YORK, THOUGH. SIT STILL FOR LONG ENOUGH AND...
I SHOULD HAVE KNOWN SOMETHING WAS OFF RIGHT FROM MY FIRST SWING.
GOLDIE
GOLDIE
MY SPIDEY-SENSE WENT OFF LIKE A THREE-ALARM FIRE...
...AND THESE GUYS WOULDN'T WARRANT A ONE-ALARM.

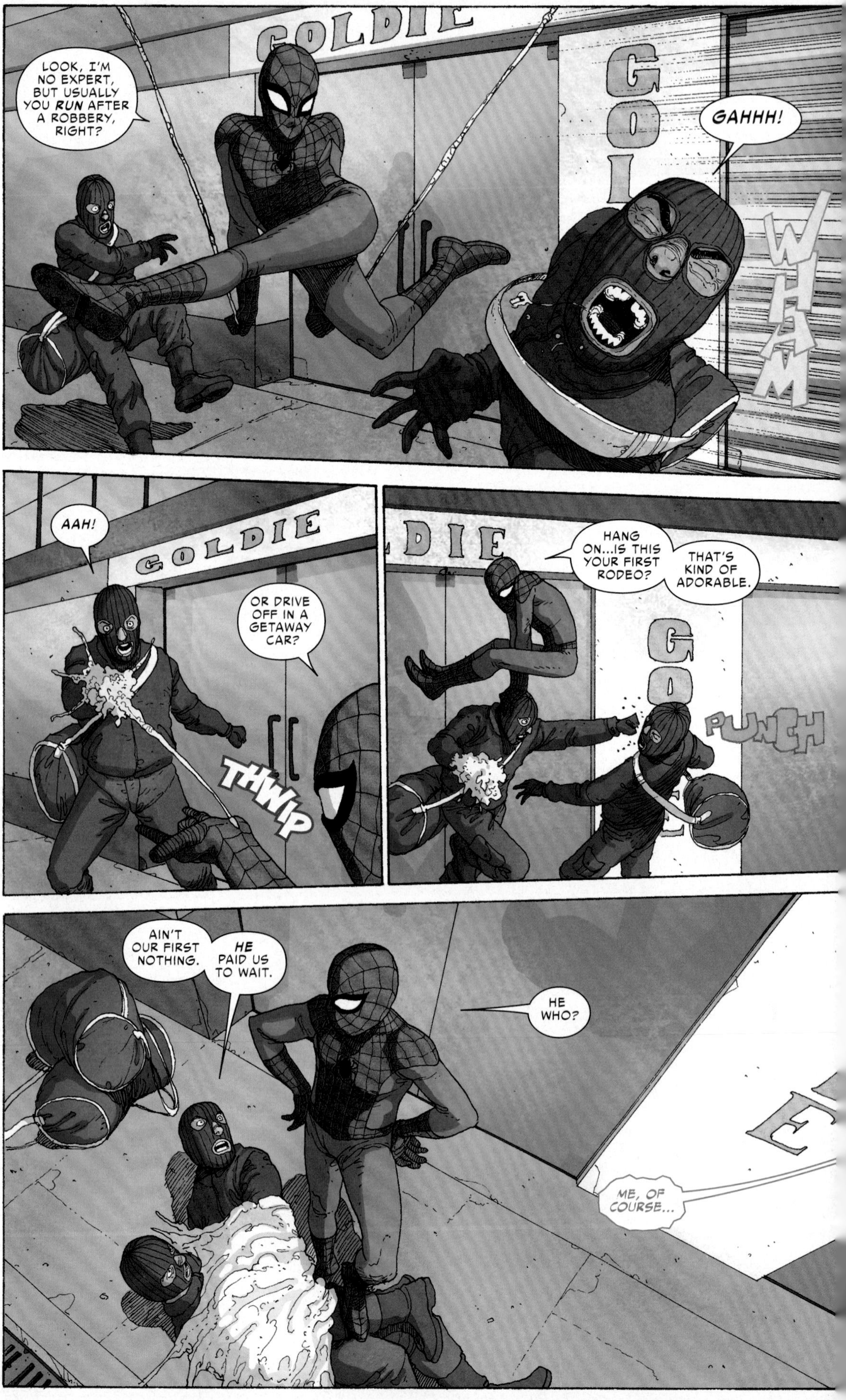

GOLDIE
LOOK, I'M NO EXPERT, BUT USUALLY YOU RUN AFTER A ROBBERY, RIGHT?
GAHHH!
WHAM
AAH!
OR DRIVE OFF IN A GETAWAY CAR?
THWIP
HANG ON...IS THIS YOUR FIRST RODEO?
THAT'S KIND OF ADORABLE.
PUNCH
AIN'T OUR FIRST NOTHING.
HE PAID US TO WAIT.
HE WHO?
ME, OF COURSE...

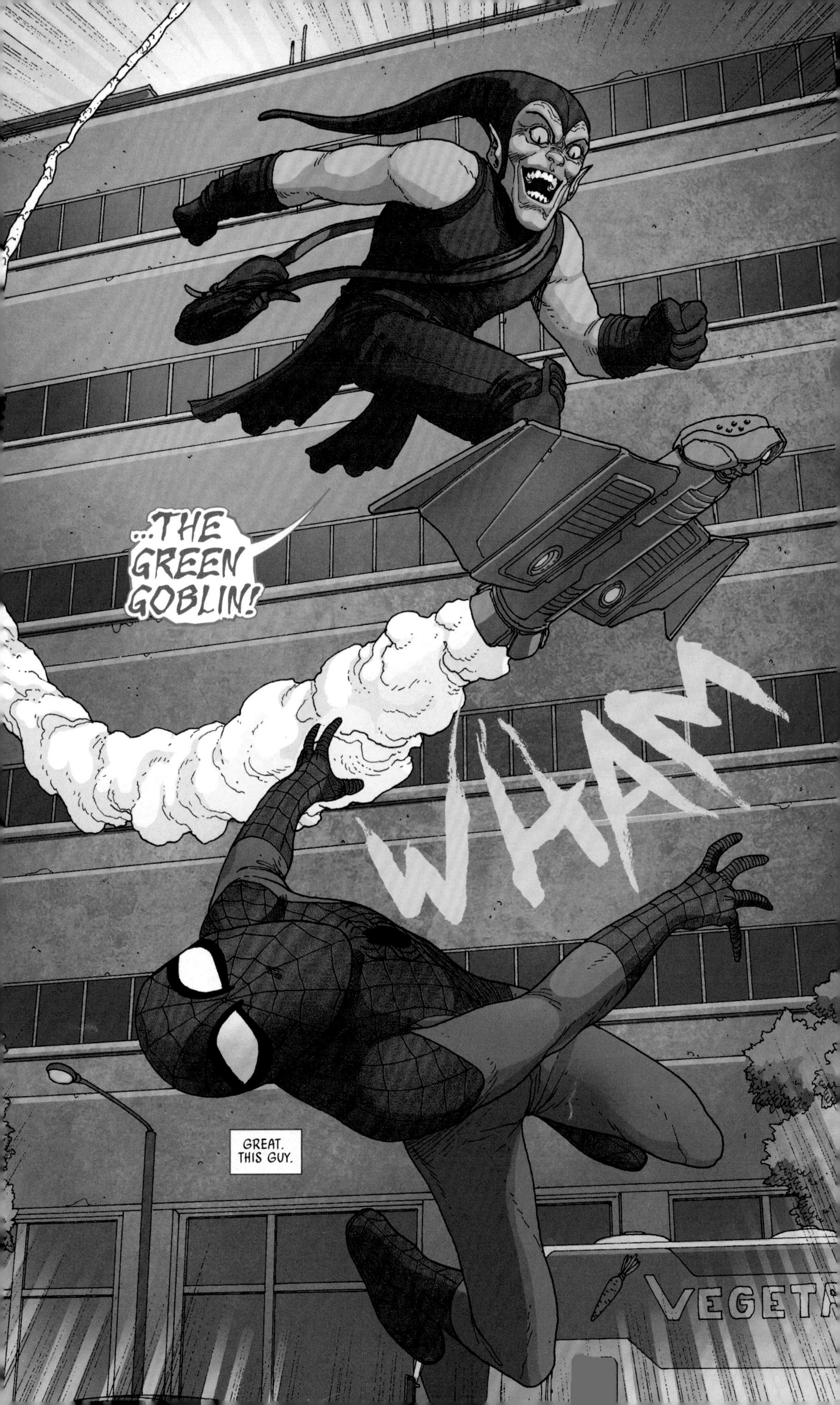
...THE GREEN GOBLIN!
WHAM
GREAT. THIS GUY.
VEGETA

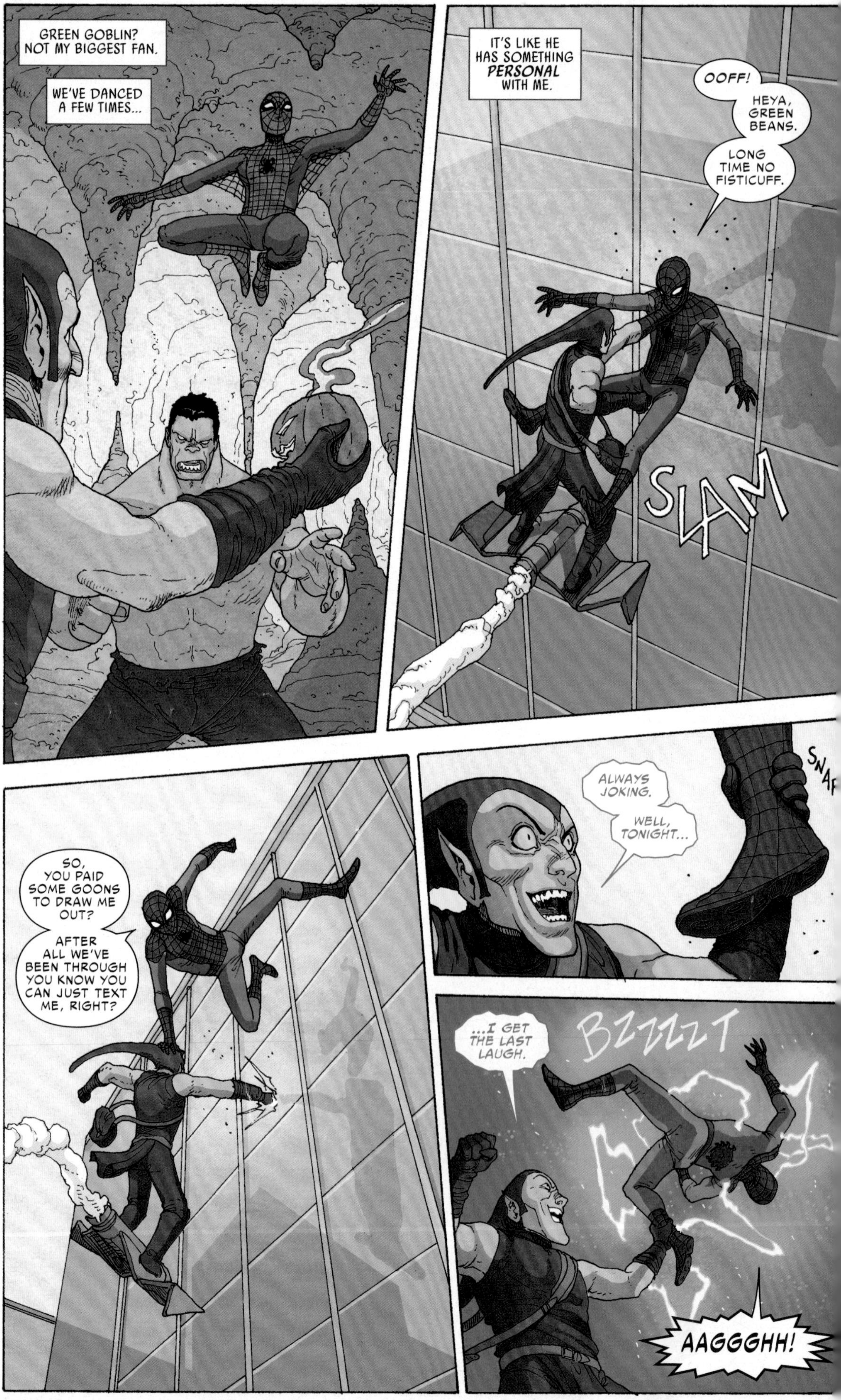

GREEN GOBLIN? NOT MY BIGGEST FAN.
WE'VE DANCED A FEW TIMES...
IT'S LIKE HE HAS SOMETHING PERSONAL WITH ME.
OOFF!
HEYA, GREEN BEANS.
LONG TIME NO FISTICUFF.
SLAM
SO, YOU PAID SOME GOONS TO DRAW ME OUT?
AFTER ALL WE'VE BEEN THROUGH YOU KNOW YOU CAN JUST TEXT ME, RIGHT?
ALWAYS JOKING.
WELL, TONIGHT...
...I GET THE LAST LAUGH.
BZZZZT
AAGGGHH!

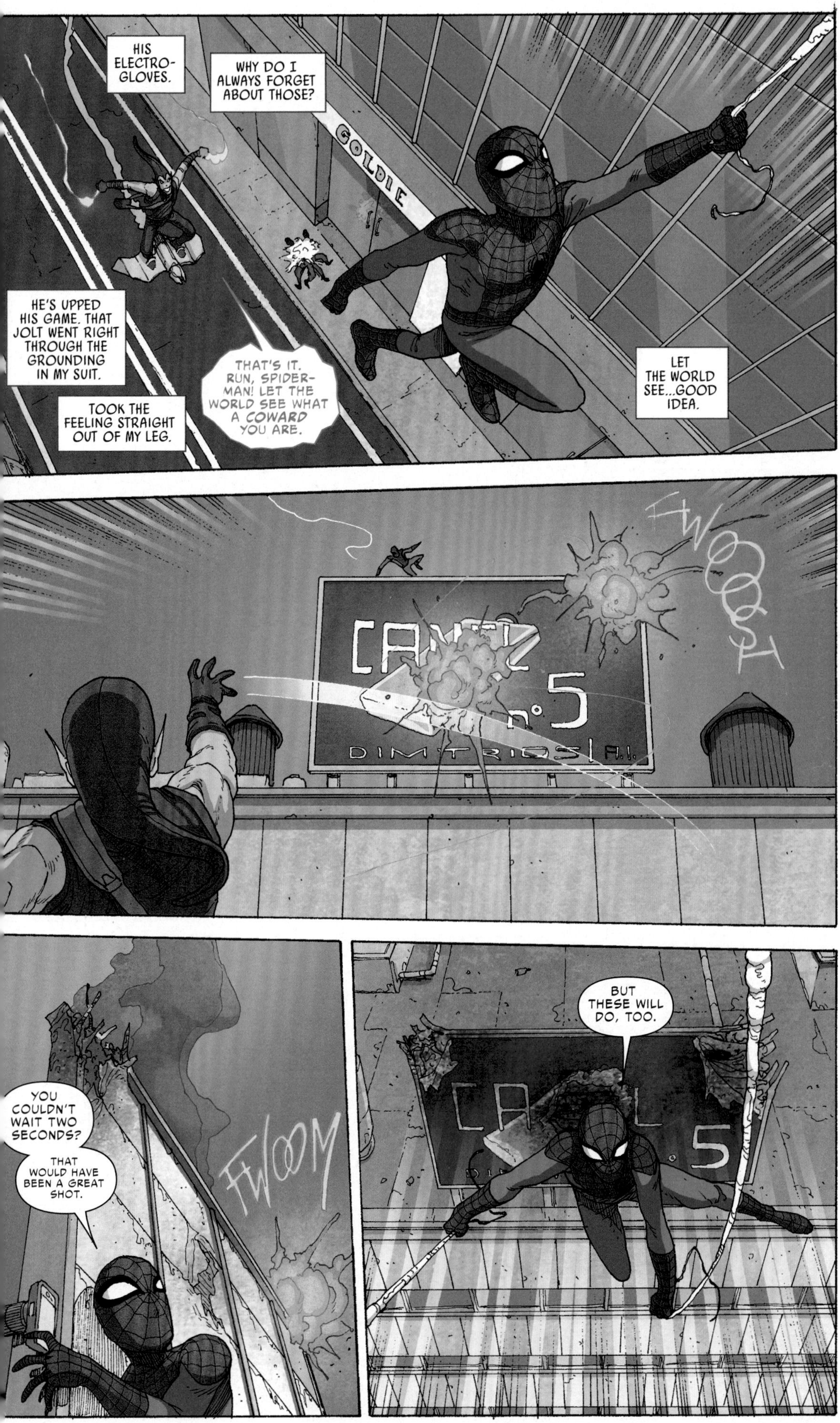
HIS ELECTRO-GLOVES.
WHY DO I ALWAYS FORGET ABOUT THOSE?
GOLDIE
HE'S UPPED HIS GAME. THAT JOLT WENT RIGHT THROUGH THE GROUNDING IN MY SUIT.
TOOK THE FEELING STRAIGHT OUT OF MY LEG.
THAT'S IT. RUN, SPIDER-MAN! LET THE WORLD SEE WHAT A COWARD YOU ARE.
LET THE WORLD SEE...GOOD IDEA.
FWOOOOSH
n°5
YOU COULDN'T WAIT TWO SECONDS?
THAT WOULD HAVE BEEN A GREAT SHOT.
FWOOM
BUT THESE WILL DO, TOO.

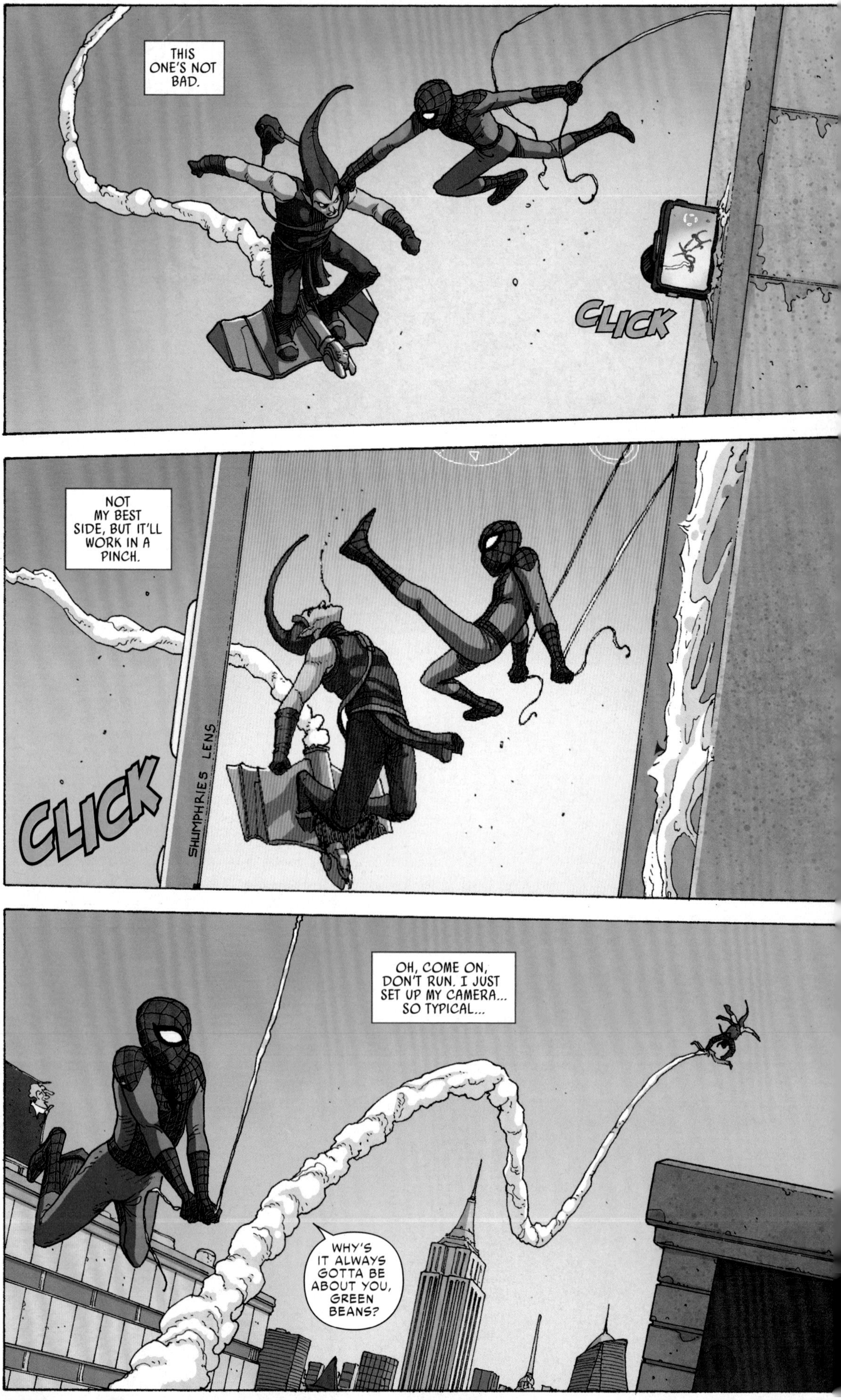
THIS ONE'S NOT BAD.
CLICK
NOT MY BEST SIDE, BUT IT'LL WORK IN A PINCH.
CLICK
SHUMPHRIES LENS
OH, COME ON, DON'T RUN. I JUST SET UP MY CAMERA... SO TYPICAL...
WHY'S IT ALWAYS GOTTA BE ABOUT YOU, GREEN BEANS?

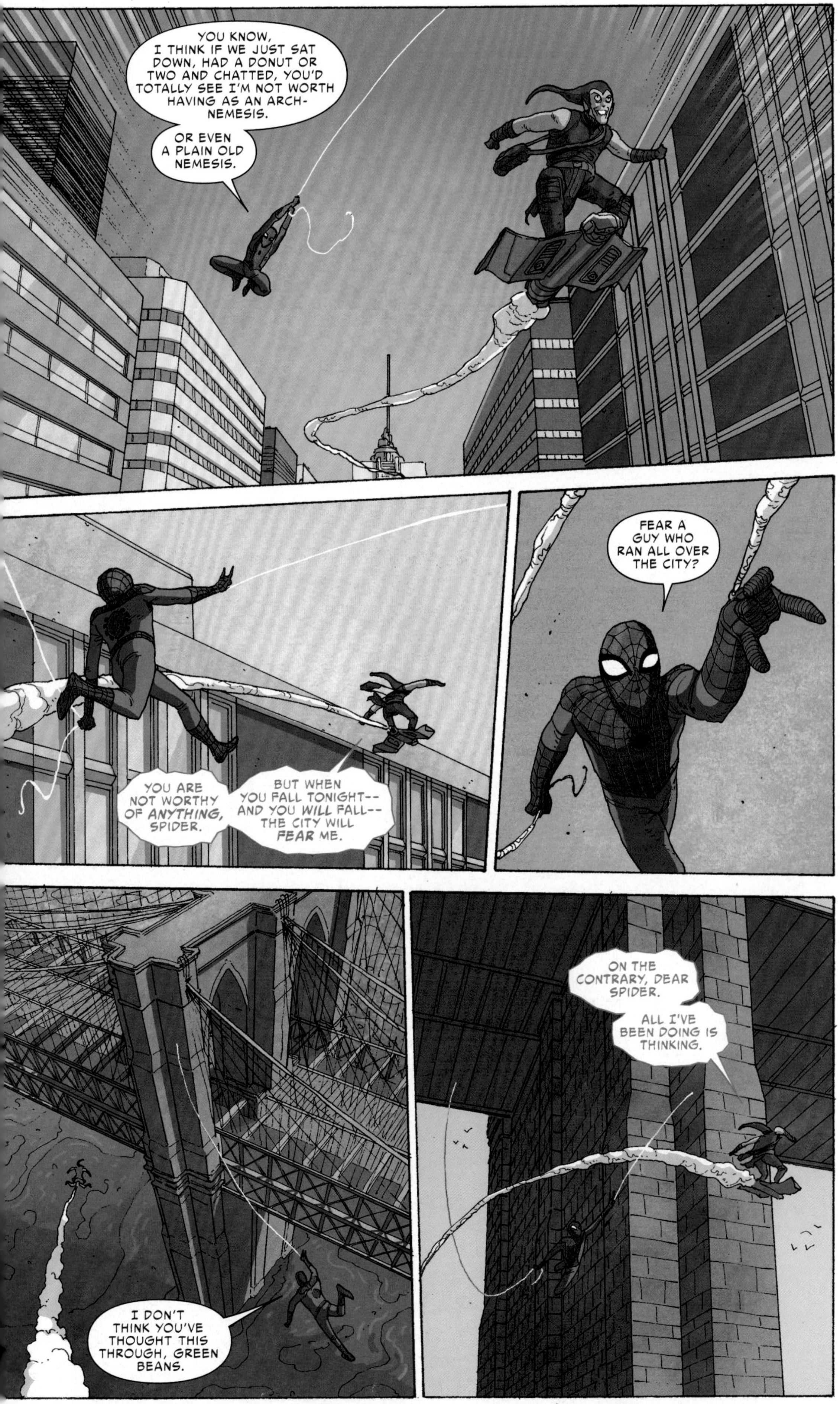
YOU KNOW, I THINK IF WE JUST SAT DOWN, HAD A DONUT OR TWO AND CHATTED, YOU'D TOTALLY SEE I'M NOT WORTH HAVING AS AN ARCH-NEMESIS.
OR EVEN A PLAIN OLD NEMESIS.
YOU ARE NOT WORTHY OF *ANYTHING*, SPIDER.
BUT WHEN YOU FALL TONIGHT-- AND YOU *WILL* FALL-- THE CITY WILL *FEAR* ME.
FEAR A GUY WHO RAN ALL OVER THE CITY?
I DON'T THINK YOU'VE THOUGHT THIS THROUGH, GREEN BEANS.
ON THE CONTRARY, DEAR SPIDER.
ALL I'VE BEEN DOING IS THINKING.

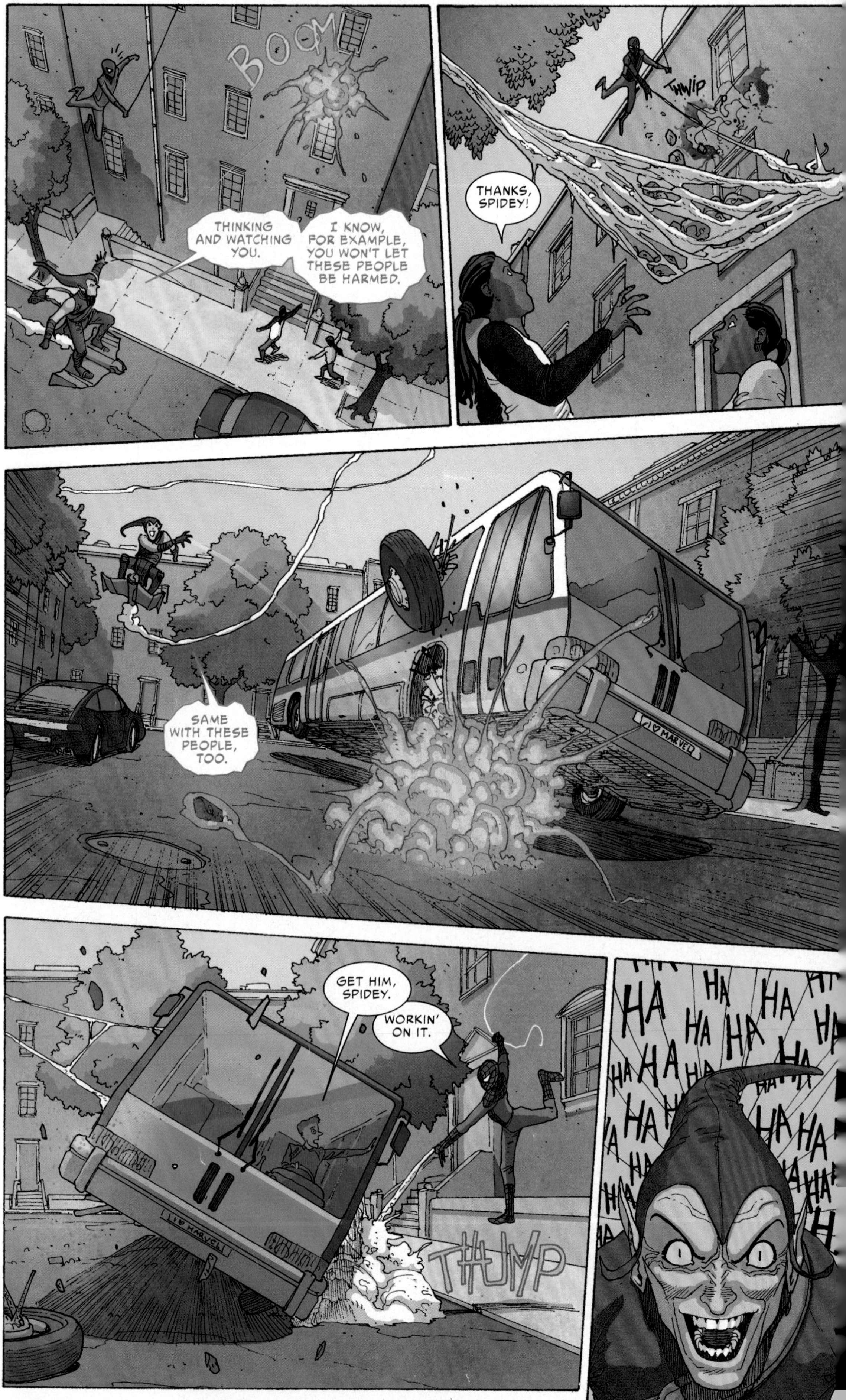

BOOM
THINKING AND WATCHING YOU.
I KNOW, FOR EXAMPLE, YOU WON'T LET THESE PEOPLE BE HARMED.
THWIP
THANKS, SPIDEY!
SAME WITH THESE PEOPLE, TOO.
I ♡ MARVEL
GET HIM, SPIDEY.
WORKIN' ON IT.
THUMP
HA HA HA HA HA HA HA HA HA HA HA HA HA HA

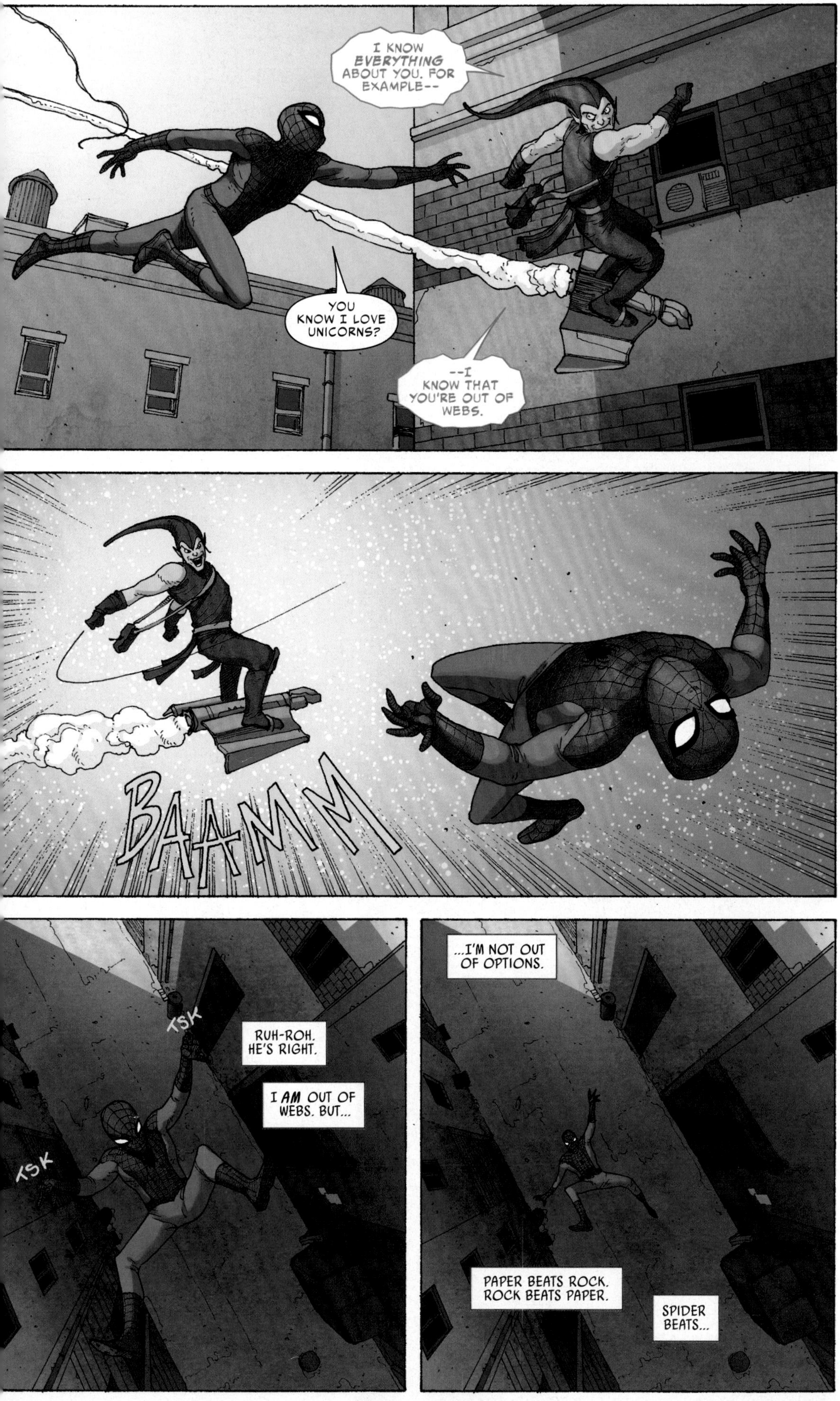
I KNOW EVERYTHING ABOUT YOU. FOR EXAMPLE--
YOU KNOW I LOVE UNICORNS?
--I KNOW THAT YOU'RE OUT OF WEBS.
BAAMM
TSK
TSK
RUH-ROH. HE'S RIGHT.
I AM OUT OF WEBS. BUT...
...I'M NOT OUT OF OPTIONS.
PAPER BEATS ROCK. ROCK BEATS PAPER.
SPIDER BEATS...

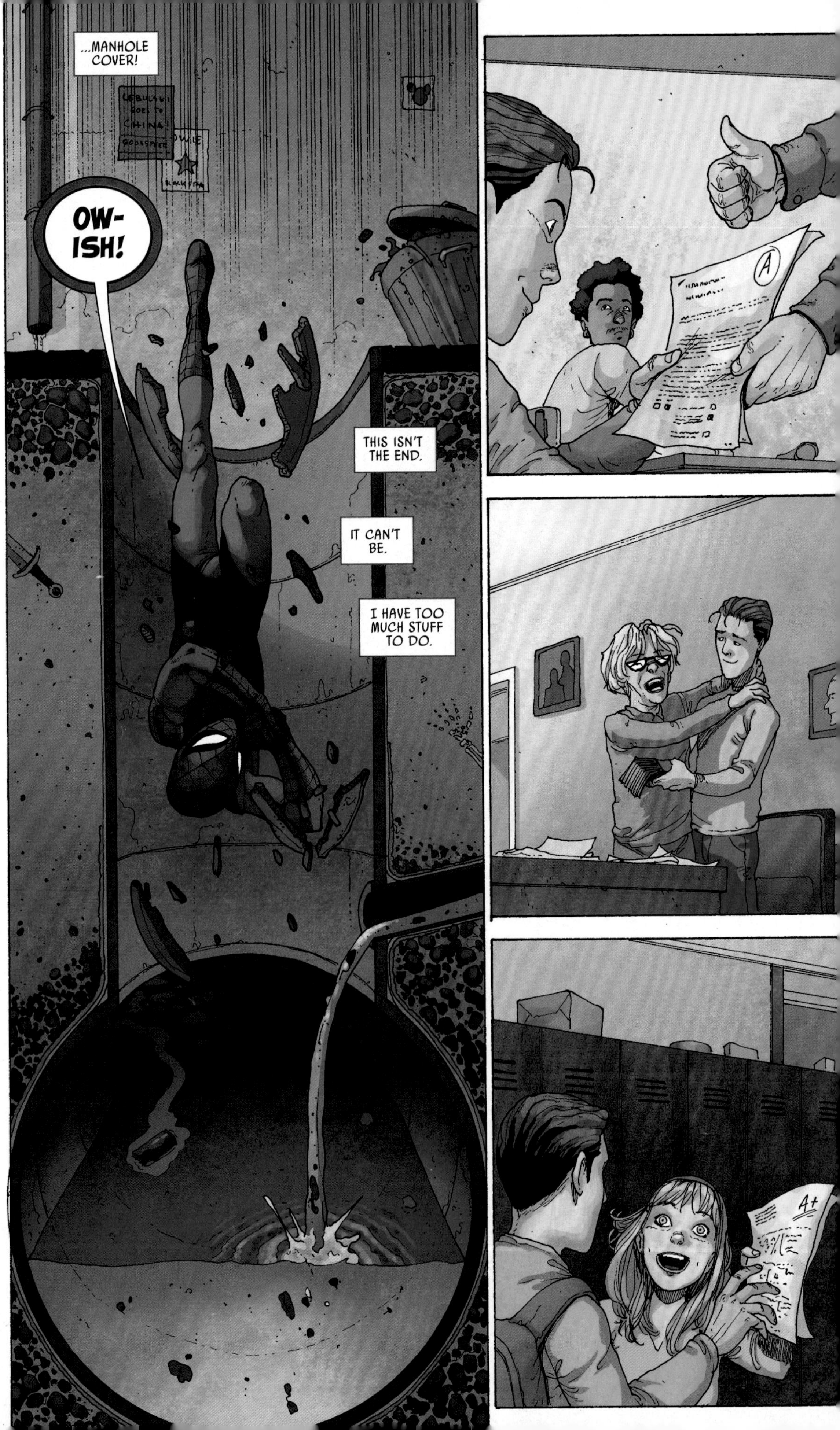
...MANHOLE COVER!
OW-ISH!
THIS ISN'T THE END.
IT CAN'T BE.
I HAVE TOO MUCH STUFF TO DO.

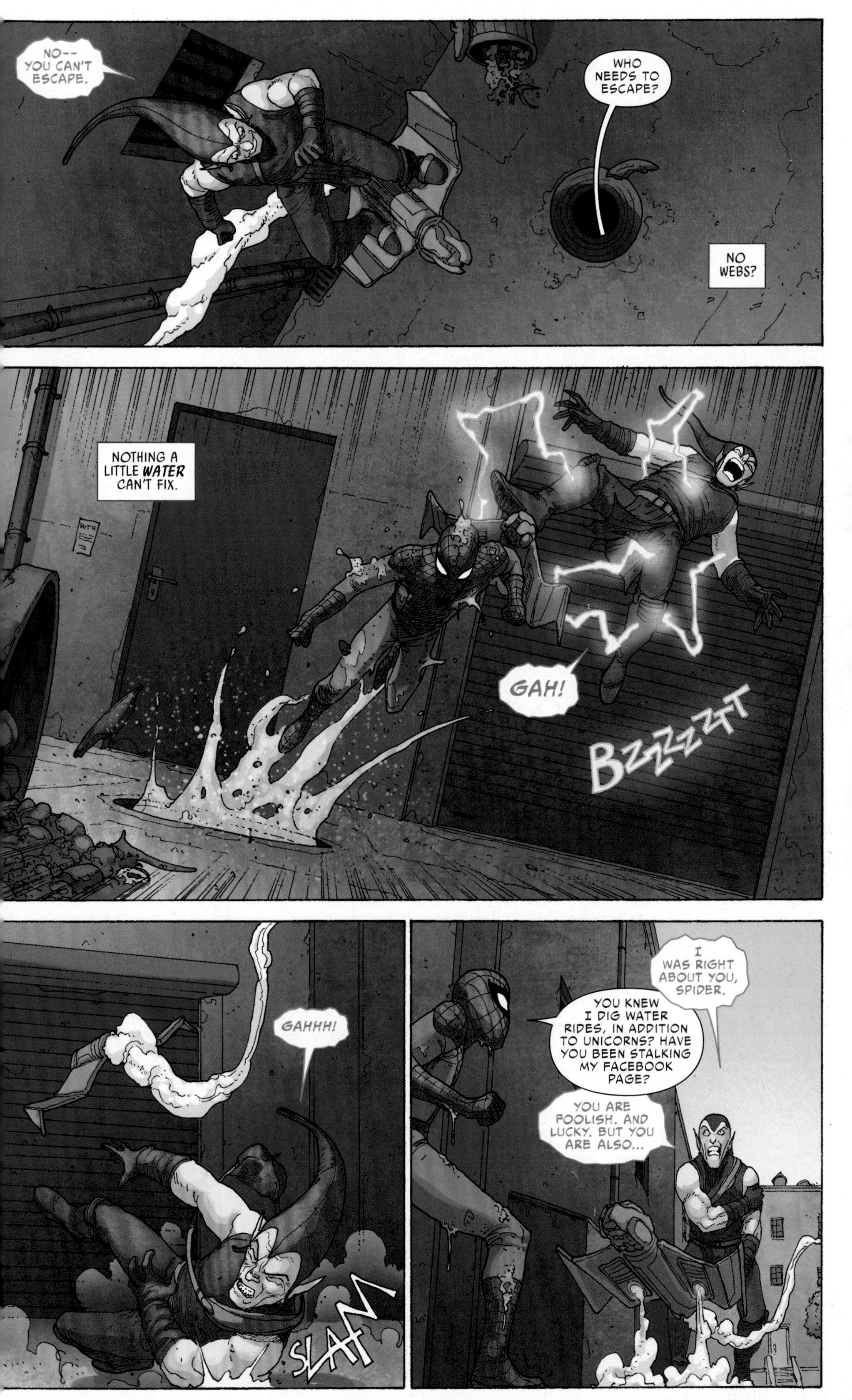
NO-- YOU CAN'T ESCAPE.
WHO NEEDS TO ESCAPE?
NO WEBS?
NOTHING A LITTLE WATER CAN'T FIX.
GAH!
BZZZZZT
GAHHH!
SLAM
I WAS RIGHT ABOUT YOU, SPIDER.
YOU KNEW I DIG WATER RIDES, IN ADDITION TO UNICORNS? HAVE YOU BEEN STALKING MY FACEBOOK PAGE?
YOU ARE FOOLISH. AND LUCKY. BUT YOU ARE ALSO...

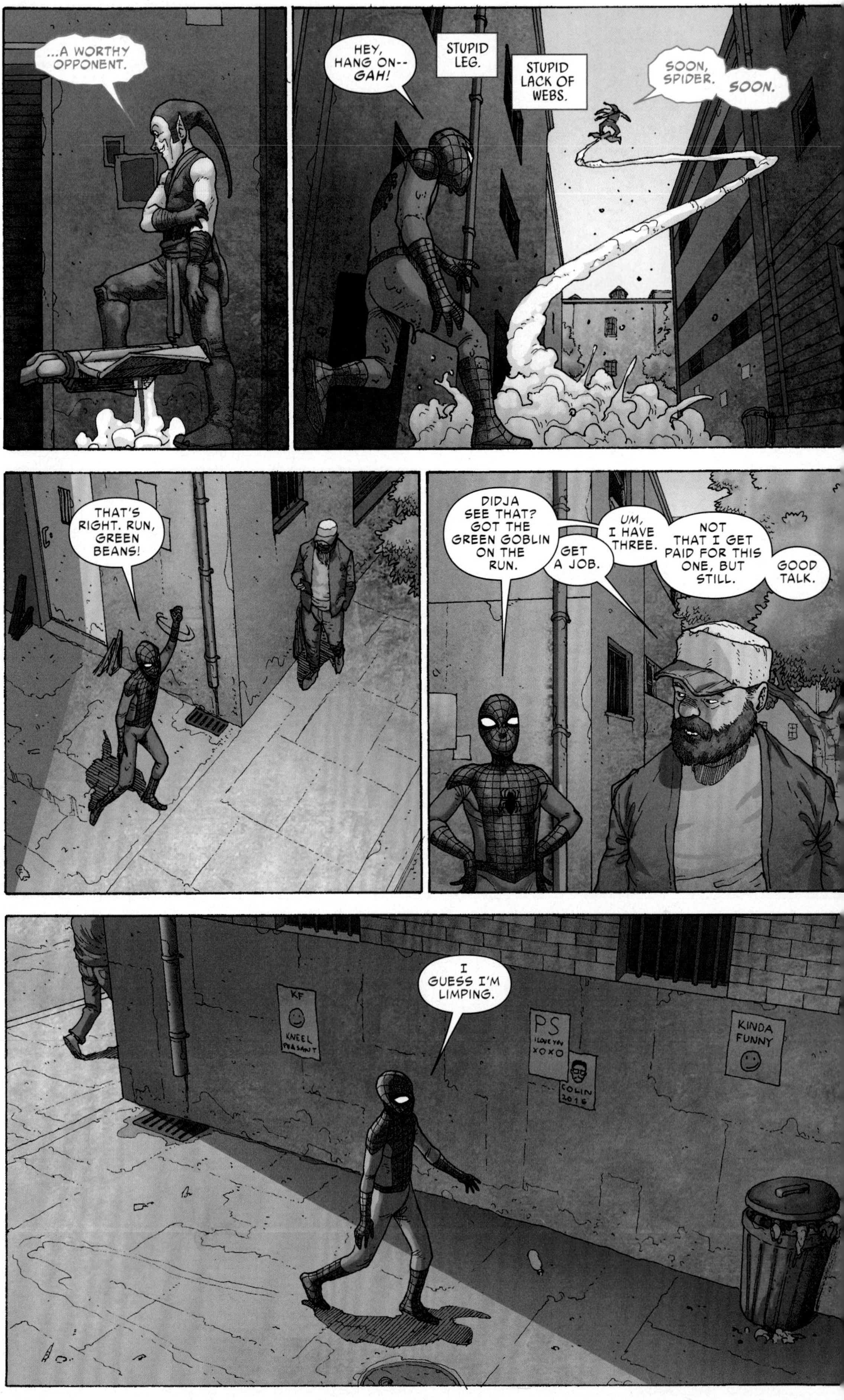
...A WORTHY OPPONENT.
HEY, HANG ON-- GAH!
STUPID LEG.
STUPID LACK OF WEBS.
SOON, SPIDER.
SOON.
THAT'S RIGHT. RUN, GREEN BEANS!
DIDJA SEE THAT? GOT THE GREEN GOBLIN ON THE RUN.
GET A JOB.
UM, I HAVE THREE.
NOT THAT I GET PAID FOR THIS ONE, BUT STILL.
GOOD TALK.
I GUESS I'M LIMPING.
KF
KNEEL PEASANT
PS
I LOVE YOU
XOXO
COLIN 2016
KINDA FUNNY

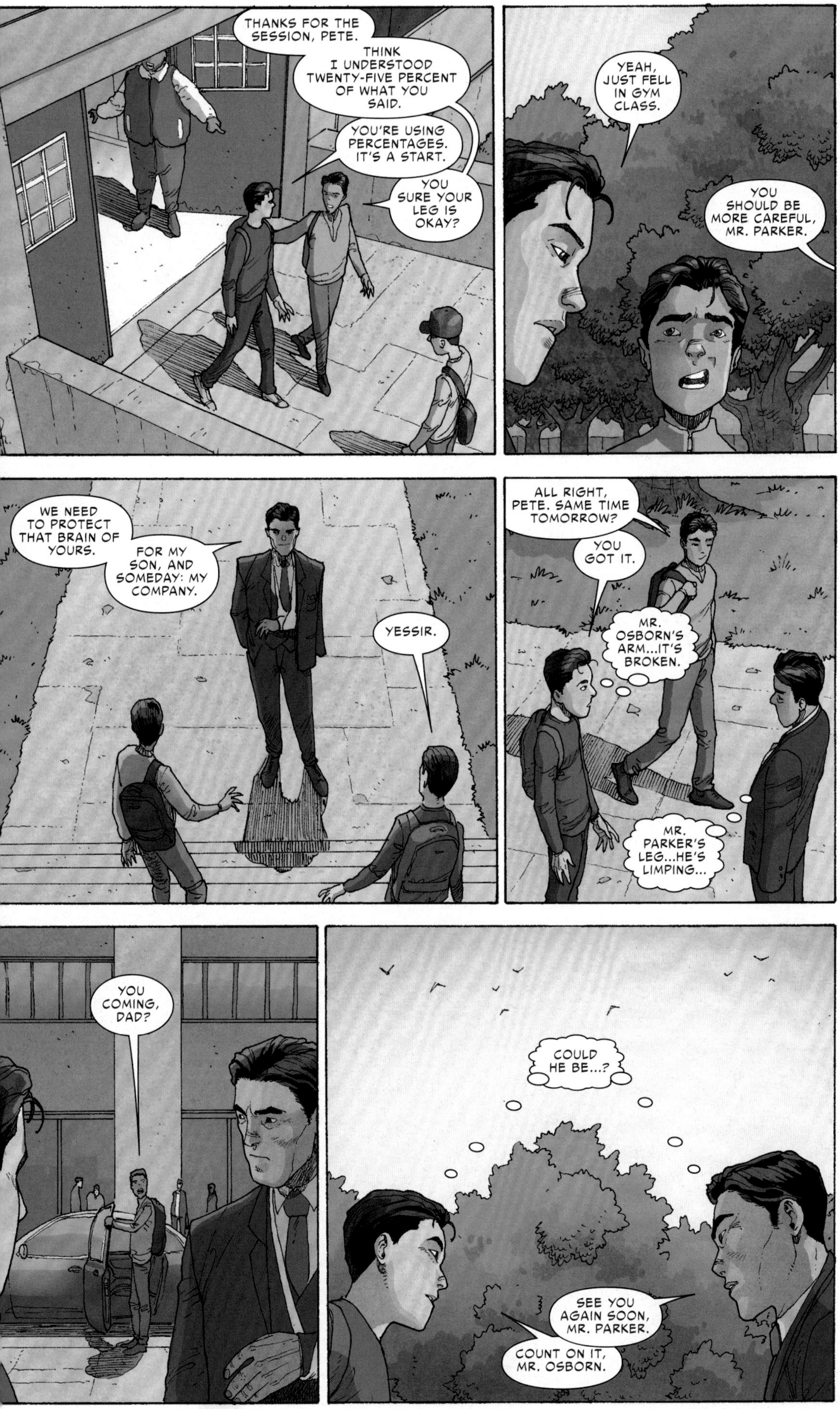
THANKS FOR THE SESSION, PETE.
THINK I UNDERSTOOD TWENTY-FIVE PERCENT OF WHAT YOU SAID.
YOU'RE USING PERCENTAGES. IT'S A START.
YOU SURE YOUR LEG IS OKAY?
YEAH, JUST FELL IN GYM CLASS.
YOU SHOULD BE MORE CAREFUL, MR. PARKER.
WE NEED TO PROTECT THAT BRAIN OF YOURS.
FOR MY SON, AND SOMEDAY: MY COMPANY.
YESSIR.
ALL RIGHT, PETE. SAME TIME TOMORROW?
YOU GOT IT.
MR. OSBORN'S ARM...IT'S BROKEN.
MR. PARKER'S LEG...HE'S LIMPING...
YOU COMING, DAD?
COULD HE BE...?
SEE YOU AGAIN SOON, MR. PARKER.
COUNT ON IT, MR. OSBORN.

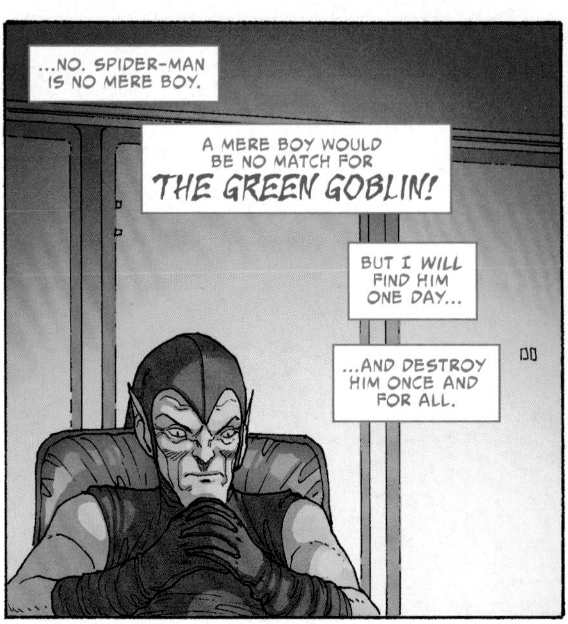
...NO. SPIDER-MAN IS NO MERE BOY.
A MERE BOY WOULD BE NO MATCH FOR THE GREEN GOBLIN!
BUT I WILL FIND HIM ONE DAY...
...AND DESTROY HIM ONCE AND FOR ALL.

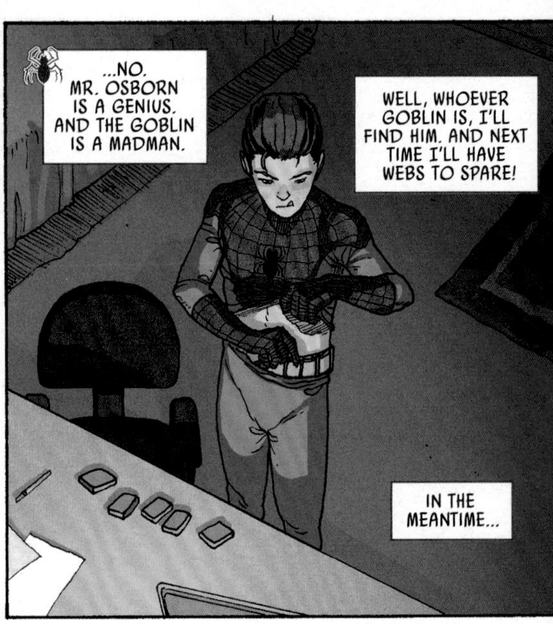
...NO. MR. OSBORN IS A GENIUS. AND THE GOBLIN IS A MADMAN.
WELL, WHOEVER GOBLIN IS, I'LL FIND HIM. AND NEXT TIME I'LL HAVE WEBS TO SPARE!
IN THE MEANTIME...

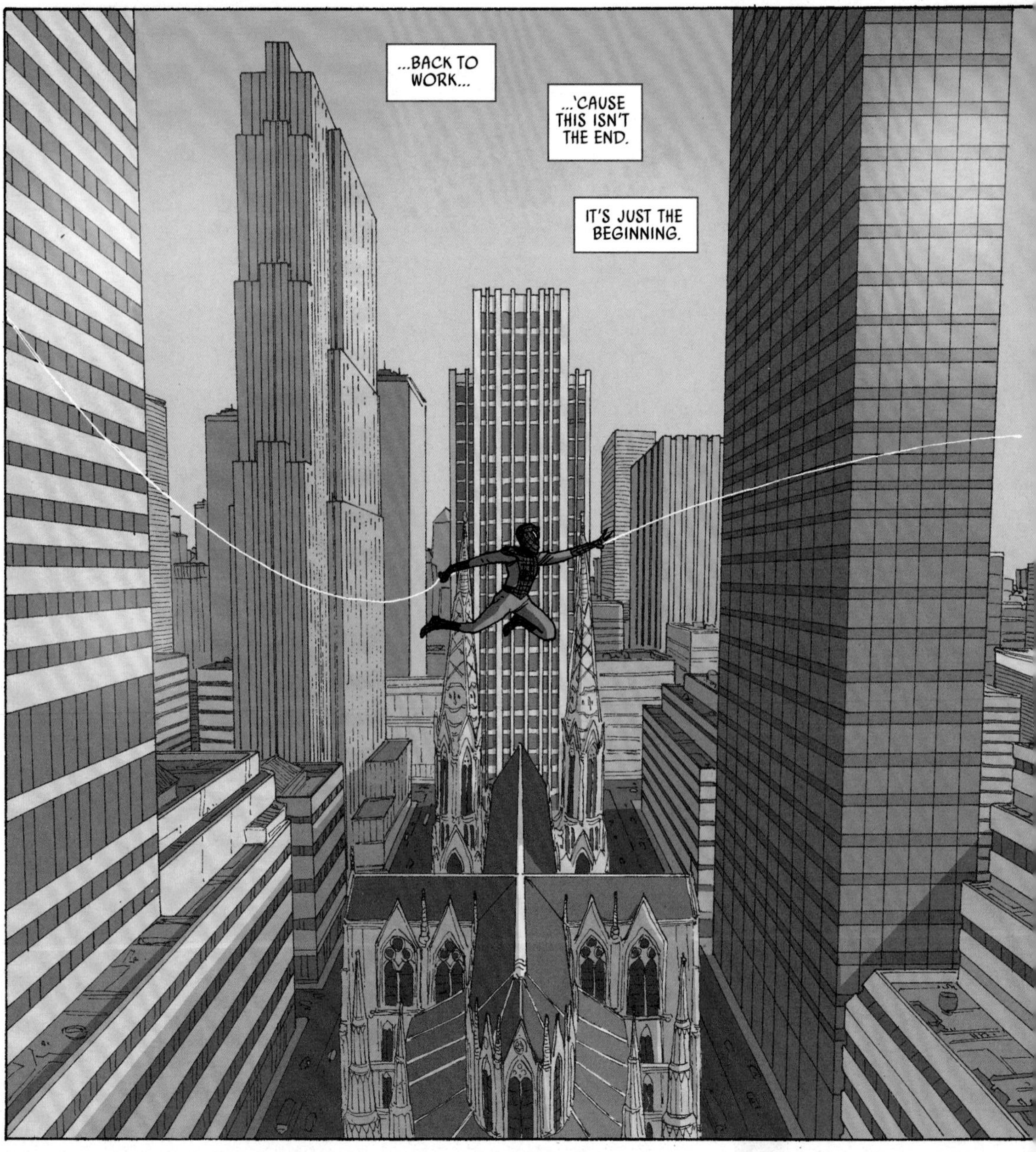
...BACK TO WORK...
...'CAUSE THIS ISN'T THE END.
IT'S JUST THE BEGINNING.

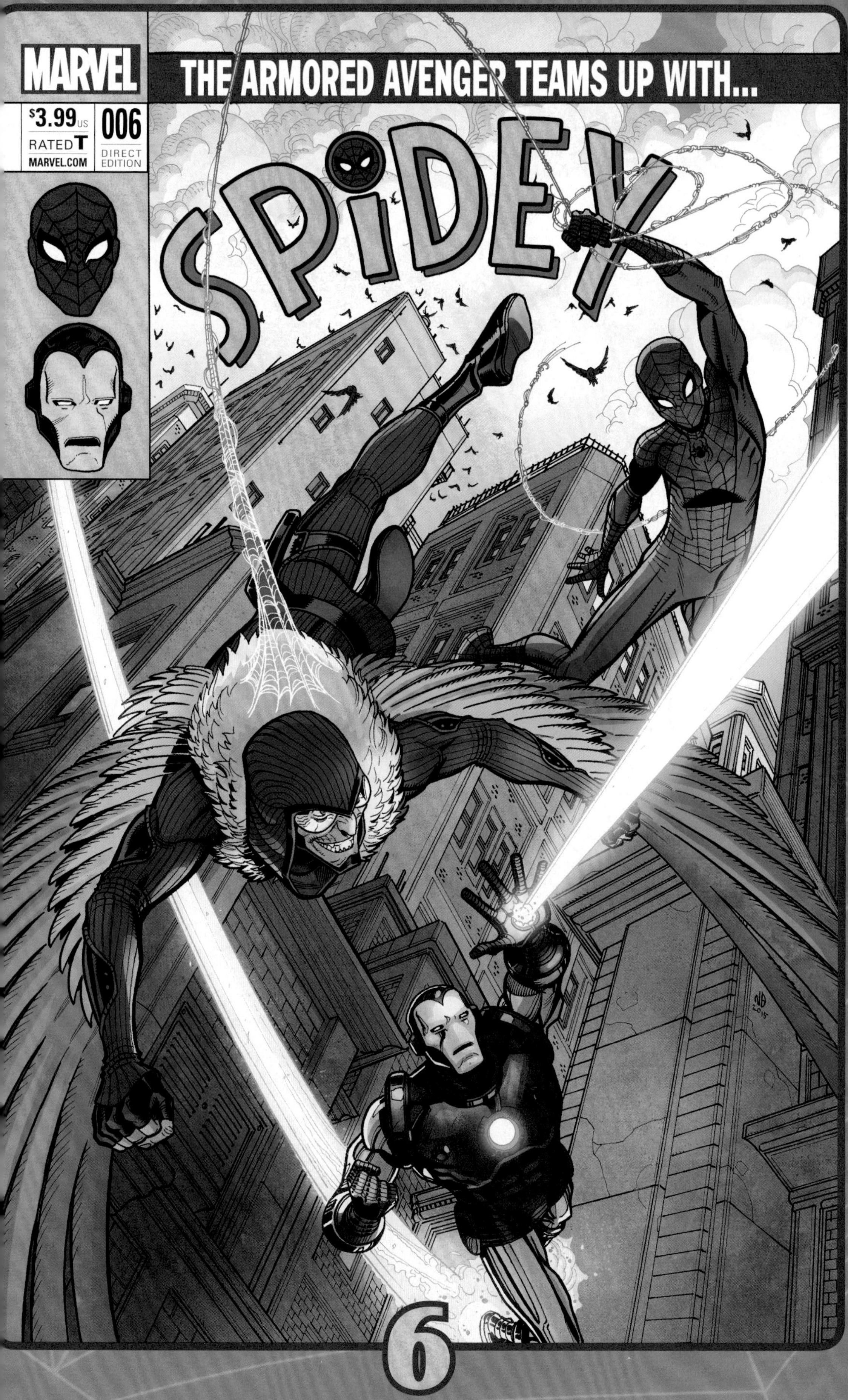
MARVEL
THE ARMORED AVENGER TEAMS UP WITH...
$3.99 US
006
RATED T
MARVEL.COM
DIRECT EDITION
SPIDEY
6

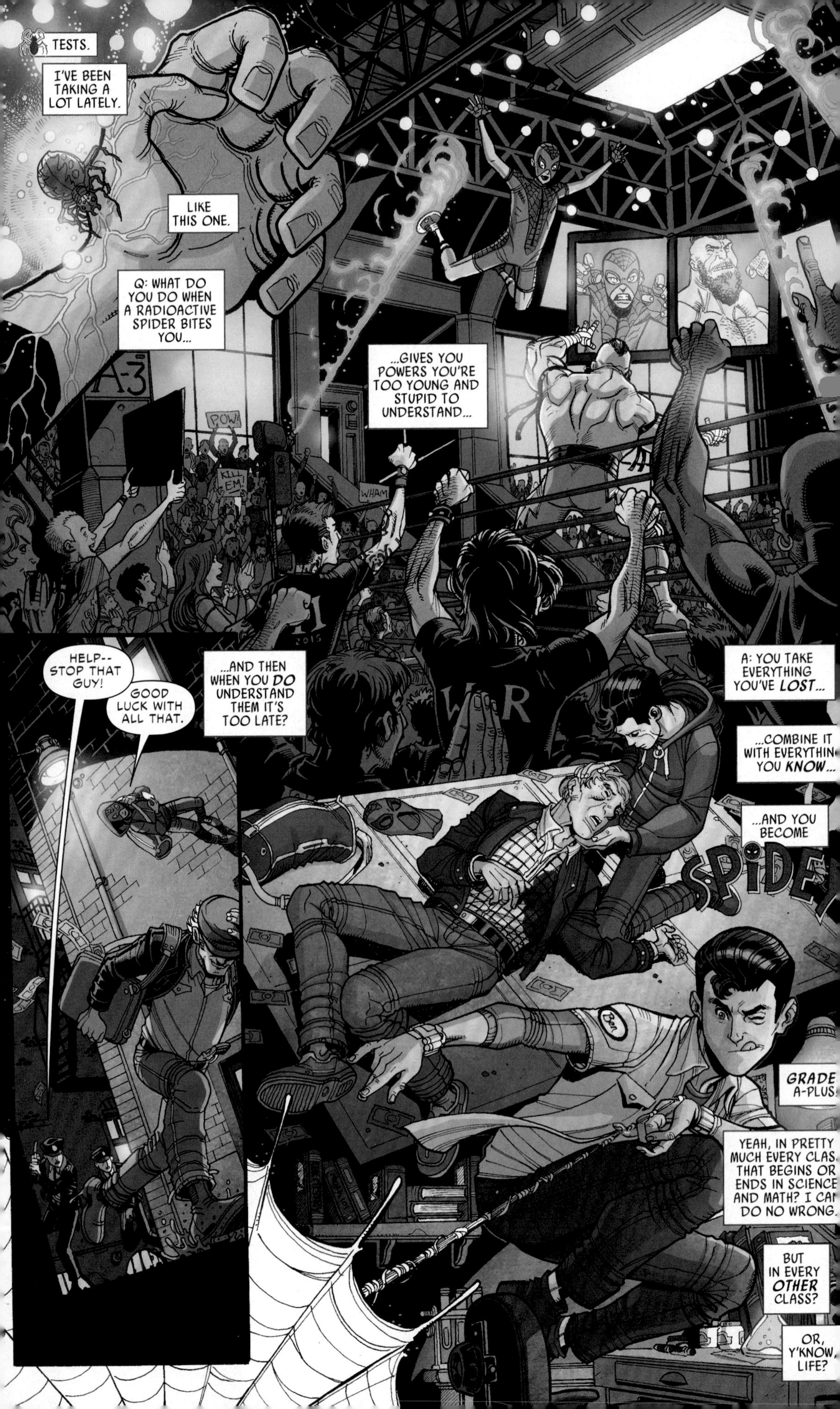
TESTS.
I'VE BEEN TAKING A LOT LATELY.
LIKE THIS ONE.
Q: WHAT DO YOU DO WHEN A RADIOACTIVE SPIDER BITES YOU...
...GIVES YOU POWERS YOU'RE TOO YOUNG AND STUPID TO UNDERSTAND...
POW!
KILL 'EM!
WHAM
HELP-- STOP THAT GUY!
GOOD LUCK WITH ALL THAT.
...AND THEN WHEN YOU DO UNDERSTAND THEM IT'S TOO LATE?
A: YOU TAKE EVERYTHING YOU'VE LOST...
...COMBINE IT WITH EVERYTHIN YOU KNOW...
...AND YOU BECOME
SPIDE
GRADE A-PLUS.
YEAH, IN PRETTY MUCH EVERY CLAS THAT BEGINS OR ENDS IN SCIENCE AND MATH? I CA DO NO WRONG.
BUT IN EVERY OTHER CLASS?
OR, Y'KNOW LIFE?

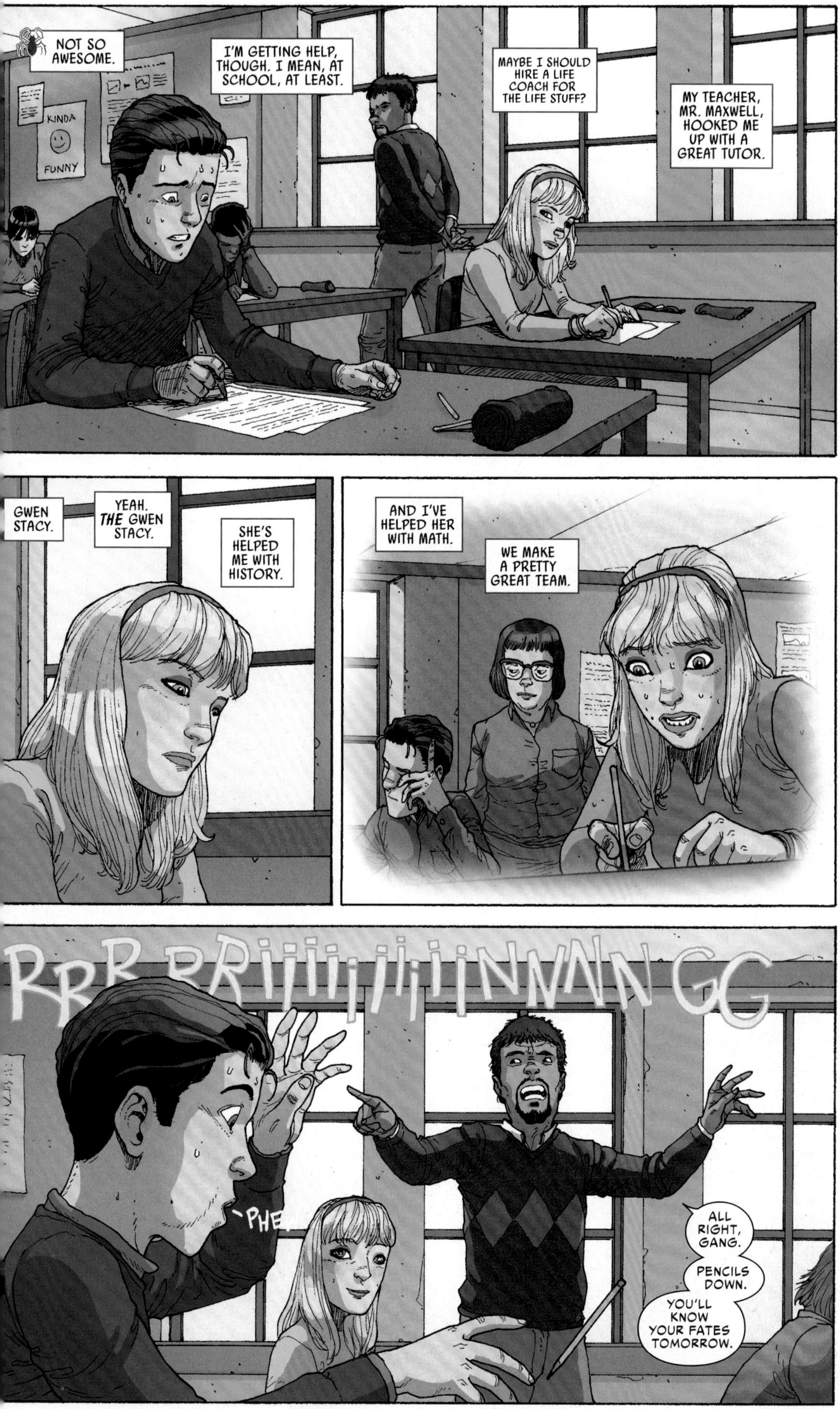

NOT SO AWESOME.
I'M GETTING HELP, THOUGH. I MEAN, AT SCHOOL, AT LEAST.
MAYBE I SHOULD HIRE A LIFE COACH FOR THE LIFE STUFF?
MY TEACHER, MR. MAXWELL, HOOKED ME UP WITH A GREAT TUTOR.
KINDA
FUNNY
GWEN STACY.
YEAH. THE GWEN STACY.
SHE'S HELPED ME WITH HISTORY.
AND I'VE HELPED HER WITH MATH.
WE MAKE A PRETTY GREAT TEAM.
RRRRRIIIIIIIIINNNNNGG
PHEW
ALL RIGHT, GANG.
PENCILS DOWN.
YOU'LL KNOW YOUR FATES TOMORROW.

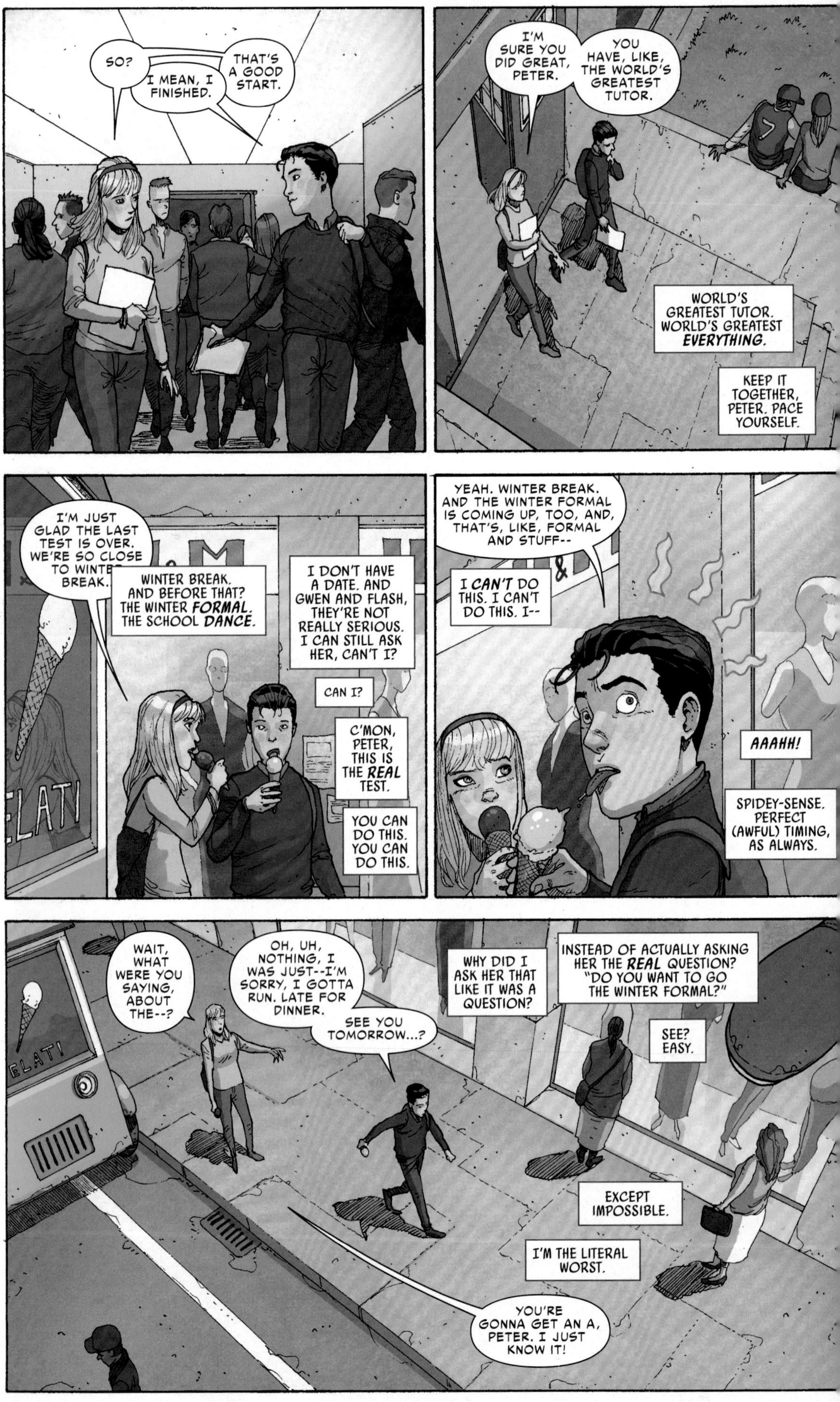
SO?
I MEAN, I FINISHED.
THAT'S A GOOD START.
I'M SURE YOU DID GREAT, PETER.
YOU HAVE, LIKE, THE WORLD'S GREATEST TUTOR.
WORLD'S GREATEST TUTOR. WORLD'S GREATEST EVERYTHING.
KEEP IT TOGETHER, PETER. PACE YOURSELF.
I'M JUST GLAD THE LAST TEST IS OVER. WE'RE SO CLOSE TO WINTER BREAK.
WINTER BREAK. AND BEFORE THAT? THE WINTER FORMAL. THE SCHOOL DANCE.
I DON'T HAVE A DATE. AND GWEN AND FLASH, THEY'RE NOT REALLY SERIOUS. I CAN STILL ASK HER, CAN'T I?
CAN I?
C'MON, PETER, THIS IS THE REAL TEST.
YOU CAN DO THIS. YOU CAN DO THIS.
YEAH. WINTER BREAK. AND THE WINTER FORMAL IS COMING UP, TOO, AND, THAT'S, LIKE, FORMAL AND STUFF--
I CAN'T DO THIS. I CAN'T DO THIS. I--
AAAHH!
SPIDEY-SENSE. PERFECT (AWFUL) TIMING, AS ALWAYS.
WAIT, WHAT WERE YOU SAYING, ABOUT THE--?
OH, UH, NOTHING, I WAS JUST--I'M SORRY, I GOTTA RUN. LATE FOR DINNER.
SEE YOU TOMORROW...?
WHY DID I ASK HER THAT LIKE IT WAS A QUESTION?
INSTEAD OF ACTUALLY ASKING HER THE REAL QUESTION? "DO YOU WANT TO GO THE WINTER FORMAL?"
SEE? EASY.
EXCEPT IMPOSSIBLE.
I'M THE LITERAL WORST.
YOU'RE GONNA GET AN A, PETER. I JUST KNOW IT!

Q: HOW DO YOU ASK A GIRL OUT?
A:...
GRADE: EPIC FAIL.
ZOMBIES THE MOVIE
WHY IS THIS SO HARD?
"DO YOU WANT TO GO TO THE WINTER FORMAL?"
IT SOUNDS EASY. IN MY HEAD ANYWAY.
MAYBE I SHOULD TRY IT OUT LOUD.
DO YOU WANT TO GO TO THE WINTER FORMAL?
(TERRIBLE)
DO YOU WANT TO GO TO THE WINTER FORMAL?
(WORSE)
BREAK-IN. WHAT BUILDING IS THIS?
WHOA. THIS IS SOME HIGH-END EQUIPMENT.
DO YOU WANT TO GO TO THE WINTER FORMAL?
I'LL PASS, THANKS.

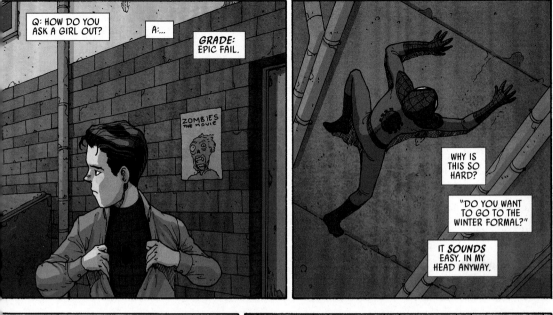

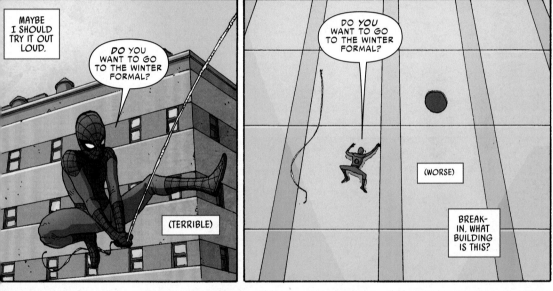

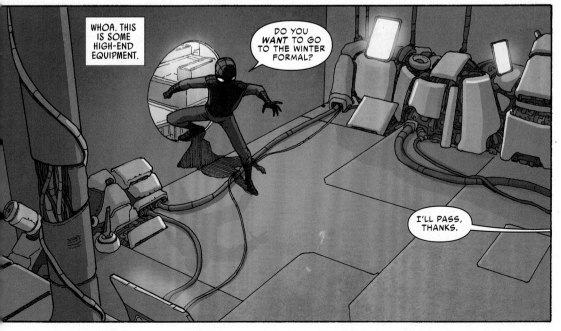

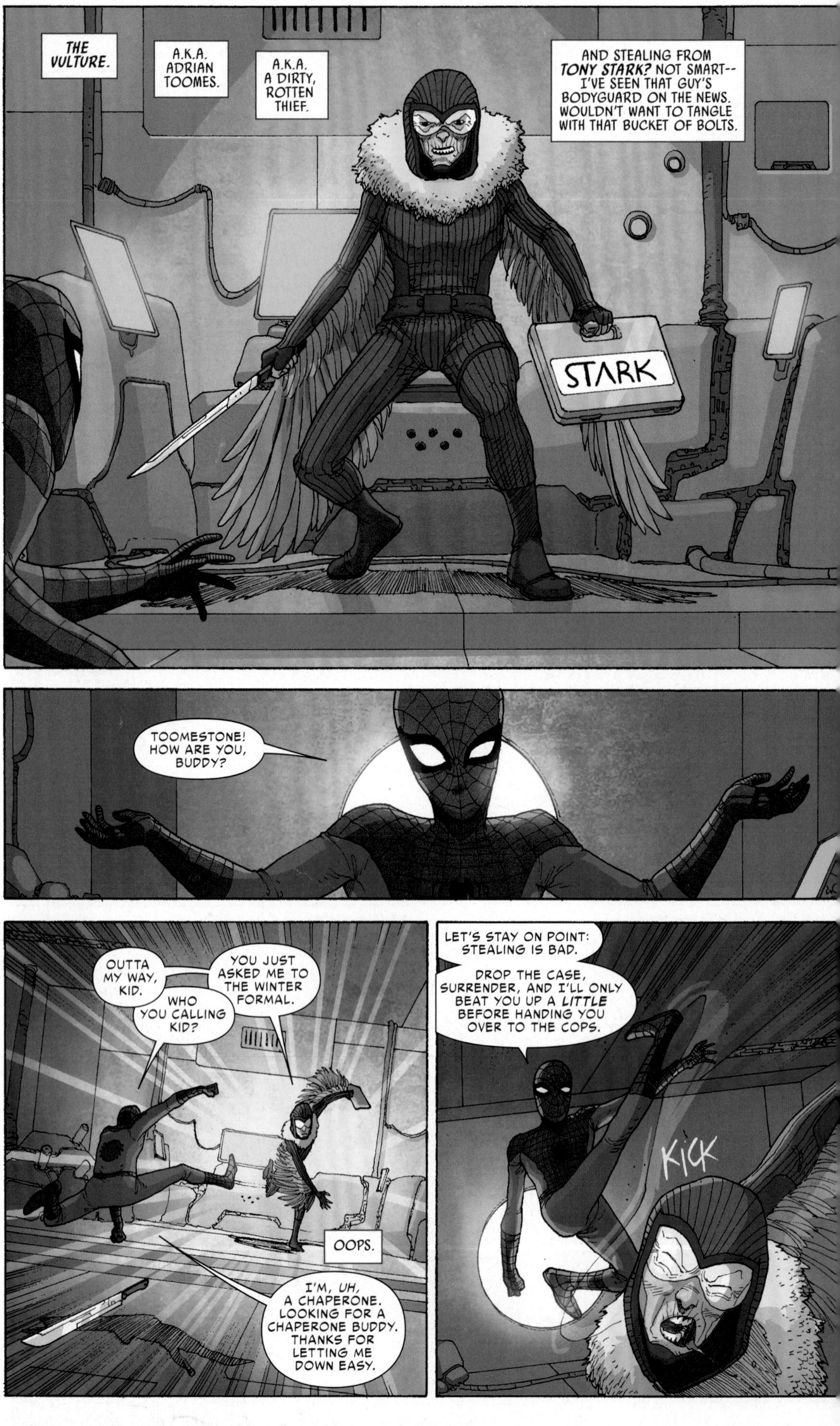

THE VULTURE.
A.K.A. ADRIAN TOOMES.
A.K.A. A DIRTY, ROTTEN THIEF.
AND STEALING FROM TONY STARK? NOT SMART-- I'VE SEEN THAT GUY'S BODYGUARD ON THE NEWS. WOULDN'T WANT TO TANGLE WITH THAT BUCKET OF BOLTS.
STARK
TOOMESTONE! HOW ARE YOU, BUDDY?
OUTTA MY WAY, KID.
WHO YOU CALLING KID?
YOU JUST ASKED ME TO THE WINTER FORMAL.
OOPS.
I'M, UH, A CHAPERONE. LOOKING FOR A CHAPERONE BUDDY. THANKS FOR LETTING ME DOWN EASY.
LET'S STAY ON POINT: STEALING IS BAD.
DROP THE CASE, SURRENDER, AND I'LL ONLY BEAT YOU UP A LITTLE BEFORE HANDING YOU OVER TO THE COPS.
KICK

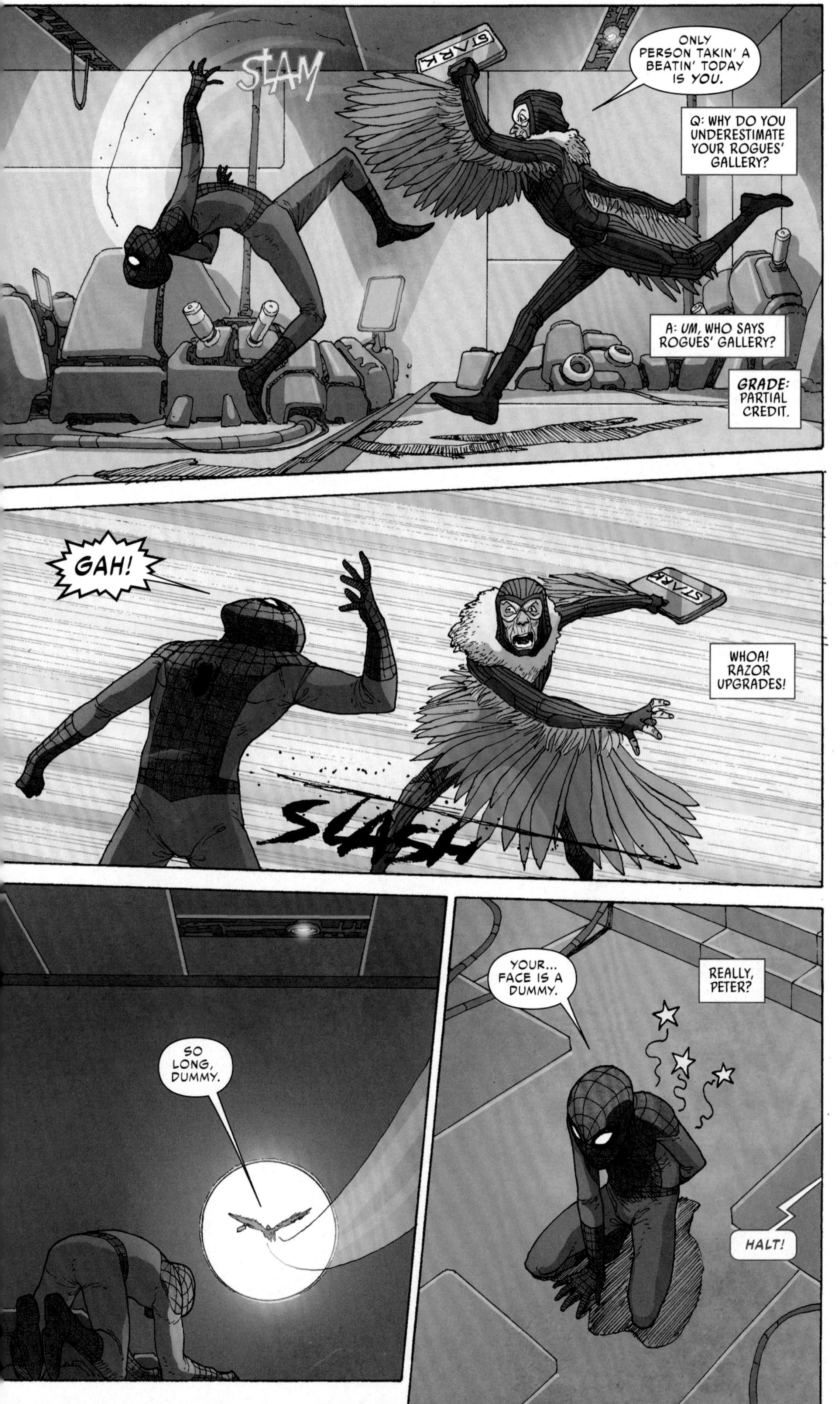
SLAM
ONLY PERSON TAKIN' A BEATIN' TODAY IS YOU.
Q: WHY DO YOU UNDERESTIMATE YOUR ROGUES' GALLERY?
A: UM, WHO SAYS ROGUES' GALLERY?
GRADE: PARTIAL CREDIT.
GAH!
WHOA! RAZOR UPGRADES!
SLASH
SO LONG, DUMMY.
YOUR... FACE IS A DUMMY.
REALLY, PETER?
HALT!

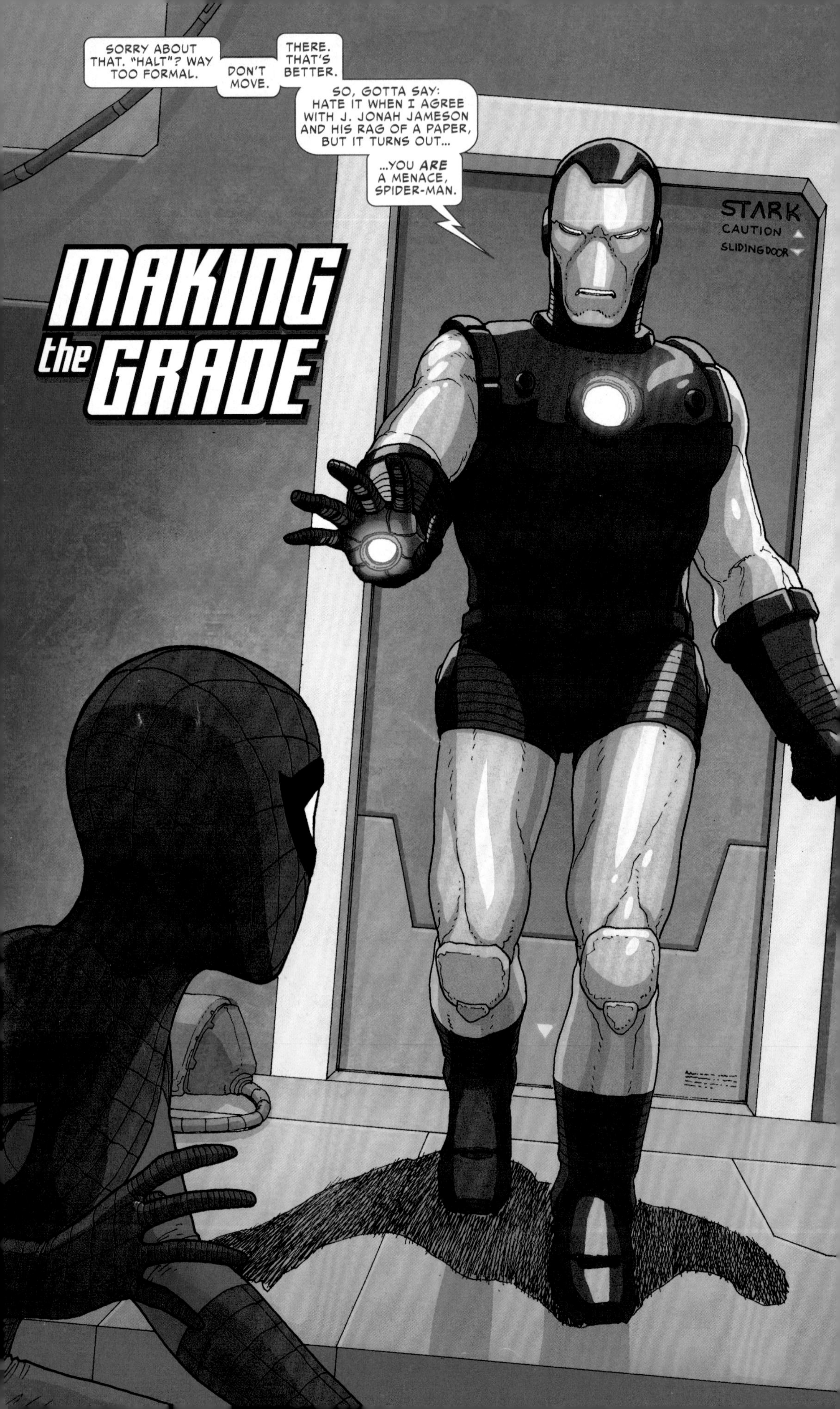
SORRY ABOUT THAT. "HALT"? WAY TOO FORMAL.
DON'T MOVE.
THERE. THAT'S BETTER.
SO, GOTTA SAY: HATE IT WHEN I AGREE WITH J. JONAH JAMESON AND HIS RAG OF A PAPER, BUT IT TURNS OUT...
...YOU ARE A MENACE, SPIDER-MAN.
MAKING the GRADE
STARK
CAUTION
SLIDING DOOR

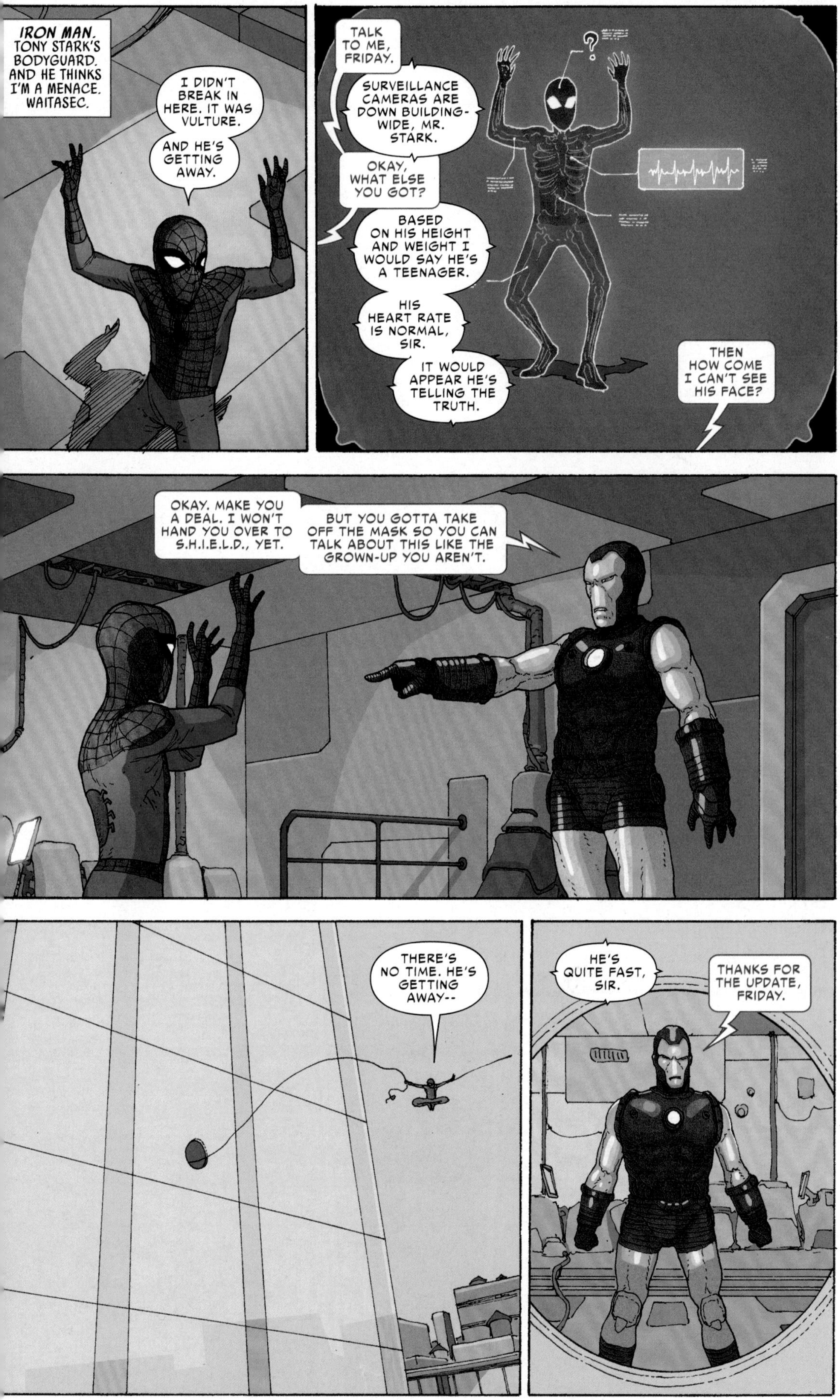
IRON MAN. TONY STARK'S BODYGUARD. AND HE THINKS I'M A MENACE. WAITASEC.
I DIDN'T BREAK IN HERE. IT WAS VULTURE.
AND HE'S GETTING AWAY.
TALK TO ME, FRIDAY.
SURVEILLANCE CAMERAS ARE DOWN BUILDING-WIDE, MR. STARK.
OKAY, WHAT ELSE YOU GOT?
BASED ON HIS HEIGHT AND WEIGHT I WOULD SAY HE'S A TEENAGER.
HIS HEART RATE IS NORMAL, SIR.
IT WOULD APPEAR HE'S TELLING THE TRUTH.
THEN HOW COME I CAN'T SEE HIS FACE?
OKAY. MAKE YOU A DEAL. I WON'T HAND YOU OVER TO S.H.I.E.L.D., YET.
BUT YOU GOTTA TAKE OFF THE MASK SO YOU CAN TALK ABOUT THIS LIKE THE GROWN-UP YOU AREN'T.
THERE'S NO TIME. HE'S GETTING AWAY--
HE'S QUITE FAST, SIR.
THANKS FOR THE UPDATE, FRIDAY.

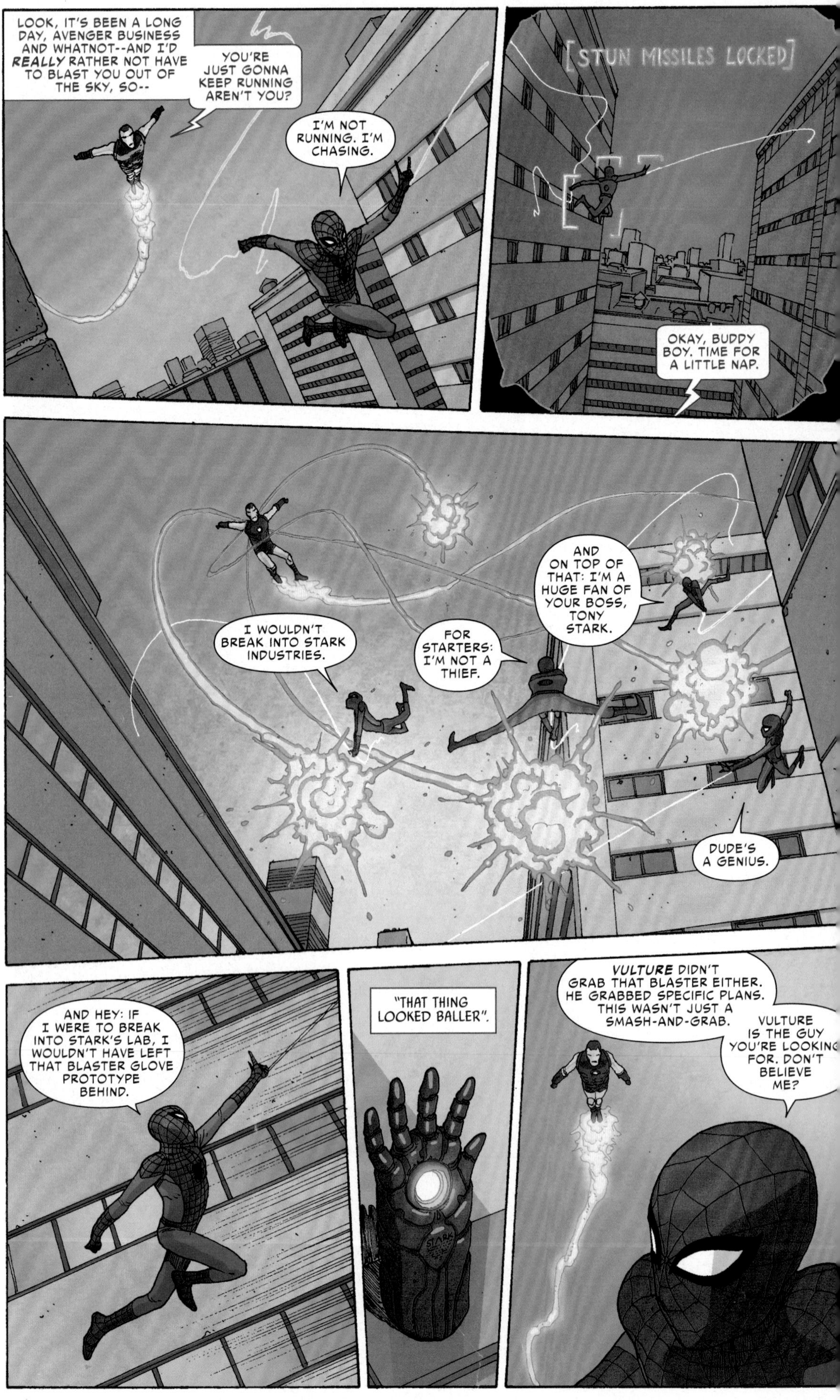
LOOK, IT'S BEEN A LONG DAY, AVENGER BUSINESS AND WHATNOT--AND I'D *REALLY* RATHER NOT HAVE TO BLAST YOU OUT OF THE SKY, SO--
YOU'RE JUST GONNA KEEP RUNNING AREN'T YOU?
I'M NOT RUNNING. I'M CHASING.
[STUN MISSILES LOCKED]
OKAY, BUDDY BOY. TIME FOR A LITTLE NAP.
I WOULDN'T BREAK INTO STARK INDUSTRIES.
FOR STARTERS: I'M NOT A THIEF.
AND ON TOP OF THAT: I'M A HUGE FAN OF YOUR BOSS, TONY STARK.
DUDE'S A GENIUS.
AND HEY: IF I WERE TO BREAK INTO STARK'S LAB, I WOULDN'T HAVE LEFT THAT BLASTER GLOVE PROTOTYPE BEHIND.
"THAT THING LOOKED BALLER".
STARK
*VULTURE* DIDN'T GRAB THAT BLASTER EITHER. HE GRABBED SPECIFIC PLANS. THIS WASN'T JUST A SMASH-AND-GRAB.
VULTURE IS THE GUY YOU'RE LOOKING FOR. DON'T BELIEVE ME?

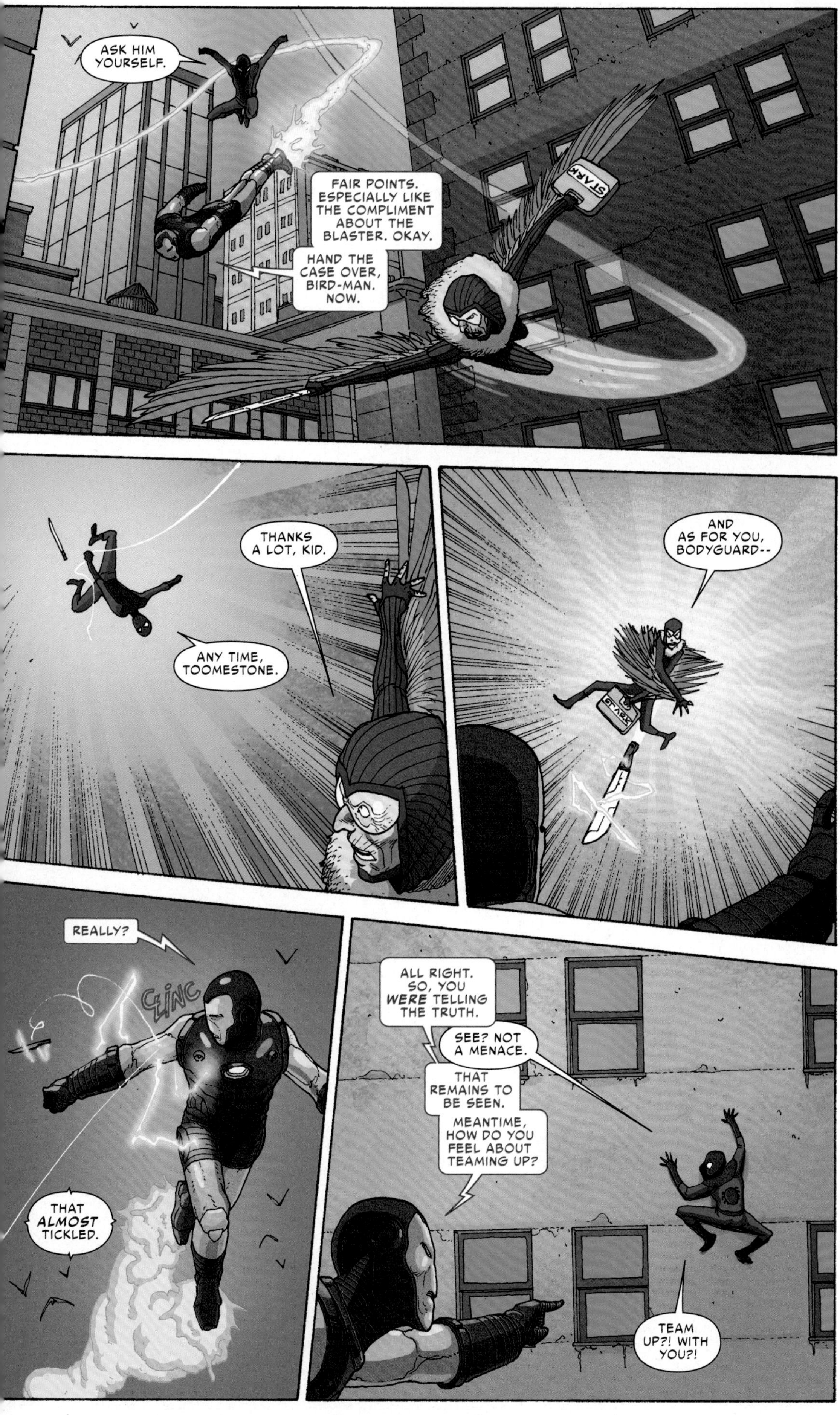
ASK HIM YOURSELF.
STARK
FAIR POINTS. ESPECIALLY LIKE THE COMPLIMENT ABOUT THE BLASTER. OKAY.
HAND THE CASE OVER, BIRD-MAN. NOW.
THANKS A LOT, KID.
ANY TIME, TOOMESTONE.
AND AS FOR YOU, BODYGUARD--
STARK
REALLY?
CLINC
THAT ALMOST TICKLED.
ALL RIGHT. SO, YOU WERE TELLING THE TRUTH.
SEE? NOT A MENACE.
THAT REMAINS TO BE SEEN.
MEANTIME, HOW DO YOU FEEL ABOUT TEAMING UP?
TEAM UP?! WITH YOU?!

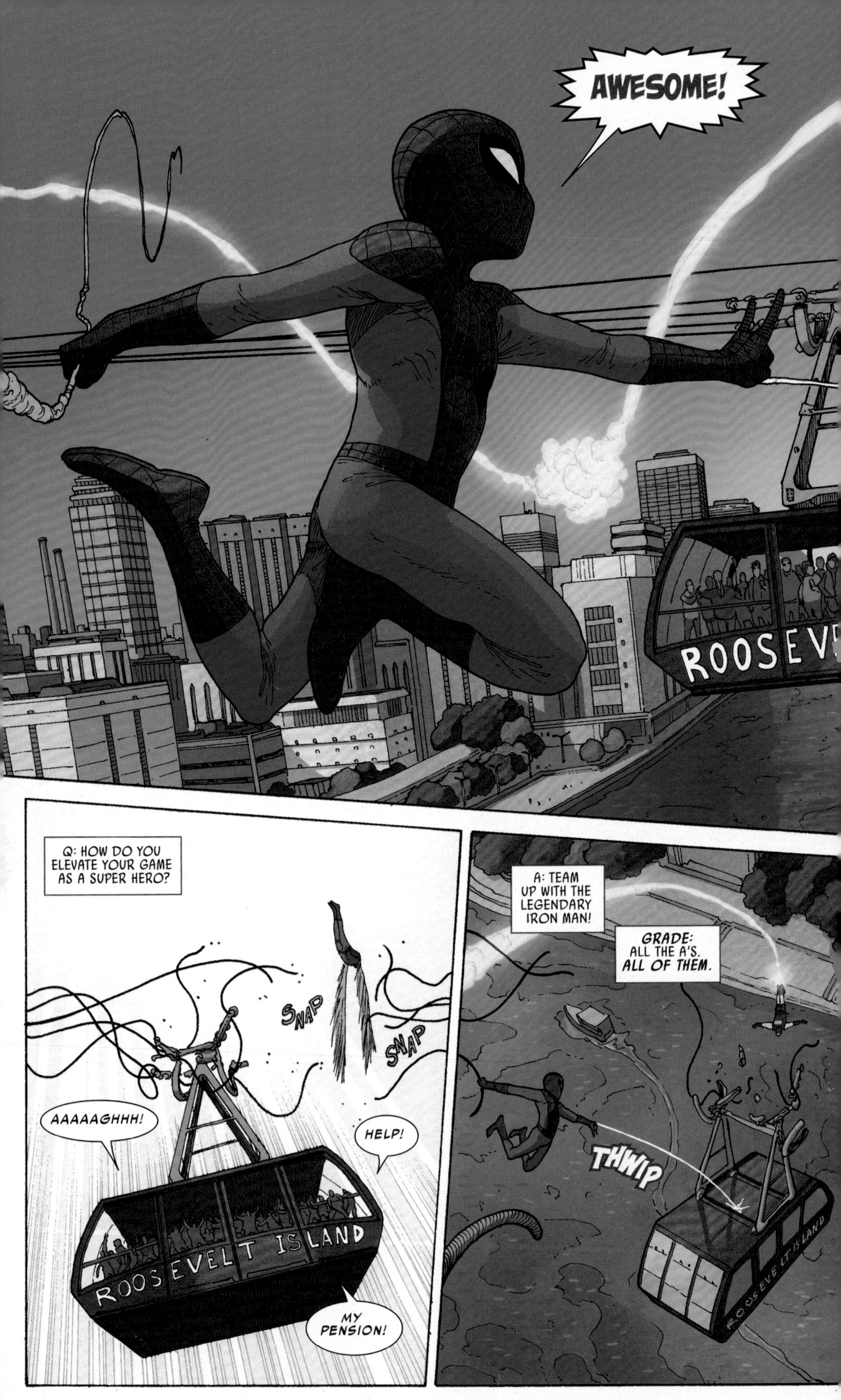
AWESOME!
ROOSEV
Q: HOW DO YOU ELEVATE YOUR GAME AS A SUPER HERO?
SNAP
SNAP
AAAAAGHHH!
HELP!
ROOSEVELT ISLAND
MY PENSION!
A: TEAM UP WITH THE LEGENDARY IRON MAN!
GRADE: ALL THE A'S. ALL OF THEM.
THWIP
ROOSEVELT ISLAND

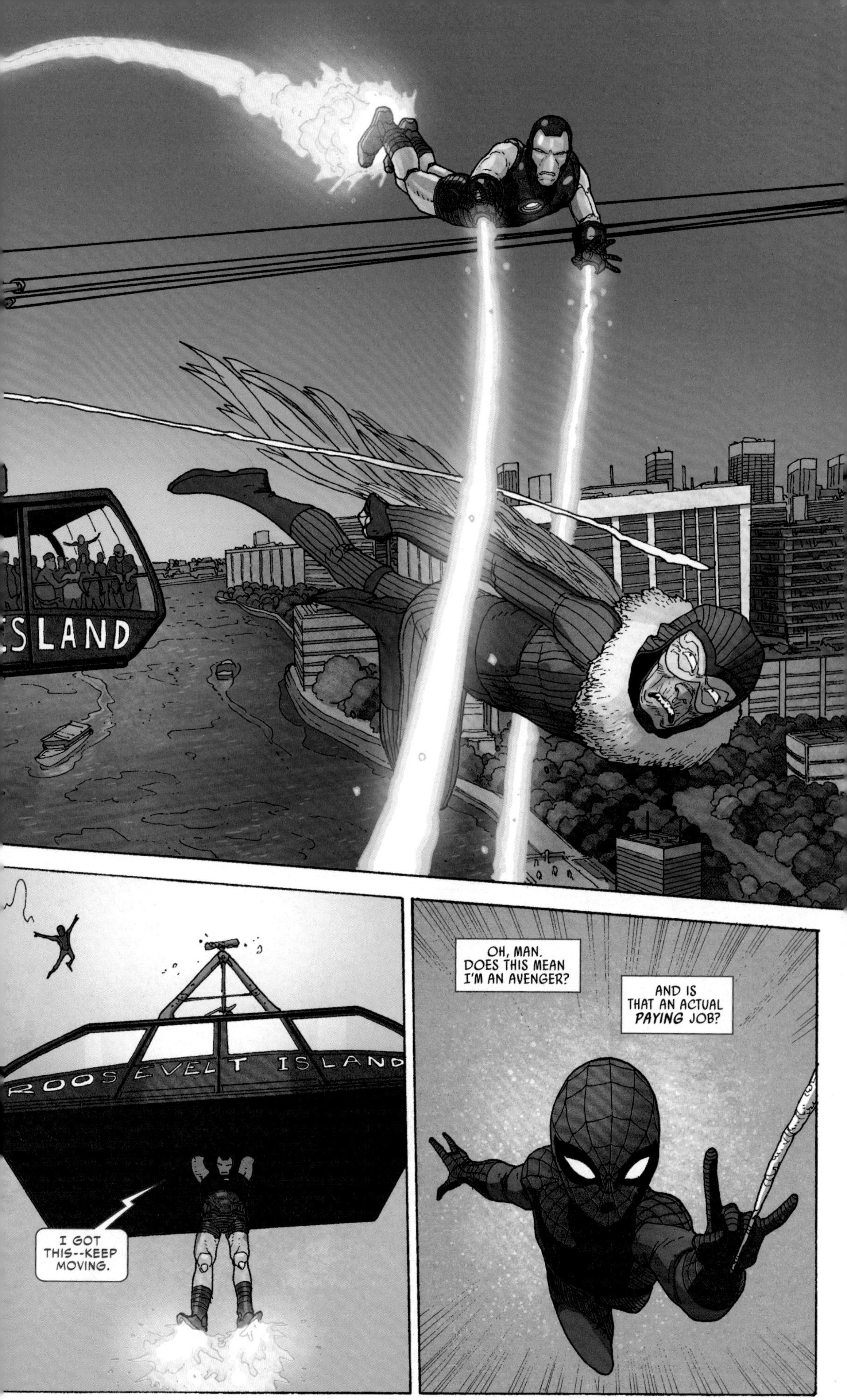
ISLAND
ROOSEVELT ISLAND
I GOT THIS--KEEP MOVING.
OH, MAN. DOES THIS MEAN I'M AN AVENGER?
AND IS THAT AN ACTUAL PAYING JOB?

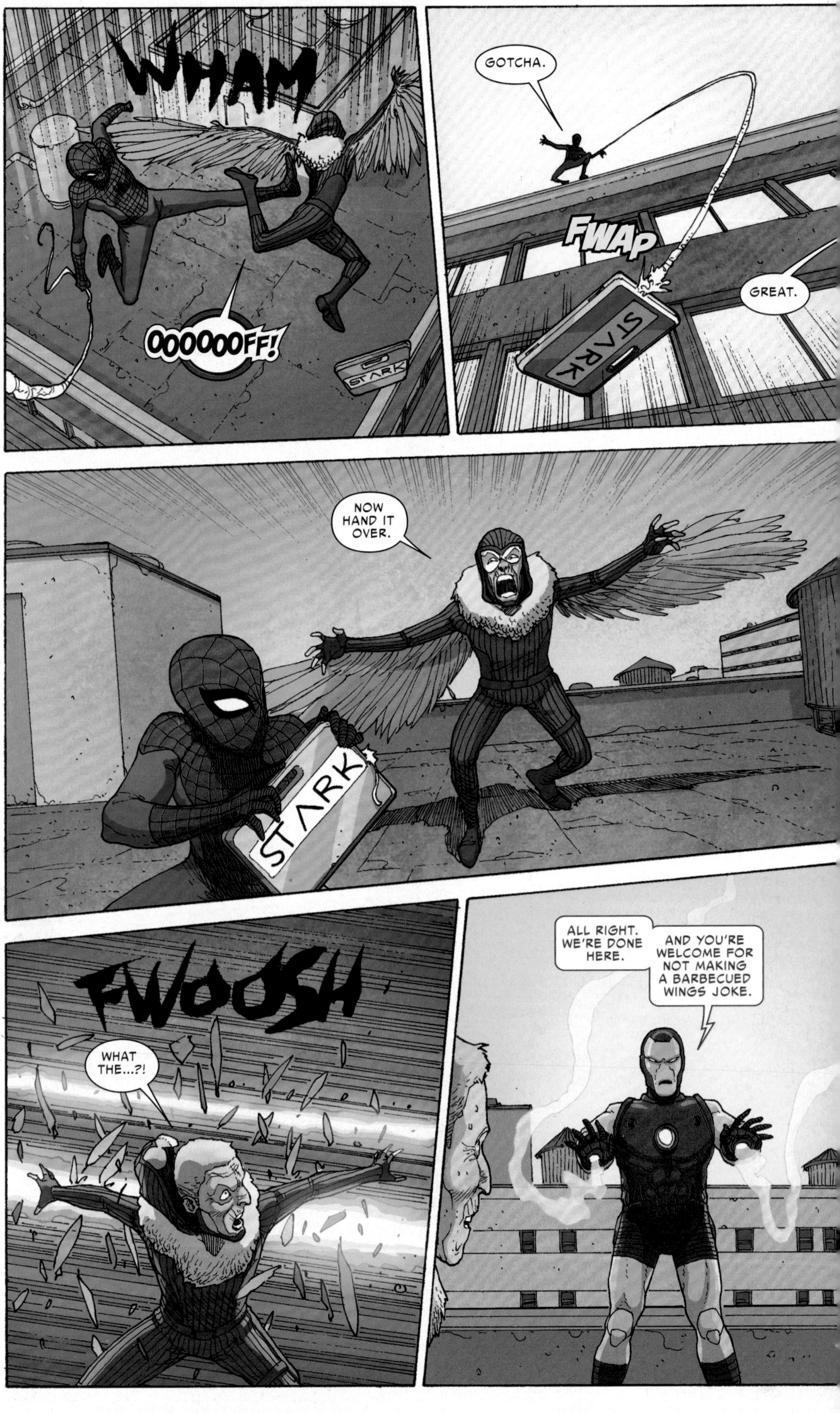
WHAM
OOOOOOFF!
STARK
GOTCHA.
FWAP
GREAT.
STARK
NOW HAND IT OVER.
STARK
FWOOSH
WHAT THE...?!
ALL RIGHT. WE'RE DONE HERE.
AND YOU'RE WELCOME FOR NOT MAKING A BARBECUED WINGS JOKE.

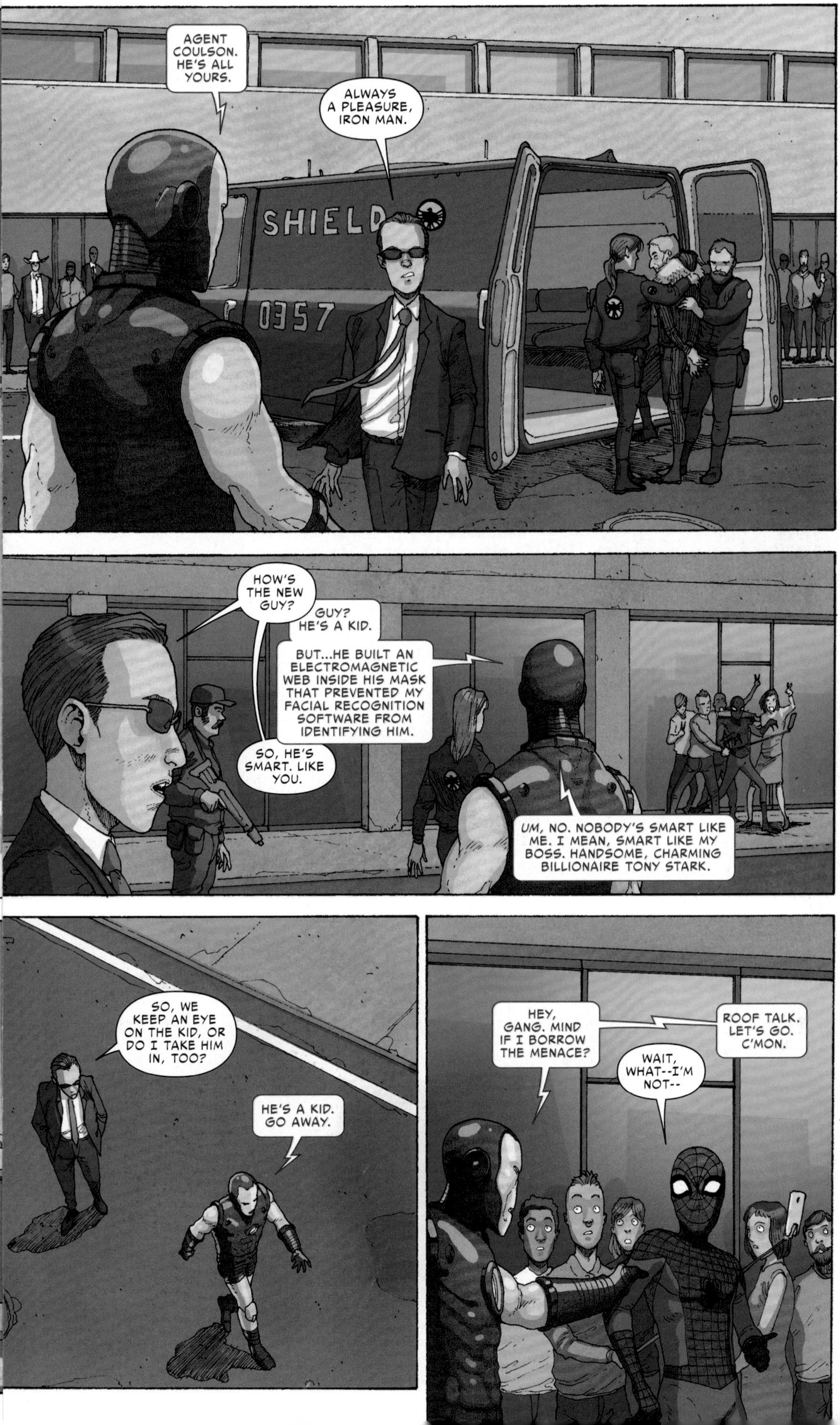
AGENT COULSON. HE'S ALL YOURS.
ALWAYS A PLEASURE, IRON MAN.
SHIELD
0357
HOW'S THE NEW GUY?
GUY? HE'S A KID.
BUT...HE BUILT AN ELECTROMAGNETIC WEB INSIDE HIS MASK THAT PREVENTED MY FACIAL RECOGNITION SOFTWARE FROM IDENTIFYING HIM.
SO, HE'S SMART. LIKE YOU.
UM, NO. NOBODY'S SMART LIKE ME. I MEAN, SMART LIKE MY BOSS. HANDSOME, CHARMING BILLIONAIRE TONY STARK.
SO, WE KEEP AN EYE ON THE KID, OR DO I TAKE HIM IN, TOO?
HE'S A KID. GO AWAY.
HEY, GANG. MIND IF I BORROW THE MENACE?
ROOF TALK. LET'S GO. C'MON.
WAIT, WHAT--I'M NOT--

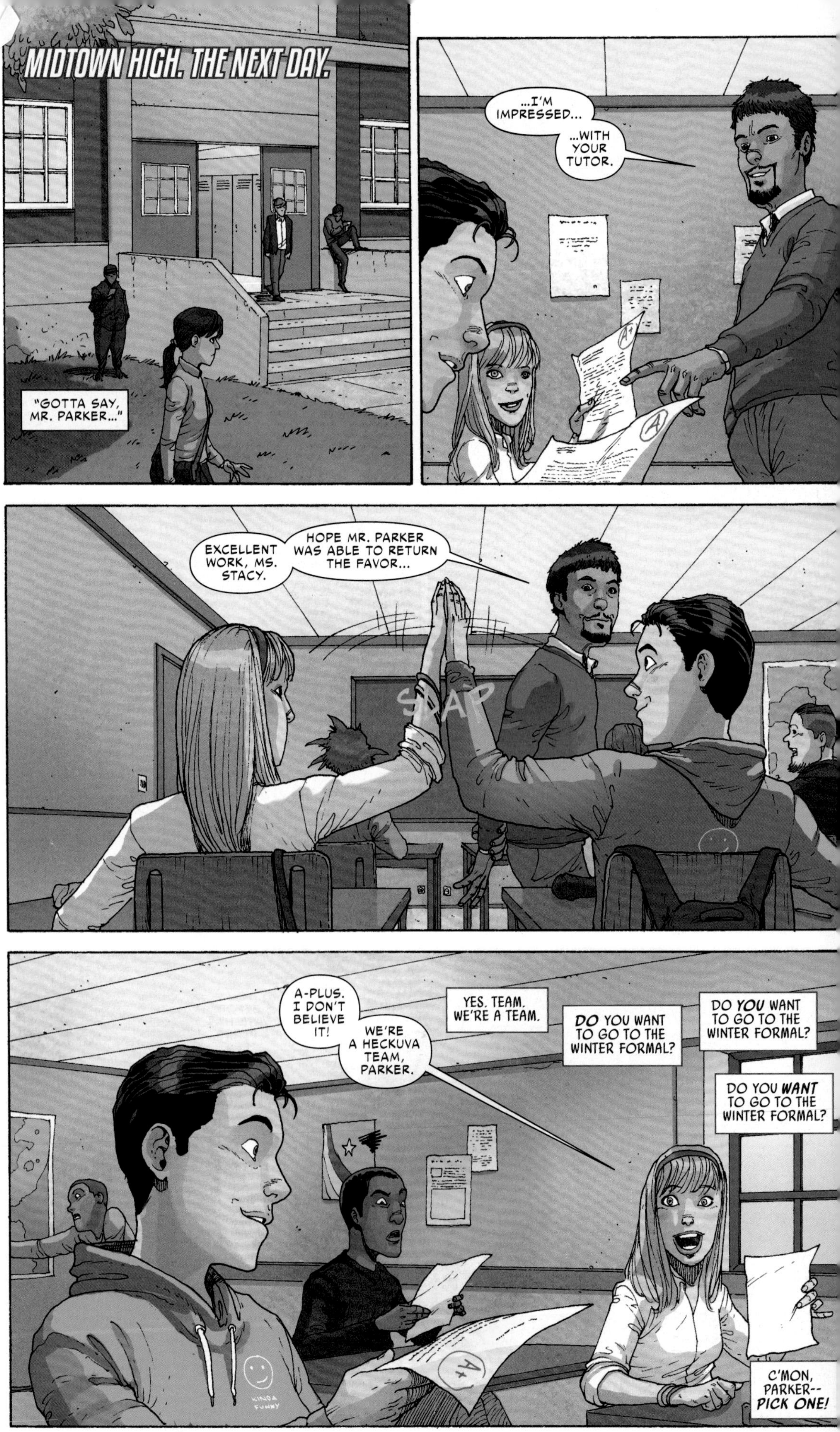
MIDTOWN HIGH. THE NEXT DAY.
"GOTTA SAY, MR. PARKER..."
...I'M IMPRESSED...
...WITH YOUR TUTOR.
EXCELLENT WORK, MS. STACY.
HOPE MR. PARKER WAS ABLE TO RETURN THE FAVOR...
SLAP
A-PLUS. I DON'T BELIEVE IT!
WE'RE A HECKUVA TEAM, PARKER.
YES. TEAM. WE'RE A TEAM.
DO YOU WANT TO GO TO THE WINTER FORMAL?
DO YOU WANT TO GO TO THE WINTER FORMAL?
DO YOU WANT TO GO TO THE WINTER FORMAL?
C'MON, PARKER-- PICK ONE!

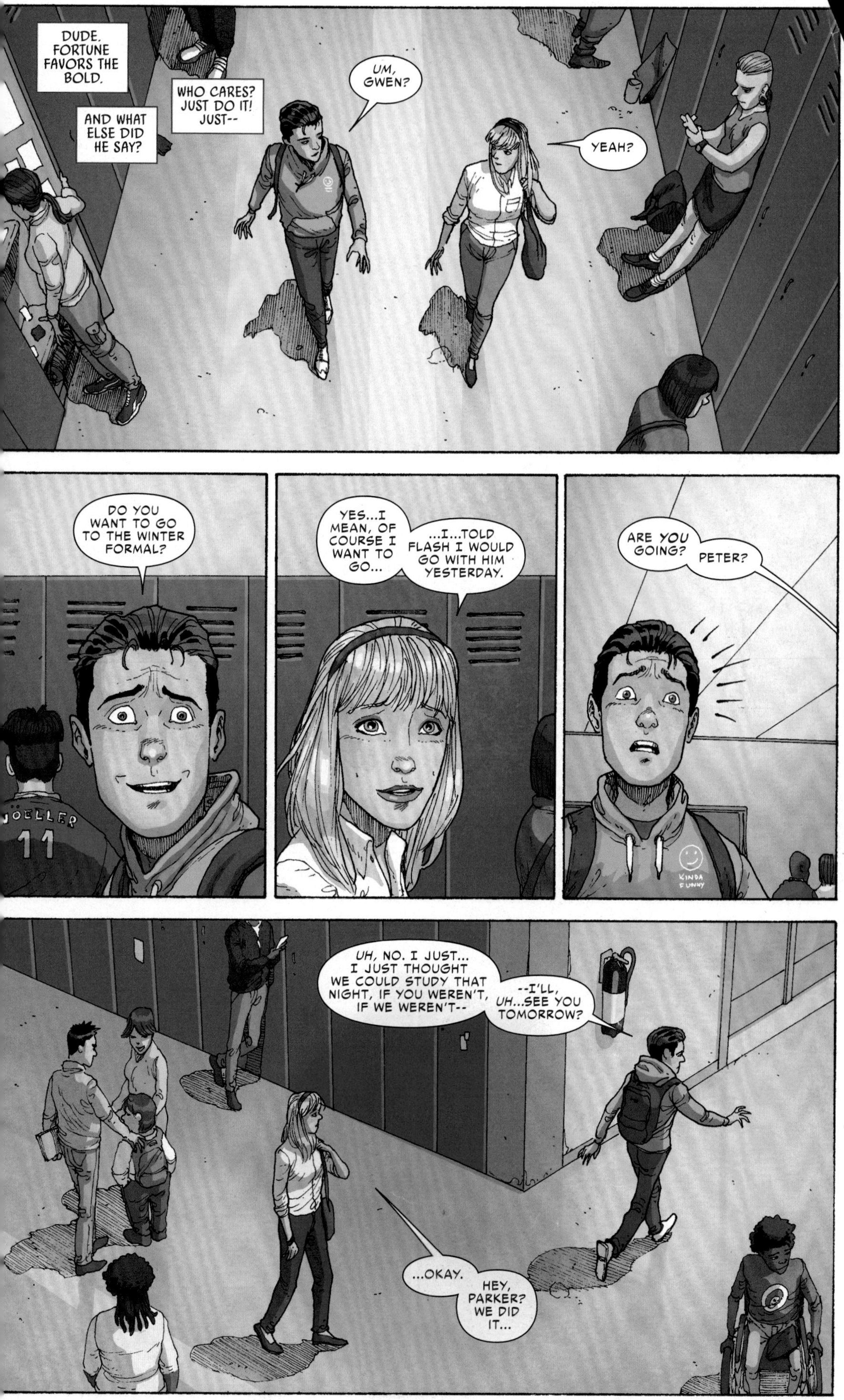
DUDE. FORTUNE FAVORS THE BOLD.
AND WHAT ELSE DID HE SAY?
WHO CARES? JUST DO IT! JUST--
UM, GWEN?
YEAH?
DO YOU WANT TO GO TO THE WINTER FORMAL?
WOELLER
11
YES...I MEAN, OF COURSE I WANT TO GO...
...I...TOLD FLASH I WOULD GO WITH HIM YESTERDAY.
ARE YOU GOING?
PETER?
KINDA FUNNY
UH, NO. I JUST... I JUST THOUGHT WE COULD STUDY THAT NIGHT, IF YOU WEREN'T, IF WE WEREN'T--
--I'LL, UH...SEE YOU TOMORROW?
...OKAY.
HEY, PARKER? WE DID IT...

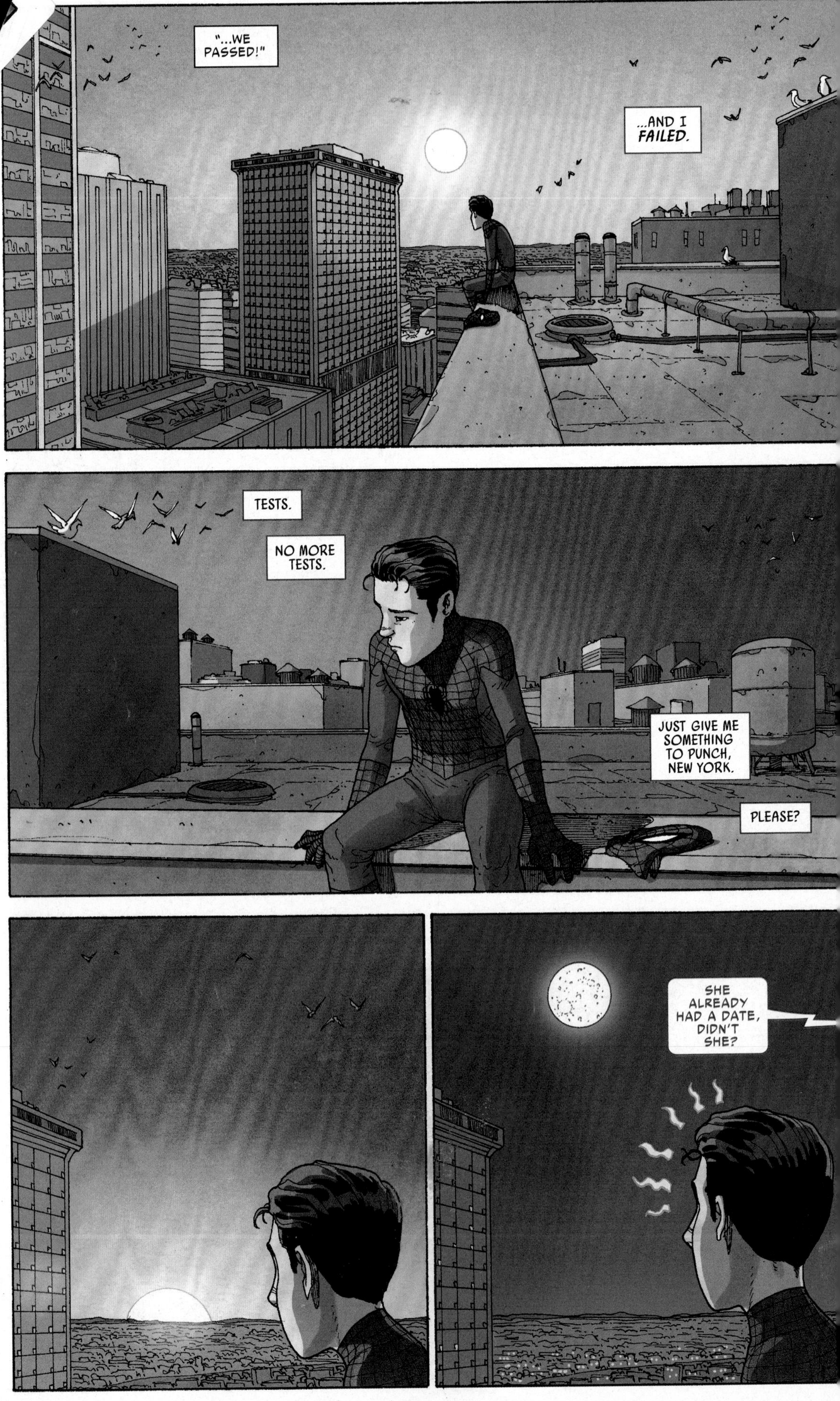
"...WE PASSED!"
...AND I FAILED.
TESTS.
NO MORE TESTS.
JUST GIVE ME SOMETHING TO PUNCH, NEW YORK.
PLEASE?
SHE ALREADY HAD A DATE, DIDN'T SHE?

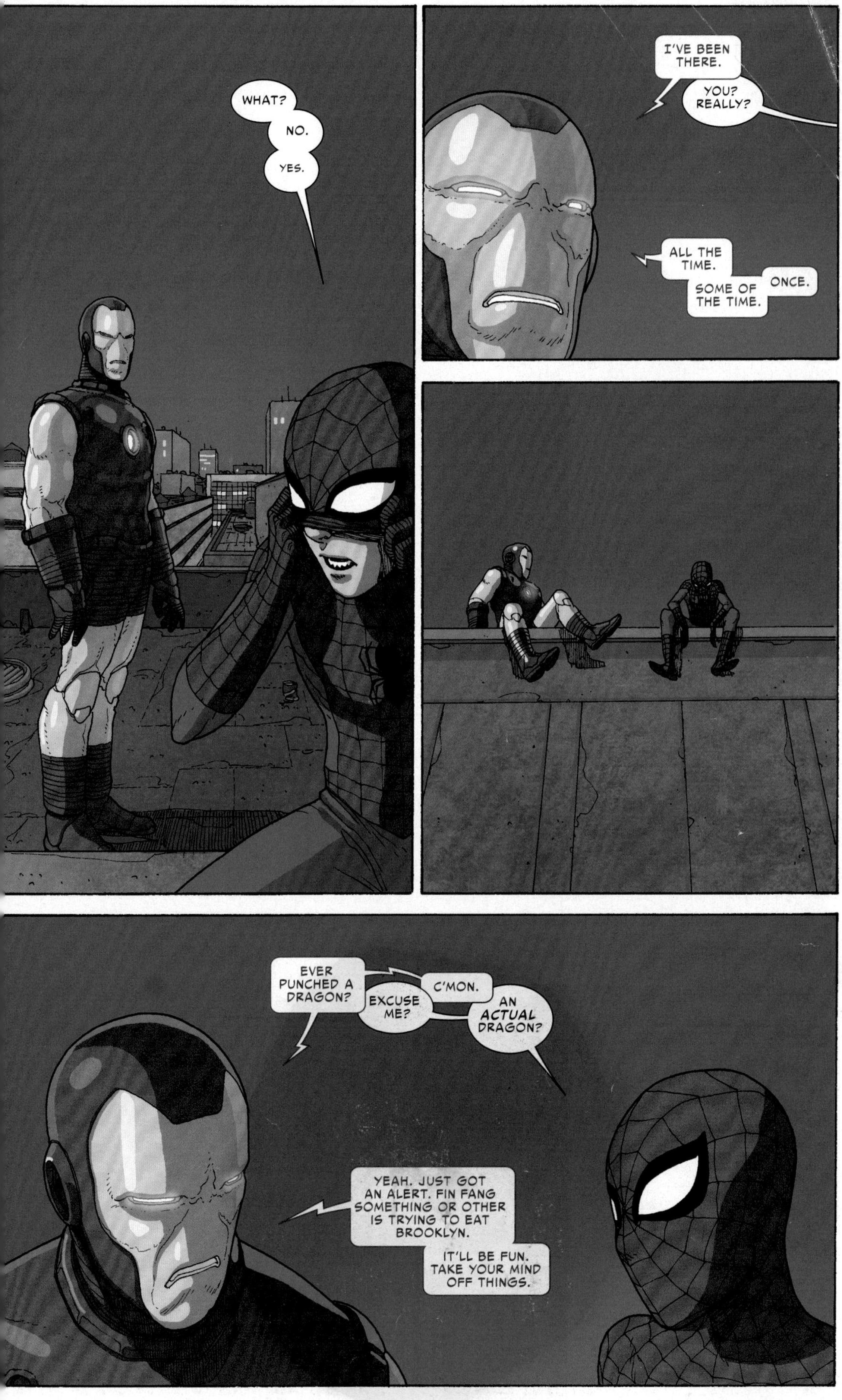
WHAT?
NO.
YES.
I'VE BEEN THERE.
YOU? REALLY?
ALL THE TIME.
SOME OF THE TIME.
ONCE.
EVER PUNCHED A DRAGON?
EXCUSE ME?
C'MON.
AN *ACTUAL* DRAGON?
YEAH. JUST GOT AN ALERT. FIN FANG SOMETHING OR OTHER IS TRYING TO EAT BROOKLYN.
IT'LL BE FUN. TAKE YOUR MIND OFF THINGS.

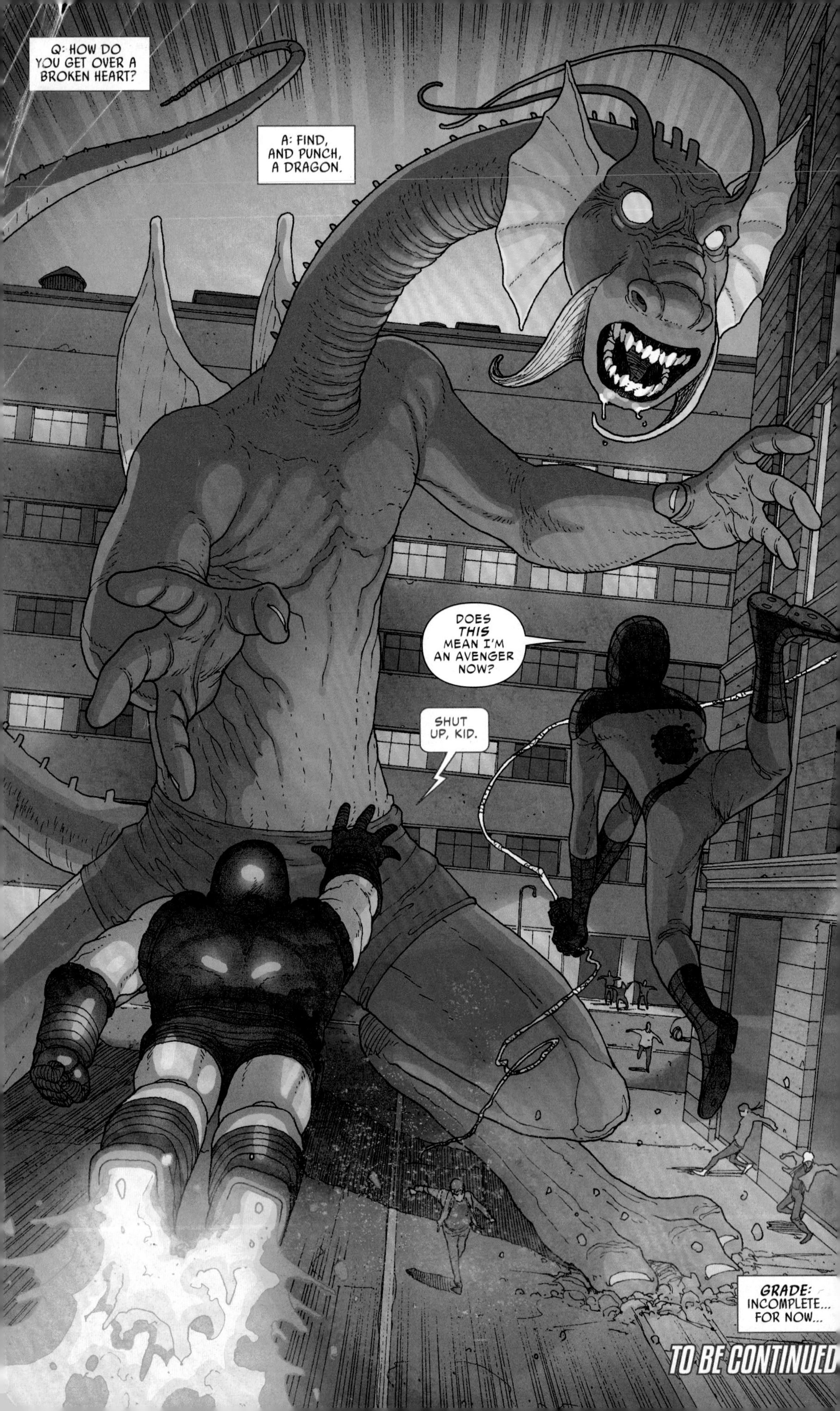

Q: HOW DO YOU GET OVER A BROKEN HEART?
A: FIND, AND PUNCH, A DRAGON.
DOES THIS MEAN I'M AN AVENGER NOW?
SHUT UP, KID.
GRADE: INCOMPLETE... FOR NOW...
TO BE CONTINUED

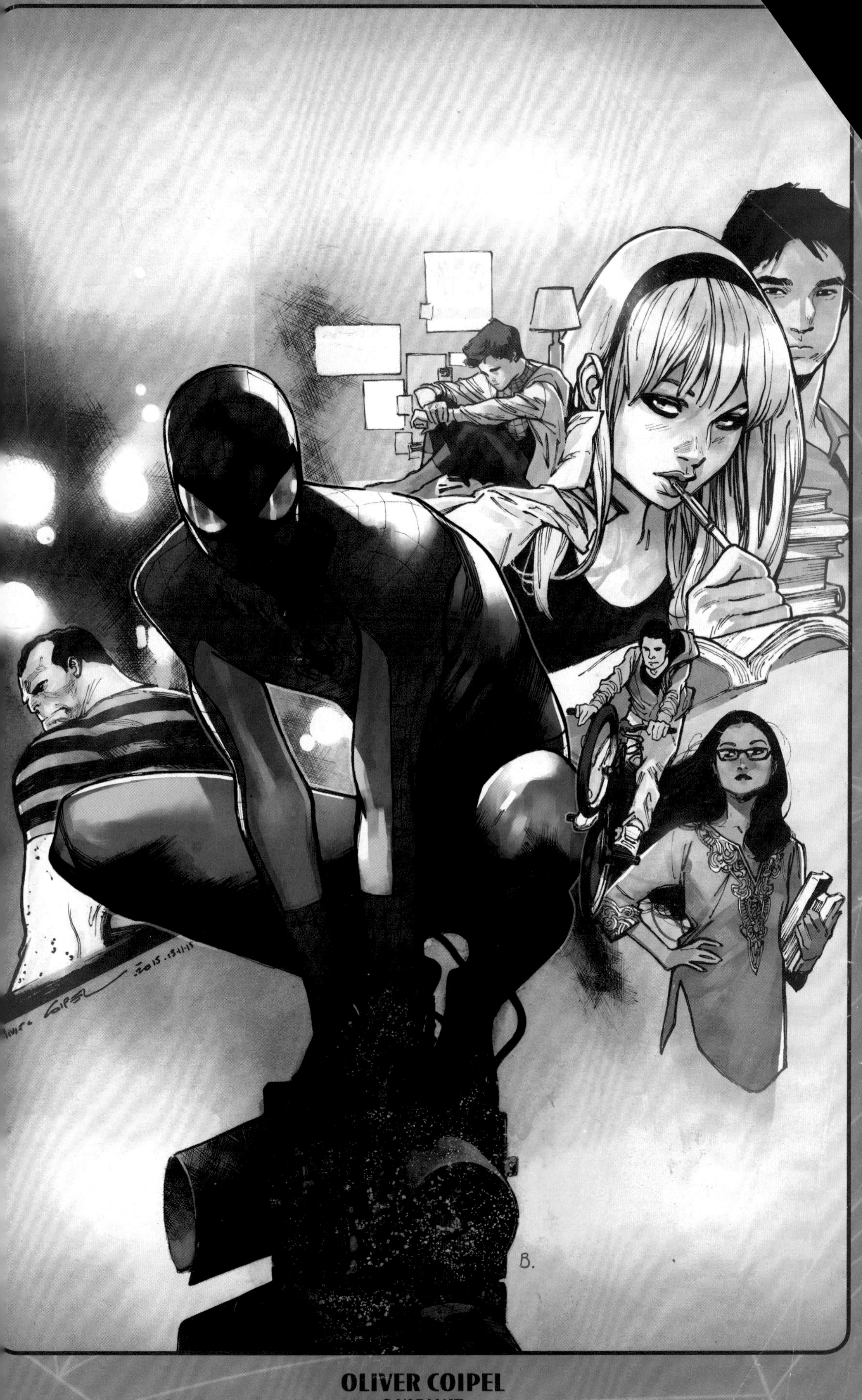

**OLIVER COIPEL**
**2 VARIANT**

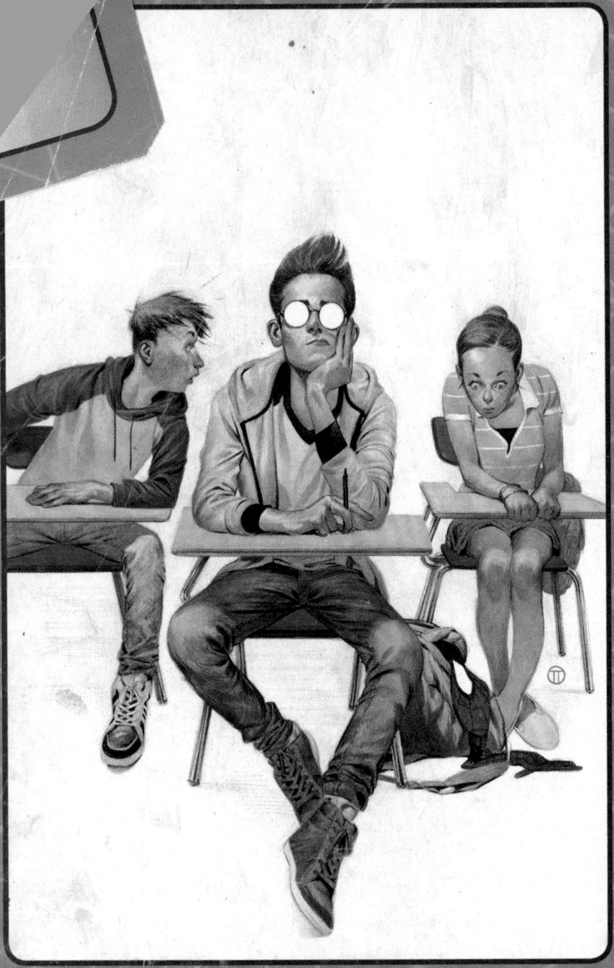

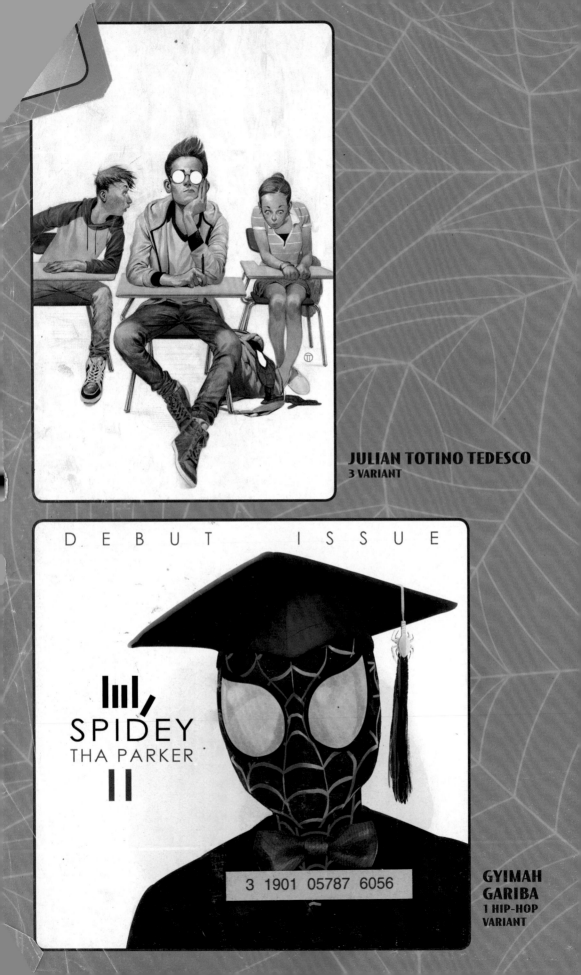

**JULIAN TOTINO TEDESCO**
**3 VARIANT**

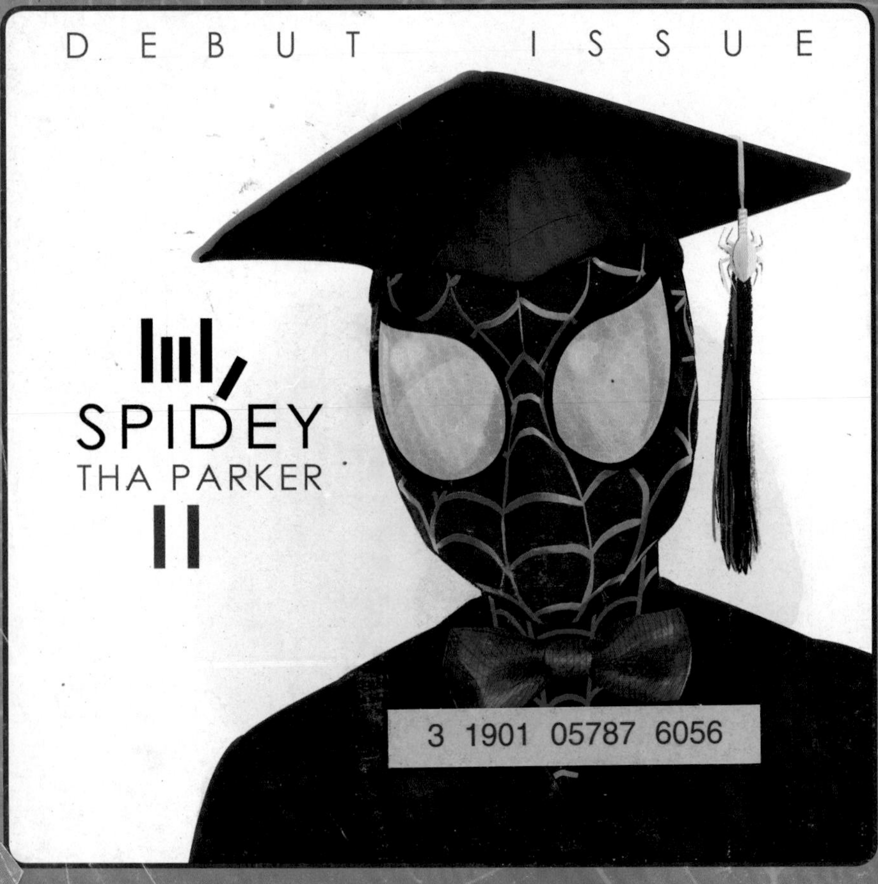
DEBUT ISSUE
SPIDEY
THA PARKER
II



**GYIMAH GARIBA**
**1 HIP-HOP VARIANT**